]

JUMBO

THE GREATEST ELEPHANT IN THE WORLD

Paul Chambers

André Deutsch

2 4 6 8 10 9 7 5 3 1

Text copyright © Paul Chambers 2007
Design copyright © Carlton Publishing Group 2007

Plate-section picture credits: page 1: *top & bottom* author's collection; page 2:
top London Stereoscopic Company/Getty Images; *bottom* The Stapleton
Collection/The Bridgeman Art Library; page 3: *top* Culver Pictures/The Art
Archive; *bottom* The Print Collector/Alamy; page 4: The Print Collector/Alamy;
page 5: *top* Hulton-Deutsch Collection/Getty Images; *bottom* The Print Collector/
Alamy; page 6: *top* Corbis; *bottom* Three Lions/Getty Images; page 7: *top* Swim
Link/Corbis; *bottom* Circus World Museum, Baraboo, Wisconsin, USA, with
permission from Ringling Bros and Barnum & Bailey; page 8: *top* Zoological
Society of London; *bottom* Digital Collections and Archive/Tufts University

All in-text line illustrations are from the author's collection

Every effort has been made to acknowledge correctly and contact the source
and/or copyright holder of each picture, and Carlton Books Limited apologises
for any unintentional errors or omissions, which will be corrected in future
editions of this book.

A catalogue record for this book is available from the British Library

ISBN 978-0-233-00222-4

Typeset by E-Type, Liverpool
Printed and bound in Great Britain by Mackays

CONTENTS

ACKNOWLEDGEMENTS

I am grateful to all those people who offered and gave me assistance while I was researching and writing Jumbo's story. I am especially grateful to the staff at the following institutions for their patience and assistance: the British Library, British Newspaper Library, Cambridge University Library, D.M.S. Watson Science Library (University College London), Family Records Centre, Hertfordshire Library Services, Institute for Historical Research, National Archives: Public Record Office, Society of Genealogists and Zoological Society of London.

I should like to offer particular gratitude to Michael Palmer, the archivist at the Zoological Society of London, for his advice and for his good humour when faced with dozens of requests for archive material. I must give a big thank you to my agent Isabel Atherton, of Watson, Little Ltd, for her advice, patience and considerable negotiating skills. I am also very grateful to Penny Phillips of André Deutsch for her professionalism, support and outstanding good humour.

Finally, the support of my family has, as ever, been absolutely wonderful and has frequently provided me with the will and the energy to keep going. I am grateful to my father, brother and John, Elizabeth and Sarah Baxter, all of whom selflessly gave up their own time in order to help me. The biggest thank you of all must, as ever, go to my wife Rachel and daughter Eleanor; it is their sense of humour and lust for life that keep me going. I love you both, always and for ever.

PREFACE

"Jumbo landed in safety. He celebrates his arrival in a bottle of whiskey."

Thus ran the *New York Times*'s headline on 10 April 1882. The announcement ended weeks of nervous speculation and offered reassurance to readers that the world's first international animal superstar had survived the sea voyage from London and arrived safely in the United States. A few hours later Jumbo, the largest elephant in the world, disembarked on American soil; he did so in front of the largest crowd ever seen in New York. The streets were lined with thousands of people who cheered and waved as the elephant made his way along Broadway toward Madison Square Garden. The scenes were unprecedented in the United States – yet they were no less spectacular than the send-off that Jumbo had been given in London a couple of weeks earlier.

Many predicted that the blaze of publicity surrounding the elephant would soon burn itself out and that the "Jumbo craze" would be a short-lived affair. Such pessimism was unfounded: this humble elephant was to end up so famous that his name is still a household word used to describe any big object. Throughout his life – and beyond – Jumbo was the subject of adulation across the world.

In a remarkable career spanning three decades Jumbo not only thrilled countless people and bore children without number on his massive back but rubbed shoulders, metaphorically, with the likes of Queen Victoria, the Prince of Wales, the young Winston Churchill and P.T. Barnum. His fame spread across Europe, the entire United States, Canada, and even reached southern Africa and the Indian subcontinent. But sadly, like many of the stars, both human and animal, who have come and gone since his day, Jumbo was to pay a high price for the greatness that was thrust upon him.

7

PART ONE

AFRICA

The Elephant Hunters

"I believe that I am the oldest acquaintance of Jumbo, as I knew him in his early youth." So wrote the explorer Samuel White Baker, whose unkempt hair, flowing white beard and double-barrelled rifle marked him out as something of an eccentric character in Victorian Britain. Baker had spent over 30 years exploring Africa and Asia, during which time he had accumulated several volumes' worth of anecdotes and adventures, but it was his association with Jumbo, the world's most famous elephant, that persuaded the retired explorer to write to the newspapers to proclaim his long-term friendship with this animal superstar. We must be grateful to Baker, for if he had not chosen to break his silence, the world would never have learned anything of Jumbo's traumatic introduction to human society.

Baker first met Jumbo in February 1862, in the remote desert highlands that straddle the border between eastern Sudan and Abyssinia (now Eritrea). This area was about as far from civilization as it was possible for an English gentlemen to get: there were no roads, railways or even permanent rivers and, aside from the harsh climate and wild animals, Baker had to contend with hostile tribes, flash floods and bush fires. It was the prospect of adventure that drew people like him to the African interior, and for several months he had been in Sudan exploring the Setite basin in the hope of finding a connection to the River Nile. So it was pure chance that while making his way along the dried-up bed of the River Royan he stumbled across the camp of a party of Hamran tribesmen.

The Hamran were Arabians and, as a fluent Arabic speaker, Baker was able to offer a friendly greeting to the group's leader, Taher Sheriff. Pleasantries were exchanged and Baker was invited to spend the night with the Hamran. Given the dangers present in the area, such as lions, hyenas and the aggressive Basé tribe, Baker happily accepted the offer, and he was taken on a tour of the camp.

Taher Sheriff's appearance told the explorer that he was an Aggageer, or elephant hunter. Much revered in Sudan, the Aggageers could be distinguished from other tribesmen by the extraordinary length of their hair, which was arranged in long ring- lets and always parted straight down the centre of the head. Their renown came from their ability to hunt large animals, including elephants and rhinoceroses, using just a horse, a two-edged sword and a small shield. Death and serious injury were common, and it was said that a true Aggageer would die not peacefully in his bed but beneath the feet of a rampaging elephant.

Baker was perfectly aware of the Aggageers' reputation and knew that they made a living from selling ivory, bone and hides from the elephants they killed. So he was somewhat surprised to see at their camp several temporary pens holding a variety of live wild animals, including three giraffes, several young antelopes, a juvenile rhino and two baby elephants. Baker had never heard of the Hamran taking the trouble to capture their prey alive, and as they all settled down to a dinner of wild partridge he asked his hosts what purpose the little menagerie could possibly serve.

Taher Sheriff explained that he and his men had been con- tracted to capture living animal specimens for export to European zoos. The man who had hired them was one Johan Schmidt, who lived in Kassala, a frontier military town about a hundred miles to the north. Schmidt was prepared to pay a few dollars for an antelope or bird of prey, up to $20 for a good giraffe and as much as $50 for an elephant calf. To the Hamran such sums were a fortune, so they had happily set off into the desert in search of live prey.

Baker had been to Kassala several times and knew Johan Schmidt to be a Bavarian who had come to Sudan in search of his fortune. However, Schmidt, who was a skilled carpenter, ended up working as an odd-job man for other Europeans, most of whom did not linger long in the area. In a region beset by war and political turmoil, he was considered an honest and dependable character whose word could be relied upon. Baker was able to assure his hosts that they were working for a good boss.

The presence of two elephant calves in the Hamran camp excited the Englishman. His travels in the region had imbued him with a passion for these large animals and he had taken delight in observing their behaviour in the wild, something few Europeans had ever had the opportunity to do. The specimens captured by the Hamran, however, were less than impressive in Baker's eyes. Both were smaller than a pit pony and looked severely undernourished. One was especially scrawny and was later described as having been a runt who had not been expected to survive for long after his capture.

It was the same scrawny runt that would become both the first living African elephant to reach modern Europe and the first international animal superstar. He would also grow to such an extraordinary size that he was hailed as the largest animal on Earth. This runt was Jumbo – a name he would not be known by for several years yet. At the time, in the fading light of day, the little elephant looked far from remarkable; terrified, he stood motionless inside the temporary corral, unsure where he was and where his mother had gone.

Taher Sheriff could answer this last question: both elephants' mothers were dead. As he explained to Baker, in order to secure the capture of any elephant calf, he had first to kill its mother. If he did not, then the female, or cow, would not desist from protecting her offspring – and there are few animals of any species more dangerous than a mother elephant bent on defending her calf.

The talk of hunting excited the Englishman, for although he enjoyed observing elephants in their habitat he also had a passion for shooting them. In common with many Victorian explorers, Baker viewed the African elephant – which is the world's largest living land animal – as the ultimate hunting challenge. But while he preferred to blast at them with his trusty rifle, he knew that the Aggageers could achieve the same end using just a sword. To Baker it seemed an impossible feat and one that was surely fraught with danger. He pleaded with Taher Sheriff to be allowed to accompany the group on one of their elephant hunts.

The leader was pleased to oblige. "We will start before sunrise tomorrow," he said, adding that they would be riding for a full day and that success was far from guaranteed. Baker did not care; his only desire was to bear witness to the manner in which the Hamran had hunted down and killed Jumbo's mother. In doing so he became one of only a handful of Europeans who would ever witness the Aggageers' traditional hunting methods, for in a few years' time the gun would replace the sword as their weapon of choice.

As night fell the camp grew silent, except for the noise of restless shuffling from the pens as the elephants and other captive animals tried to make sense of the strange situation in which they found themselves.

Baker's discovery of the Hamran's camp was fortunate in occurring only a few days after Jumbo was captured. Had the explorer not come across it, Jumbo's early history would have been lost in the desert sands of his birth. We can deduce much from Baker's account of his stay. For example, he estimated Jumbo's height to be around four feet, which, according to modern observations, would have made him just over a year old and approximately 500 lb in weight. This dates Jumbo's birth to around Christmas 1860, which coincided with the start of the dry season in that part of Sudan.

Elephants have one of the longest gestation periods of all mammals; Jumbo would have spent around 22 months in the womb before the contraction pains began. Elephantine birth is not a protracted affair; after pacing restlessly, but silently, back and forth for several minutes, Jumbo's mother – still standing – would have given several final grunts as the calf dropped to the ground. Jumbo would have weighed around 265 lb and would have lain in a large puddle of embryonic fluid. The birth would most likely have taken place in the presence of several other elephants, including a bull (male) and one or more aunts. While Jumbo took his first breaths, the other elephants would have crowded round, protecting him from predators and nudging him with their trunks in an effort to get him on to his wobbly legs. Within hours Jumbo would have been an accomplished walker, capable of following his mother almost anywhere. Within weeks he would have been able to run, and after several months he would have started using his trunk to grasp plants and drink water.

Elephants have one of the most complicated societies in the animal world, although our understanding of their behaviour has many gaps. They are emotionally reliant on one another and display reassurance and affection by mutual touching, grooming and grasping with their trunks. They are also very vocal, capable of producing a wide repertoire of noises, some of which are too low for human ears but can be heard many miles away by other elephants. The function of these sounds is little understood, but scientists are in the process of creating dictionaries of the elephantine language. Jumbo would have had little time to learn these communication skills or indeed the other complex behavioural traits of his family unit.

Whatever aspects of elephantine culture Jumbo did manage to absorb would have come mostly from his mother. As with humans, much time and effort is devoted to the task of parenting and for the first six months elephant calves are almost entirely dependent on their mother for food, protection and physical stimulation. After this period they start to gain some independence; by its first birthday the average calf can feed and groom itself, although it is still dependent on the nutrients in its mother's milk and remains so until it is at least two years old.

Jumbo lived in the security of his mother's protection until he was about a year old; in all this time he would not have strayed further than five yards from her side. So remote was the area in which they lived that they could conceivably have never seen a human being before. If so, their first contact with mankind was to be a bloody and brutal encounter. The day that Jumbo's family strayed into the path of Taher Sheriff's men was to have a profound effect not just on Jumbo himself but on the lives of millions of people across the globe. There is no first-hand account of the moment when the hunters separated Jumbo from his mother's care, but it is known how the feat was accomplished.

The morning after Baker first met Jumbo he was taken by Taher Sheriff to the area where the calf had been captured and was shown exactly how the Aggageers had killed his mother. The location, about 25 miles from the camp in a highland area at the head of a dry river bed, was very remote indeed. Baker describes the early part of the journey as passing through a magnificent landscape of lofty, overhanging rocks, wide tracts of fine forest and groves of enormous baobab trees. As the group moved further up the valley, so the river bed narrowed until it became a steep mountain gully where the rock surfaces had been worn smooth by flash floods. When the terrain started to become impossibly steep, they turned away from the river and into a wide, sandy valley lying at the foot of a mountain. Taher Sheriff explained to Baker that elephants would come to the valley in order to drink, and that by following their footprints it was possible to catch up with the herds.

The journey had already taken several hours, during which time the ambient temperature had become uncomfortably hot. It is not just humans that dislike the sun's direct heat; elephants also avoid it and often move about by night or at dawn or dusk, when the risk of sunstroke is greatly reduced. From mid-morning they seek out the shade of trees and rock overhangs; this makes the hunters' task easier as it allows them to track a static target. The dry season also helped the Aggageers as, according to Baker, it was usual for the Sudanese elephants to move in smaller clans or as individuals rather than in larger herds.

Unintentionally demonstrating how Jumbo's mother had been killed, the Hamran tracked and confronted a lone elephant that stood drinking from a shallow puddle. "It was a fine bull," recalled Baker. "The enormous ears were thrown forward, as the head was lowered in the act of drawing up the water through the trunk; these shaded the eyes, and, with the wind favourable, we advanced noiselessly upon the sand to within twenty yards before we were perceived."

The bull elephant spotted the hunters and made off in the opposite direction at speed; this is the reaction of almost all elephants when confronted with a perceived threat. Jumbo's family would have attempted to flee as well, but with the small calf between her legs his mother would have become separated from the herd and so been easier to hunt. Faced with the Hamran and their horses, she would have turned to face them and become very aggressive in defence of her calf. This is what Taher Sheriff wanted: the Aggageers' hunting technique relied on riling an elephant to such a degree that it would charge at them in a blind rage. To Baker this seemed an odd idea: few people who witnessed an elephant charging at them lived to tell the tale. An enraged elephant will ram, gore and stamp on its victim until it is absolutely certain that all life has been extinguished. Baker knew this only too well, having watched a man die after being impaled on the tusks of a charging elephant. Even the Aggageers didn't always get it right – as evinced by the crushed and withered arm of one of Taher Sheriff's brothers.

The Aggageers always hunted on horseback and usually in a group of four men. They preferred to go after bull elephants, but if they wanted to capture a live calf they would have to engage its mother in battle and persuade her to attack them. In all probability little provocation was ever needed. Game hunters like Baker often observed that a cow elephant with a calf is a far more dangerous prospect than an elephant on its own. Even though an adult bull can stand 12 feet tall, weigh over five tons and attack extremely aggressively, hunters consider them to be predictable when alarmed, which makes it easy to avoid their headlong charges. However, a cow defending her calf is a different matter; she will tend to be younger and fitter than the bulls and more easily agitated. She may charge without warning and will sometimes refuse to break off an attack even if her pursuers are fleeing in the opposite direction. If severely threatened, she will become frenzied and attack anything within reach.

Jumbo's mother would have been goaded by the Hamran until, with a shrill scream, she ran at them in fury. It was at this point that the hunters would have entered the highly choreographed display of horseback hunting for which they were famed. Baker was lucky to witness the Aggageers at work and, by recording what he saw, he has given us details of how Jumbo would have become separated from his mother. What follows is his account of the Hamran hunting a bull elephant, but their technique would have been identical to that used to kill Jumbo's mother.

"The elephant stood facing us like a statue," wrote Baker in his memoirs; "it did not move a muscle beyond a quick and restless action of the eyes, that were watching all sides."

While the explorer watched from the sidelines, two of the Aggageers remained directly in front of the elephant, distracting its attention. As they did so, Taher Sheriff and his youngest brother, Ibrahim, positioned themselves about 20 yards behind the animal. With everyone in place, one of the two hunters in front of the prey started to ride slowly and purposefully toward its head. Baker held his breath, waiting for the animal to make its move: then he saw its eye twitch.

"Look out! He's coming!" shouted Baker – and with that the elephant charged headlong at the rider, who turned his horse as though on a pivot and rode away at speed. "For a moment I thought he must be caught," recalled Baker. "Had the mare stumbled, all would have been lost; but she gained in the race and kept the rider's distance so close to the elephant that its outstretched trunk was within a few feet of the mare's tail."

Samuel Baker is chased by an elephant.

With the elephant chasing one of the men, Taher Sheriff and his brother started to chase the animal from behind. They caught up with it and positioned themselves right next to its hind legs.

By now the animal was in such a blind rage that it did not even notice their presence. Baker takes up the story again: "When close to the tail of the elephant, the sword of Taher Sheriff flashed from its sheath. Grasping his trusty blade he leapt nimbly to the ground, while Ibrahim caught the reins of his horse; two or three bounds on foot, with the sword clutched in both hands, and he was close behind the elephant. A bright glance shone like lightning, as the sun struck upon the descending steel. This was followed by a dull crack as the sword cut through skin and sinews and settled deep in the bone, about twelve inches above the foot. At the next stride, the elephant halted dead in the midst of its tremendous charge. Taher vaulted back into the saddle with his naked sword in hand. The elephant's foot was dislocated, and turned up in front like an old shoe. In an instant Taher was once more on foot, and again the sharp sword slashed the remaining leg. The great elephant could not move!"

While hanging from their galloping horses, the Sheriff brothers had sliced through the elephant's hamstrings, rendering it unable to even walk. Then they severed an artery and left the animal to bleed to death. This shocked even Baker, who begged to be allowed to shoot the elephant, but his host refused, saying that it would quickly bleed to death without pain.

Jumbo's mother suffered the same fate. She too would have lain helpless for several minutes while a fatal quantity of her 790 pints (450 litres) of blood – the amount the average elephant holds – drained from her wounded body and into the sandy soil beneath. This process takes about 20 minutes, and she would have heard Jumbo pathetically bellowing for help. She may even have had time to watch Taher Sheriff approach the stricken calf, throw ropes about his neck and secure him to one of their horses. With his mother prostrate, Jumbo would have been helpless, rooted to the spot and unable to move or act independently. Capturing Jumbo and leading him back to the camp would not have been a problem, although the distance probably called for a stay overnight *en route*.

After his return, Taher Sheriff had no further interest in the animals he captured. Jumbo would have been handed to one of the African helpers who had been hired to care for them.

Although the young calf was capable of gathering and eating plants by himself, he was still dependent on the fat and other nutrition found in his mother's milk and was a year from being weaned. In the absence of milk, a calf will quickly weaken and die. Johan Schmidt was aware of this and had directed Taher Sheriff to take with him a large number of goats whose milk could be used to feed the unweaned captive animals. This, at least, was the theory; nobody had ever attempted before to capture and transport a young African elephant any great distance – let alone take one halfway across the world to Europe.

For all Baker's later enthusiasm about his desert encounter with Jumbo, his acquaintance was a brief one. Satisfied with his day's hunting, he soon took leave of Taher Sheriff's company and started to make his own way through the wilderness once more. He remained in the area for many months and was to meet Taher Sheriff again and, some time after this, even employed Johan Schmidt for one of his own expeditions. Schmidt was able to tell Baker what had happened to the two elephants after his departure and it is because of this, and other documentary evidence, that we can be certain that the miserable animal seen by Baker on the banks of the River Royan is the hero of our story.

After their brief encounter, the young elephant and the English explorer separated and for two decades followed their own destinies before eventually meeting again. The reunion did not take place in a parched desert landscape but in a colder, more formidable land where elephants were not hunted to death but worshipped by crowds of curious onlookers.

⚘ An Exotic Commodity ⚘

To a Hamran tribesman the idea of moving desert animals 3,000 miles north to the cold, wet climate of Europe must have seemed very odd indeed. Despite explanations from people like Baker and Schmidt, the Aggageers could hardly have envisaged the gulf that existed between their nomadic lifestyle and the more rigid, urbanized existence of the average European citizen. It would have been especially hard to learn that in other parts of the world the elephant was such a rare and extraordinary animal that people would pay good money just to stand and stare at one.

At the time of Jumbo's capture elephants were a rarity in Europe and, as a consequence, zoological gardens and private menageries would pay handsomely to obtain one. In the industrialized world exotic animals had become a commodity that, like rice and tea, could be shipped in from foreign countries and traded for profit. Rarer and larger animals were difficult to obtain but they attracted large crowds and so were expensive to buy; this was why Schmidt had specifically asked Taher Sheriff to collect some young elephants. It was his hope that these animals would not only fetch a high price when sold, but would cause a stir among Europe's scientific community. He reasoned that, should either of his elephants make it to Europe alive, they would be the first of their species to be seen outside Africa for nearly 2,000 years.

Individual living elephants had been brought to Europe for centuries and were often to be found at various royal courts and in private menageries. Indeed, when Jumbo was taken from the wild there were around 20 captive elephants in various parts of Britain, France and Germany. However, none of these was

African in origin but all had come instead from Asia and were a completely different species from any elephant that lived in Africa. Because of unreliable trade routes and the barrier presented by the Sahara Desert, African elephants had not been seen outside their native continent since the days of the Roman empire. It was for this reason that Jumbo's capture was so special and also why his new owners expected to make a small fortune from selling him on if he could be returned to Europe safely.

The Asian elephant that populated Europe's zoos in the nineteenth century is known to scientists as *Elephas maximus*; it is native to the Indian subcontinent, as well as many parts of the Far East, and has been domesticated by humans for millennia. Good trade links with Asia meant that for years zoologists, anatomists and other scientists had been able to observe Asian elephants at close quarters, both in the wild and as working animals. By the 1860s the biology of *Elephas maximus* was well understood, as were some aspects of its behaviour; specimens imported into European zoos allowed further studies to be made and in some instances the animals had even been persuaded to breed. By contrast, the African elephant remained an enigma, so obscure that it did not receive a formal scientific name (*Loxodonta africana*) until 1797, some 40 years after its Asian counterpart. In the absence of specimens, living or dead, zoologists had to base their knowledge of the African elephant on descriptions given to them by nineteenth-century explorers, many of whose tales were exaggerated or lacked useful detail.

For example, Major Dixon Denham, who explored west and central Africa in the 1820s, was able to state (correctly) that the African elephant is taller, heavier and more aggressive than the Asian species. But his only other comments were that it could not be domesticated and that its meat was "better flavoured than any beef". Explorers' conflicting descriptions made separating fact from fiction very difficult; a popular encyclopedia of the day was able to devote two pages to the characteristics and habits of the Asian elephant but just a single paragraph to those of the African species and even that is erroneous, stating, for example, that "it is smaller than the Asiatic".

The popular press did not know what to make of the African

elephant either, but, in true journalistic fashion, explorers' descriptions were fashioned so that *Loxodonta africana* became an oversized, bloodthirsty monster that could reach 16 feet in height, weigh 10 tons and rip up trees and buildings with its tusks and trunk. Like the shark today, the African elephant would crop up as the bad guy in sensational newspaper stories and cheap novels, giving the public an irrational fear of the animal.

"The enraged elephant instantly seized the unhappy huntsman with its trunk," wrote Oliver Goldsmith in a posthumously published work, "flung him up to a vast height in the air, and received him upon one of his tusks as he fell; and then turning towards the other two brothers, as if it were an aspect of revenge and insult, held out to them the impaled wretch, writhing in the agonies of death."

The notion of the African elephant as a gigantic, murderous beast increased its appeal to the many people who longed to see one of these remarkable animals in the flesh. Unfortunately the few attempts that had been made to transport elephants from the colonies in eastern and southern Africa had all ended in failure. Being confined in a hold throughout a long sea voyage was more than these animals could endure and at some point in the journey their carcasses would end up being dumped into the Indian or the Atlantic Ocean.

The public's desire to see an African elephant was so great that when a stuffed female specimen was exhibited in Britain at the Great Exhibition of 1851 crowds flocked to see it. This was the only African elephant on display anywhere in Europe and, despite being just nine feet tall, it attracted so much press attention that its origins became the subject of speculation. Some claimed that the animal had been part of a travelling menagerie; others that it had been the personal pet of one of the Great Exhibition's officers which had died in mysterious circumstances. The truth was more mundane. A village museum in Saffron Walden in Essex had paid for the skin and bones to be imported directly from Africa but had agreed to loan them to the Great Exhibition.

The hysteria that surrounded the stuffed elephant highlighted the public's fascination with the species. At the time there was fierce rivalry between Europe's zoological gardens, and the prestige of being the first institution to obtain a living African elephant became a matter of great importance, but nowhere was this urgency felt more keenly than at the Regent's Park Zoological Gardens in London.

The Zoological Society of London had been founded in 1826 in direct competition with the Jardin des Plantes in Paris, which was then considered to possess the finest menagerie in Europe. By 1828 the Society had opened its own Zoological Gardens in Regent's Park, which it populated with such novelties as giraffes, ostriches, hyenas, zebras and birds of prey. The venture was a success and in its first year of operation was visited by almost 200,000 people at a cost of 1 shilling. each. Before long commentators were saying that London Zoo, as the Zoological Gardens were popularly known, "far surpasses the Jardin des Plantes of Paris".

Most of the Zoo's early exhibits had been donated or borrowed from private menageries, but in time the Zoological Society routinely obtained its specimens from commercial animal traders, several of whom operated in London's East End. As the collection of animals grew, so did the Zoological Gardens, and by 1834 they were an impressive tourist attraction occupying 36 acres of Regent's Park. Keeping wild animals is an expensive business, and the Zoological Society soon realized that, in order to keep the paying public flowing through its gates, it would have to offer an ever-increasing selection of new and unusual animals imported from exotic and distant parts of the world. The problem was that finding such creatures was neither cheap nor easy.

Across the Channel the star attraction at the Jardin des Plantes was the Asian elephants, which were drawing large crowds to see them frolic about their enclosure. London Zoo was envious of its French rival but during its early years all its attempts to obtain an elephant were frustrated. Britain was home to several Asian elephants but these were all in private collections and unavailable for loan. As a result, in 1830 the Zoological Society reluctantly paid £420 (around £28,000 today) to a Captain Smith for an 11-year-old Asian bull elephant which was at that time resident in Madras.

The unfortunate animal had to endure a gruelling nine months on a ship which sailed to London the long way round the world, via the Pacific Ocean. After arriving at the East India Docks on 11 May 1831 the elephant was so pleased to be allowed to stretch his legs that he veritably trotted through the streets of the capital to his new home in Regent's Park. The Zoological Society had been given plenty of time to build, in the centre of the Gardens, a generous Elephant House and fenced enclosure, modelled on that in Paris, which included a sizeable bathing pond. The arrival of an elephant at the Zoo was widely welcomed, and as one London journalist wrote: "In the Jardin des Plantes at Paris the elephant has long enjoyed advantages proportionate to his importance in the scale of creation. This example has been rightly followed in our Zoological Gardens."

The Asian elephant, named Jack, soon became the star of the Zoo, bringing in thousands of new visitors. A few months later he was joined by a younger elephant, a present from the Governor of Ceylon, and from now on the Zoological Society strove to ensure that it had at least two elephants in residence.

People delighted at the elephants' tricks, such as spraying water from their trunks, and took even greater pleasure in sticking their hands through the railings to feed them with cakes and buns. Sadly, some abused this privilege by inserting pins and other foreign objects into the buns, which greatly upset, but fortunately rarely injured, Jack and his cohorts. To put a stop to the problem, one lucky woman was given the exclusive right to sell elephant buns outside the compound, and it was said that on a good day she would make as much as 36 shillings. (£120 today).

Over the years the Zoological Society bought and sold several elephants but it never dared to get rid of Jack, who was the public's favourite of all the Zoo's animals and much loved for his comic antics. "I gazed on the greatest brute under Heaven," wrote one visitor. "His begging trunk before him conveyed every article within his reach into his mouth, regardless from whom it came. He yelled most hideously when refused contribution; he plunged into the unrippled bed of waters within his confines and raised a mimic storm there. He threw a mass of mud and dirt around him (much of which attached itself to his own back) and he quailed with evident terror when the lash was applied to his own shoulders."

What Jack particularly enjoyed was to torment his neighbour, an Indian rhinoceros, by pressing him to the ground with his tusks. Unfortunately, this led to the rhino's death when, as a result of a particularly vigorous pressing, one of its ribs fractured and pierced the animal's lung. The playful, albeit lethal, Jack is credited by some with securing the early financial success of London Zoo; he was certainly an ambassador for the Zoo and generated much publicity.

For over 15 years Jack was the Zoo's prize attraction, but in 1847 he began to show signs of age, and early on the morning of 6 June he sank slowly to the ground and lay with his legs stretched out, his trunk resting on one of his front legs. At exactly 7 a.m. Jack's trunk relaxed and his head sank to the ground – the great elephant was dead. "The doors were all closed," wrote one witness, "and the morning sun, which could struggle but dimly through a high window, rested gloomily on the dark, mighty form, which had lost none of its dignity in death."

The most famous resident of the Zoological Gardens might have died, but the British public's passion for elephants did not subside and a female given by King William IV in 1836 absorbed some of the affection that had hitherto been lavished on Jack, until she died of shock after a violent thunderstorm in July 1855. Over the years various species of animal had come into fashion, and for a while a new exhibit could always be relied upon to pull in the crowds, but the popularity of elephants was constant. To Victorian tourists a trip to Regent's Park without seeing the elephants was like visiting the Tower of London without seeing the Crown Jewels.

Although popular, the mother and daughter that followed Jack lacked the impressive dimensions of the deceased star, who had been not only the largest elephant in Europe but also a magnificent "tusker", the possessor of a full set of tusks. This deficiency was even more apparent when comparisons were made with the pair of magnificent Asian elephants then at the Jardin des Plantes, both bigger than their counterparts in London.

Obtaining large elephants was a tricky and expensive process but in the late 1850s the Zoological Society decided that its priority was to obtain a living African elephant as these were larger and more impressive than the Asian species. Size apart, the novelty of such a rare animal would be a crowd pleaser, but how should the Zoo go about acquiring one? In the absence of any other ideas, the Society's Council decided to contact the most famous African explorer of the day. "The Secretary be directed to write to Dr Livingstone," record its minutes in February 1858, "and authorise him to offer £150 on the part of the Society for the first elephant, and £150 for the first rhinoceros, brought down fit for shipment at Quillimane [in Mozambique], and £100 for the second animal of each species, provided it be of the opposite sex."

At this time David Livingstone, having just embarked on a long expedition starting at the Zambezi River, had more pressing matters on his mind. The trip was beset with problems and the explorer did not have the time to capture and transport elephants, even at £150 (about £10,000 today) each. The Society's offer was declined and its members, unsure where else to look, put on hold their plan to obtain an elephant. They resolved to wait for an enterprising animal trader to import one into Europe, at which point they would seek to buy it, no matter what the cost. But the Society and the Zoo's managers did not reckon on their rivals at the Jardin des Plantes, who also wanted an African elephant and were prepared to go to almost any lengths to get one.

∽ Crossing the Desert ∽

By late February 1862 Taher Sheriff was facing the challenge of taking his collection of animals along the network of dry river beds that led to the town of Kassala. Jumbo had been with their captors for less than a month but he and the other elephant calf were already accustomed to their new life. Elephants are highly social animals who reassure one other constantly with physical attention. The calves are especially needy and will seek some such comfort from their mother every few minutes. So the sudden absence of a mother is a highly traumatic experience for a calf and in the wild its suffering may be alleviated by another cow elephant acting as a surrogate. This remedy was not available for Jumbo, but his instincts would have told him to transfer his affection to a mother figure – in this case the man who brought them food, water and milk. This transference of affection was observed elsewhere with some amusement by one Nubian collector, who wrote: "After their arrival in the camp, the young elephants quickly became accustomed to their black keeper and would follow him about like dogs."

The majority of the animals taken by the Aggageers were juvenile specimens and, like Jumbo, were easy to coerce. This was just as well given that the plan was to form the giraffes, antelopes, ostriches and other animals into a large train and lead them through the desert. The hunters achieved this by loosely tethering the larger creatures to their camels or horses, while the smaller, less mobile ones, such as porcupines and birds of prey, were bagged and/or tied to the backs of the camels.

It was the largest captives, the two elephants and the two rhinoceroses, that were the cause of most concern. Although young and already semi-tamed, they were still powerful and quite capable of inflicting damage on people, horses or one another. Capturing and transporting these animals alive was not something that the Aggageers were accustomed to, and there was no established practice for their safe transportation. Taher Sheriff's solution was bold but simple. Instead of tethering the elephants and rhinos, he turned them loose, allowing them to walk freely alongside the cavalcade of camels, horses, giraffes and other animals. It worked, and the procession of tethered animals with elephants and rhinos trotting free alongside must have been quite a sight as it wound its way back along the beds of the Royan and Setite to Kassala. Progress would have been painfully slow but the skill of the Aggageers delivered the majority of the beasts to their destination alive.

Taher Sheriff must have been delighted to offload his troublesome living cargo on Johan Schmidt, especially as it meant he and his men would be paid. The trip must have been profitable to the Aggageers, not least because the additional ivory they had collected was sold separately from the living specimens delivered to Schmidt.

Although Taher Sheriff's role in Jumbo's life was over, his success in securing so many animals ensured that in subsequent years other animal traders came in search of local Aggageers, creating a new and lucrative industry in one of the remotest parts of the world. Later in the century, however, the arrival of European game hunters, soldiers and an assortment of revolutionaries would reduce the rich wildlife of the Sudanese–Abyssinian borderlands to a fraction of its former glory. Many of the larger species were hunted to the point of extinction, including the elephants, which had once travelled in herds of 50–100 but had all but disappeared by the end of the Second World War. In 2001 a small group of elephants was spotted in the region where Taher Sheriff and his men used to hunt; they were the first herd to be seen in the area for over 40 years and their return is seen as a sign that after decades of war the local wildlife is starting to recover.

Back in 1862 Johan Schmidt found himself in charge of the largest collection of African wildlife ever seen on Earth. He was, nevertheless, only the middleman in this venture; his boss was an Italian named Lorenzo Casanova, an "enterprising traveller" who had gambled his entire fortune on the Sudanese expedition. Casanova's origins are obscure but it is known that during the 1850s he operated a "dog and monkey show" in St Petersburg which burned to the ground in 1859, forcing him to find an alternative income. In 1858 the African explorer Dr Josef Natterer had returned from eastern Sudan with a small consignment of wild animals which he sold at a considerable profit. Inspired by this, Casanova decided to risk an all-or-nothing animal-collecting venture to Kassala, employing Schmidt as his agent in the town, although the Italian himself would be in charge of transporting the animals from Kassala back to Europe.

Before travelling to Kassala, Casanova studied Natterer's methods and route. One of the remotest towns in colonial Africa, Kassala was in Egyptian-occupied territory on the eastern fringe of the Sahara Desert. The next sizeable town was over 30 miles away and the closest port, Suakin, was on the Red Sea coast over 300 miles to the north-east. This was the only place from which the animals could be exported to Europe, but the only route between Kassala and Suakin was a dirt track that was constantly in a state of disrepair. Furthermore, over 200 miles of this track ran through hot desert in which there were only two small settlements. Never before had such a large consignment of wildlife been moved so far and across such a harsh landscape, so it was appropriate that Casanova arrived in Kassala well equipped.

The Italian traveller brought with him perhaps as many as 100 camels, a quantity of rope and dozens of iron bars. These bars were to be fashioned into sturdy cages for some of the smaller animals, including the birds of prey. The cages could then be secured to the camels, while the larger animals, such as the elephants, rhinos, giraffes, antelopes and ostriches, would make the journey on foot.

Following Taher Sheriff's method of bringing the animals to Kassala, Casanova allowed the rhinos and Jumbo and the other elephant calf to walk untethered, while the more flighty animals, such as the antelopes and giraffes, were loosely tied behind the camels. In this fashion his gigantic caravan made slow but steady progress across the burning desert towards the Red Sea coast.

Such a large operation called for a substantial retinue of staff. An identical expedition mounted two years later would require 300 men to accompany the camels and wild animals. And this was by no means the only logistical issue: sufficient quantities of hay, bread and vegetables had to be transported for both men and animals, and around 100 goats were purchased to provide milk for the unweaned large mammals. These also served as a supply of meat for the carnivores and men. But, even with all these precautions, there was no guarantee that all (or indeed any) of the animals would survive the hazardous journey to Europe.

In late March 1862 Casanova paid off Schmidt and urged his travelling menagerie northwards into the sandy plains of the Sahara. There was no question of either beasts or men travelling in the heat of the day and so the entire operation was nocturnal, the caravan moving off into the desert as the sun started to set and then, several hours later, coming to a halt as the first rays of light appeared over the eastern horizon. Progress was excruciatingly slow and Casanova considered himself lucky if they covered more than about eight miles a day, although bad weather and illness must sometimes have made the daily distance considerably less than this.

The journey from Kassala to Suakin would typically take a man on horseback 16 days. Casanova and his men took six weeks to cross the desert, but by not forcing the pace they achieved reasonable success in that very few of the animals succumbed. Jumbo survived the ordeal, but his fellow calf did not; unable to contend with the stress and heat of the journey, he was left to die in the desert. The loss was a financial blow for Casanova as it left him with just a single elephant, and a scrawny and unhealthy-looking one at that.

While there was surely some relief to have got Jumbo as far as Suakin, the desert march had been the easiest and least risky part of the entire voyage to Europe. Of more concern was the 800-mile journey by boat from Suakin up the Red Sea to the Egyptian port of Suez. It was expected that this voyage would produce a greater number of fatalities, especially among the larger animals, which would be more susceptible to the stifling heat of the cargo hold.

Suakin was Sudan's principal port and a few years earlier had been the scene of fierce fighting between the invading Egyptian forces and the Sudanese Arabs, who, using only swords and lances, kept the enemy at bay for weeks. The port was notably picturesque, constructed mainly from blocks of coral covered in a façade of mud. Along the quayside were large warehouses that held all manner of goods, such as gum arabic, ivory, senna and animal hides, all waiting to be shipped to Europe. Despite its importance to the Sudanese economy, Suakin was poorly served by cargo boats, with the only regular service being operated by the Abdul Azziz Company, whose steamers were supposed to stop there while travelling from Suez to Jeddah. In practice, they often failed to call in, enraging local traders, diplomats and travellers because the cost of both accommodation and warehousing in the town was high.

How long Casanova and his party had to wait before boarding a northbound coastal steamer to Suez is not known, but when a suitable ship did arrive they must have coaxed and dragged the animals on board with a sense of trepidation. The voyage from Suakin to Suez took less than a week but, trapped below decks in one of the hottest regions of the world, the animals faced a great risk of death through exhaustion, thirst or overheating. Exact details of Casanova's losses are not known, but when making the same voyage six years later he reported the loss of "many animals during this voyage by the heat"; his stock of elephants, for example, was reduced by half from 32 to 16. It is fairly certain that the 1862 journey was just as costly as he arrived in Suez with neither of the young rhinos, both of which must have died at sea. Jumbo, however, was not among the casualties and the lone elephant calf was able to disembark at Suez with the rest of the surviving wildlife. The animals were temporarily housed in the courtyard of a local hotel while Casanova made arrangements to have them transported by train 200 miles north to the Mediterranean port of Alexandria.

The renowned German animal dealer Carl Hagenbeck witnessed one of the Italian's subsequent stop-overs in Suez and was amazed. "I was scarcely prepared for what met our gaze when we reached the Suez Hotel," he wrote. "I shall never forget the sight which the courtyard presented. Elephants, giraffes, antelopes and buffaloes were tethered to the palms; sixteen great ostriches were strolling about loose; and in addition there were no fewer than sixty cages containing a rhinoceros, lions, panthers, cheetahs, hyaenas, jackals, civets, caracals, monkeys and many kinds of birds."

The train journey to Alexandria on that occasion was no less exciting: "On the way to the station the ostriches escaped and were only recovered after considerable delay. One of the railway trucks caught fire, endangering the entire menagerie; and finally we were furnished for the last part of the journey with a drunken driver who nearly burst his boiler. Moreover, the poor creatures were so closely packed together that it was impossible to feed them."

Fortunately for Jumbo, the train travelled overnight and not during the heat of the day; it arrived in Alexandria at 6 a.m. and, after a day's recovery, the animals were loaded on to a cargo boat with a crane. The sight of "long-legged giraffes" and "cumbersome elephants" suspended in a sling over the sea gave Casanova palpitations, but the operation was accomplished quickly and safely.

The boat travelled directly from Suez to Trieste in Italy, from where the animals would be transported once more by train to their ultimate destination in Germany. Casanova's menagerie was by far the largest consignment of animals to have been taken from the Dark Continent and by some miracle included the diminutive Jumbo, the first living African elephant to set foot on European soil for almost 2,000 years. All this brought great delight to those who witnessed the collection *en route*.

"Pretty nearly the whole population of Trieste must have turned out to watch us unload," wrote Hagenbeck of a later expedition. "And whenever an elephant or a giraffe came sprawling across in the crane a roar of delight would go up from the multitude on shore. It was truly marvellous that we ever reached the railway station without an accident, for the crowd in the streets was enormous, and we had the greatest possible difficulty in making our way through."

Passing via Vienna, the train carried the animals to Casanova's headquarters in Dresden, where he planned to house his exotic livestock while seeking out a buyer. That he should have entered into such a risky venture without first finding a market for the animals is somewhat surprising, especially given his dire financial predicament. Casanova's need for cash was such that he did not have time to break up the collection and sell the animals individually, which would have been more profitable. Carl Hagenbeck complained to Casanova that the consignment was so large that

"My name is Schmidt. I am travelling for the firm of Hagenbeck. Permit me to show you my samples."

The trade in foreign animals was a lucrative business.

he "could not afford to buy his collection", although he was interested in individual animals, including Jumbo; but the Italian was offering them as a job lot.

With creditors knocking on the door, Casanova sold his animals to Gottlieb Kreutzberg, a middle-aged and very over-weight Prussian who travelled about the countryside exhibiting a large collection of wild and domestic animals. Kreutzberg's travelling menagerie was part circus, part roving pet shop; for a fee the public could view the animals, the central attraction being the sight of lions, panthers and other carnivores being fed. This element of the business was somewhat theatrical, with the lions occasionally paraded about an enclosure in a horse-drawn cart. (The practice once prompted a lion to attack and eat one of the horses.) However, by contrast with other travelling circuses, all the animals on display were for sale. While most people could not afford to buy a lion, giraffe or elephant, they could acquire the parrots, cats, dogs and other domestic pets of which Kreutzberg kept an ample stock.

"The Grand Menagerie", as he called it, would move from town to town, staying for a few days before moving on. For those who were unable to visit more established zoological gardens, attractions such as this provided a glimpse into the world of foreign animals; one visitor commented that Kreutzberg had "about as many animals as one may see in a London furrier's shop".

That such an unusual enterprise should have been the first institution to receive Europe's first and only African elephant up to that date is remarkable, but Jumbo did not remain with Kreutzberg for long. With African wildlife in such great demand, soon the Grand Menagerie was disposing of its new stock to zoos across Europe. The price tag placed on Jumbo remains unknown but it must have been considerable because he ended up being bought by the Jardin des Plantes, which, as well as being the largest of Europe's zoological gardens, was also the one with the biggest budget.

It appears that the managers at the Jardin were able to cherry-pick from Kreutzberg's new acquisitions, with the unique African elephant calf probably being one of the first animals chosen. Their purchase of Jumbo was motivated not just by the wish to fill a gap in their collection; it was also a political move designed to frustrate a rival. Aware that the Zoological Society of London had been making an effort to get hold of an African elephant for its Regent's Park collection, the Jardin des Plantes concluded the deal before word of the elephant's existence could cross the Channel and spark a bidding war.

When news of Jumbo's sale finally reached London, it did not go down at all well. "The elephant was purchased before the Zoological Society had a chance to negotiate," complained Abraham Bartlett, the Superintendent of London Zoo. He had special cause to complain about the loss of Jumbo because it was on his orders that the Zoological Society had been seeking to buy an African elephant. And the missed opportunity was all the more frustrating for Bartlett as there seemed to be no immediate prospect of another African elephant coming his way. He decided instead to keep an eye on the young calf in Paris, just in case there should be another chance to buy him. Eventually Bartlett's patience paid off and he became one of the most important and controversial figures in Jumbo's life.

CHAPTER 4

ᨆ The Superintendent ᨆ

Abraham Bartlett was a resourceful, wily and determined man who could stand his ground against all comers, human or animal. He was appointed Superintendent of the Regent's Park Zoological Gardens in August 1859 and soon revealed himself to be an effective manager but also someone who was not afraid to get his hands dirty. Bartlett's exploits at the Zoo, such as wrestling an endangered baby hippo from its mother and taking two tethered rhinos for a walk, soon made him famous with the public. His habit of always wearing a top hat and tails made him easy to spot and his acute observations on the Zoo's animals found their way into dozens of newspaper articles and scientific papers. This achievement was all the more remarkable as Bartlett held no qualifications in zoology and had received no formal scientific training. Despite this, his knowledge of animal anatomy and behaviour far surpassed that of many experts.

Bartlett's love of the natural world began when he was eight years old and his father took him to see Chunee the elephant at the Exeter 'Change in the Strand. The boy watched in amazement as the elephant used his trunk to feed itself cakes and buns and then deftly take pennies offered to it by members of the public. As luck would have it, Bartlett's father worked only a few doors away from the Exeter 'Change and was friends with its owner, Edward Cross. In consequence the young Abraham was a regular visitor to the menagerie and came to know intimately its kangaroos, ostriches, emus and eagles. But it was Chunee that had captured his heart. Chunee was a large Asian bull elephant who had been imported into England to act as a living prop in theatrical productions but his stage career soon ended and he was bought by Cross. Since 1817 Chunee had been the centrepiece of

Cross's menagerie, where he occupied a large wooden cage on the first floor; his docility and playfulness were legendary and inspired the young Bartlett to learn everything he could about the behaviour of elephants.

On 26 February 1826 Bartlett was to witness an event that would change his attitude towards wildlife in general and elephants in particular. For some weeks Chunee had been restless and ill-tempered until, on that particular Sunday, he refused to obey any instructions at all. The exasperated keeper became angry and struck Chunee on the trunk with a wooden cane; the elephant immediately retaliated, striking the keeper on the head with his trunk and knocking him semi-conscious to the floor. Chunee moved forward as if to stamp on the prostate keeper but was prevented from doing so by Cross, who used a shovel to keep the elephant at bay until the injured man could be dragged clear. Chunee's mood worsened and he became so violent that Cross feared he would break the doors of his wooden cage and, in a bid to escape, would come crashing through the rickety floor into the shops beneath the menagerie. So with some reluctance he concluded that Chunee, his star attraction for over a decade, would have to be put down. "I could imagine that no person contemplating murder could endure as great an agony," he remarked of his decision.

A first attempt involved administering a huge dose of poison to Chunee; enough, according to one observer, to kill 60 men. It had no effect and served only to persuade him to charge and barge about his cage, splintering the walls and bars in an alarming manner. Cross knew that the maddened elephant would have to be shot but feared that the resources of a small army would be needed to accomplish the task. On 1 March he sent word on to the street that many guns were needed at the Exeter 'Change. In response a contingent of soldiers arrived and levelled their rifles at Chunee, firing round after round into the panic-stricken animal. Although injured, Chunee remained alive and upright enough to make continual charges at the cage, further weakening it. By this time Chunee's ordeal with the military had lasted nearly an hour, and he had absorbed around 120 shots and several sword thrusts. Wounded and exhausted, he momentarily became calm and allowed Cross to approach. The menagerie owner ordered the elephant to kneel down, which he meekly did, and a rifleman was bought forward.

"He directed his weapon constantly at one ear," recalled one witness. "One of his shots took such good effect that the elephant suddenly rushed round from the blow and made his last furious attempt at the gates. By this last effort he again dislodged them and they were kept upright by the chain and ropes. From this time the firing was directed at his gullet and at last he fell, but with so much deliberation and in a position so natural to his usual habits that he seemed to have lain down to rest himself. Four or five discharges from a rifle into his ear produced no effect. It was evident that he was without sense and had dropped dead into the posture wherein he always lay when alive."

The drawn-out, undignified and brutal manner of Chunee's death led to a minor outcry in the newspapers, in part because members of the public had been allowed into the menagerie to witness the proceedings. One of these was the 14-year-old Abraham Bartlett, who saw Chunee's destruction at close hand and watched it with both fascination and revulsion.

The memory of Chunee's death remained with Bartlett to the end of his life and instilled in him an awareness of the dangers that came with keeping wild animals captive. From that day he

Chunee meets a terrible end.

saw himself as being entirely separate from the creatures of the natural world. He did not seek to sentimentalize animals and would rarely refer to them by their pet names (Jumbo was always called "the male African elephant") or view them as being in any way endowed with human sentiments. Most of all he learned that when one is in charge of wild animals it is sometimes necessary to take tough decisions. As a result, throughout his career he did not flinch when ordering that an animal be put down and would not hesitate to get rid of a member of staff who, for whatever reason, was judged to be underperforming.

Ironically, the occasion of Chunee's death was to be one of Bartlett's last visits to Cross's menagerie as shortly afterwards he was apprenticed to his father's hairdressing shop. "It was a business I most heartily detested," he recalled in his memoirs, "although I used to amuse myself by preserving birds, etc., in my own private room in the house."

These specimens came from Cross, who provided dead birds for the boy to experiment on, so that by degrees and with no formal training Bartlett taught himself how to preserve and stuff wild animals. It was a hobby that continued throughout his time as an apprentice barber, but when, aged 22, Bartlett could no longer stand cutting hair he quit the family business and set himself up as a taxidermist. He had made a good career choice as London was home to many private collections of animals, zoological parks, menageries and museums, all of which occasionally required the skills of a competent taxidermist.

In 1846 Bartlett moved his business to Camden Town in order to foster closer contacts with staff at the Zoological Gardens, just a stone's throw away in Regent's Park. His first big opportunity came a year later, when the celebrated Asian elephant Jack died, as it was he whom the Zoo called in to skin and prepare the body.

Jack was the first large animal that Bartlett had ever been asked to preserve and mount. This was nerve-racking enough but he was also obliged to work under the watchful eye of several professional zoologists, including Professor Richard Owen, the most celebrated (and cantankerous) animal anatomist of his era. Jack was so cumbersome that his body had to be hoisted up to allow Bartlett access to the belly, but the lifting tackle gave way and sent several tons of dead elephant crashing to the ground. Bartlett was underneath Jack at the time and it was only providence that allowed him to emerge alive. Professor Owen was less fortunate: lacerations he sustained while helping with the dissection became infected and left him so ill that for a time it was thought that he would not survive.

Despite these ordeals, the mounting of Jack was a success, ensuring that Bartlett's services would be called upon whenever a large animal died at Regent's Park. It was in this way that he became closely acquainted with the management of the Zoological Society and, in time, was invited to make his own suggestions about how best to run certain aspects of the Gardens. It was, for example, Bartlett who suggested charging the public just 6d. (rather than 1s.) to see the animals on a Monday, normally a poor day for takings. This initiative was so successful that some later credited it with having secured the Zoo's long-term financial security.

Meanwhile Bartlett's career as a taxidermist continued to flourish. A particularly significant event occurred during the Great Exhibition of 1851, when his reconstruction of the long-extinct dodo won him a prize medal and the position of Naturalist to the Crystal Palace Company, the event's organizers. This proved to be a somewhat tedious job as many of the animals that he was required to mount were afterwards displayed in damp conditions that brought about their rapid decay. One senses that Bartlett had begun to tire of the taxidermy business when, in 1859, the Superintendent of the Zoological Gardens died unexpectedly. The names of several potential replacements were suggested to the Zoological Society; one of these came from a journalist at *The Times* who believed that the ideal man was Abraham Bartlett. Although he lacked any formal scientific training, Bartlett's knowledge of the natural world was encyclopedic and his ability to work with animals, alive and dead, legendary. But it was his proven talent as a manager and businessman that swung the odds in his favour. In August 1859 Bartlett and his family made the short move from Camden Town to the Superintendent's official residence in Regent's Park. The Zoological Society had made an excellent choice: Bartlett's tenure was to be the start of a golden age in the history of London Zoo.

For Bartlett one of the greatest pleasures of being Superintendent was that it brought him close to the Zoo's two elephants, Jenny and her daughter Butcher. "My fondness for elephants led me to study them and pay particular attention to their habits and treatment in captivity," he wrote, but he (and the majority of his fellow zoologists) had only ever seen the semi-domesticated Asian variety and never the wilder, supposedly more spectacular, African.

In reading explorers' descriptions of elephants Bartlett became convinced that there were substantial physiological and behavioural differences between the African and Asian species. It was the desire to see these differences for himself that gave him a compelling reason to have examples of both at Regent's Park. Bartlett had been prepared to go to some lengths to obtain an African elephant, which is why, in late 1862, he was so disappointed to learn that his rivals at the Jardin des Plantes had managed to buy the first one to reach Europe alive. The Zoological Society of London was financially well endowed and so would almost certainly have been able to beat any offer made by the French, but in 1862 it had no formal contacts with European animal traders such as Hagenbeck, Casanova and Kreutzberg and remained unaware of Jumbo's existence until it was too late.

Bartlett must have hoped that if one elephant could make it alive from Africa, then others would soon follow. His wait was in vain; it would be several years before another African elephant became available to buy. In the meantime the Jardin des Plantes could, if it wanted, boast that it was in possession of an animal that could be seen nowhere else in Europe. In fact it did not make much of a fuss about Jumbo at all and simply put him in its Elephant House without ceremony.

"The French authorities seem to have been wholly unaware of the value of their treasure," commented the naturalist Theo Johnson, who, like Bartlett, had long desired to see an African elephant in London Zoo. After an absence of nearly two millennia, the arrival of a live specimen in Europe had turned out to be something of a damp squib. Nonetheless, and after months of travelling, in the autumn of 1862 the young African elephant was given a permanent home in the manicured surroundings of Paris's famous botanical gardens.

PART TWO

EUROPE

CHAPTER 5

∽ Paris ∾

Jumbo's first settled home in Europe was an institution with a considerable pedigree, but by the time of his arrival it had become a victim of its own success. Cracks had begun to show in its day-to-day management: a situation that did not bode well for those animals which were not regarded as money-spinners, and this included Jumbo.

The Jardin des Plantes holds one of Europe's oldest public menageries. It was founded in 1626 as a medicinal herbarium for King Louis XIII but by 1640 the gardens were open to the visiting public. Over the coming century the site, which covered a space of some 280,000 square metres on the left bank of the River Seine in Paris, had been expanded to include a maze, library, hothouses and several museums, all of which concerned themselves with the study of plants. Soon after the French Revolution, the Jardin des Plantes experienced a change of direction when, in 1792, the Royal Menagerie was moved there from the palace of Versailles. From then on the Jardin was known as much for its animal life as for its magnificent collection of living plants and dried seeds and flowers.

During the nineteenth century the Jardin underwent protracted improvement which made it into Europe's largest zoological gardens but, more importantly, also the world's leading university of natural history. Many famous professors, most notably Georges-Louis Leclerc, Jean-Baptiste Lamarck and Georges Cuvier, studied in the Muséum National d'Histoire Naturelle, sited in the grounds of the Jardin, where they performed the work that would later underpin various biological sciences, including zoology, botany and palaeontology.

By the early 1860s the Jardin was in danger of overreaching itself. As well as its botanical gardens and menagerie, the site

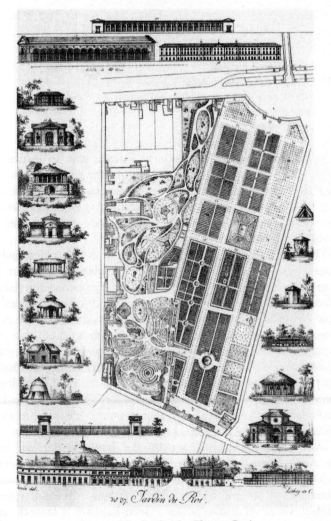

A map of the Jardin des Plantes, Paris.

contained museums and living exhibitions covering all aspects of botany, zoology and geology, both national and international. The scale of the operation as a whole was explained in a British guidebook to Paris of the day:

43

"Entering by the gate, the visitor sees on his left hand the building containing stuffed zoological specimens to the number of 200,000. On the left is the library and the museums of geology, mineralogy and botany. In front are numerous beds of foreign and indigenous plants. Further on, towards the left, are the large hot-houses... Still more to the left is the anatomical gallery. Not far from this is the entrance to the zoological collections. The birds and reptiles are to the left, the bears to the right and straight in front appear in succession the large rotunda with the hippopotami, elephants and camels, the monkey-house, and the cages of the lions, tigers, etc."

The young Jumbo was probably introduced into the already overcrowded menagerie in late 1862 or early 1863, but if the French were proud of their new acquisition they did not go out of their way to show it. The Jardin des Plantes had a tradition of publicizing the arrival of new animals, especially novel ones such as elephants, by placing advertisements or articles in newspapers exhorting the public to come and view the latest acquisitions. But, in contrast with the usual fuss, the arrival of Jumbo passed entirely without comment, which perhaps substantiates a later rumour that his Parisian owners were less than impressed with their new exhibit.

When he arrived in Paris Jumbo was just over four feet tall, about the same height as an eight-year-old child. Rumour had it that the managers had purchased him from Kreutzberg's Grand Menagerie sight unseen and had been led to expect an animal that was much larger and more impressive. This expectation certainly would have matched the perceived view of the greater size, strength and aggression of the African elephant compared with the Asian variety. If Samuel Baker's description is accurate, Jumbo would have looked anything but impressive; he was a malnourished "runt" and would have been dwarfed by the Jardin's two adult Asians, which were around 10 feet tall. In comparison Jumbo would have looked ridiculous; he was dwarfed by even the Jardin's carthorses. Thus, rather than make a big fuss over his arrival, the managers left the young African elephant to his own devices in the hope that he would rapidly gain height.

Jumbo was placed in the Rotunda for Large Herbivores, located in the central part of the gardens and already home to the two Asian elephants, several camels and giraffes and at least one hippo. The Rotunda was a tall, octagonal building which provided shelter for the animals at night and during bad weather; surrounding the animals' stables was a wide, circular fence of iron railings through which the public could gaze at the animals and even feed them. Within this stood a series of walls and fences which provided internal partitions and so prevented the different species of animal from meeting one another and fighting.

Within the Rotunda the elephants had been given by far the largest area, their exercise yard taking up a full 120 degrees of the circular enclosure. Next came the giraffes, who had an arc of around 100 degrees, while the hippos and camels had to make do with the remainder. At times overcrowding in the menagerie meant that the existing herbivores had to share their compound with alien species. For example, when the medical student Augustus Gardner visited the Jardin the elephants were in the same compound as the tapirs. "In the Rotunda," he wrote, "are confined a great many kinds of the more bulky animals, among which the lofty giraffe, and the ponderous elephant, are the most conspicuous. Both of these are extremely tame and receive liberal donations of bread with which the visitants are generally well supplied. In the company of the largest elephant are two tapirs who share with her the muddy pond in the centre of the ground."

Despite these arrangements, by 1863 conditions in the Rotunda were far from idyllic. The building had been erected half a century earlier for a much smaller number of large mammals, including the lone Asian elephant that was then held by the Jardin des Plantes. Given the difficulty of obtaining large zoological specimens, especially mammalian ones, it was thought that the Rotunda would never be short of space but the designers did not reckon on the manic livestock-buying spree embarked on by the Jardin's managers in the 1850s and 1860s. As a result, Jumbo spent his first months in Paris living in cramped conditions with the Asian elephants, sharing the same open stable area and food. His plight was made even more uncomfortable when, in October 1863, the Jardin took delivery of two more elephant calves, along with several camels, which had been sold to them by the Viceroy of Egypt for £800 (£53,000 today).

The new elephant calves were also African and, after Jumbo, were the second and third specimens of *Loxodonta africana* to reach Europe. By purchasing them, the Jardin des Plantes had retained a monopoly over this animal. The newcomers were a male and female pair and younger than Jumbo at perhaps not even a year old. They were named Castor and Pollux by the Jardin's managers and, like Jumbo, were deposited in the already overcrowded Rotunda with little ceremony. As a solitary juvenile elephant Jumbo had received little attention from the visiting public and was something of a sedentary animal who spent much of his time cowering in the stables and did not seek human affection. The same could not be said of Castor and Pollux, who soon revealed themselves to be energetic and frolicsome, to the delight of the staff and visiting public.

"The elephants are not taller than young asses," wrote a correspondent to *The Times*, "but they are as lively and playful as kittens. They gallop and strike each other with their trunks and when tired they lie down one beside the other."

Castor and Pollux were especially popular with children and became known as "the pets of young Paris" and, to the surprise of the Jardin's authorities, they began to draw in large crowds. What little limelight Jumbo had enjoyed had been stolen by his younger companions, leaving him alone and neglected in the increasingly unsanitary conditions of the Rotunda.

Endearing as the two new arrivals were, the Jardin found itself housing five elephants in a compound originally designed for just one. This was possible only because the three African elephants were juveniles; if, as was hoped, they started to undergo a growth spurt, conditions inside the Rotunda would degenerate from poor to intolerable. Nor was the problem of overcrowding specific to the elephants: across the entire Jardin animals and exhibits were being squeezed into every available nook and cranny. The managers were having difficulty coping with the expense and practicality of housing and maintaining its existing exhibits, both living and dead, and yet the acquisition policy continued apace. Conditions at the Jardin had long since reached breaking point when, in late 1864, a large collection of oxen, monkeys, tortoises, birds and stags was purchased from animal traders in Laos and Cambodia.

For decades the Jardin des Plantes had been handsomely subsidized by the taxpayer and in 1864 it was funded to the tune of some £240,000 (about £16 million today). However, the reckless expansion of the collections was leading to concerns over the quality of their management, with the result that the French government had made it clear that the directors ought to take better care of the existing specimens before setting out to acquire new ones. The revelation that there were dozens of new zoological specimens on their way from the Far East was the final straw. In the opinion of the Minister of Public Instruction this was an acquisition too far and in early 1865 he announced that there would be an official investigation into the state of the Jardin's museums and menagerie.

The inquiry was conducted during the early months of 1865 by several government commissioners, who made a nuisance of themselves by examining every glass case, cupboard, flowerbed and cage. Their report was submitted to the government in April 1865 and made public a few days later. It did not make for comfortable reading.

During 1863, it revealed, the Jardin had spent a massive £100,000 (£6.7 million today) on acquiring and tending to new stock, a figure that was topped only by its wages bill. Yet this expenditure was of secondary concern in comparison with the commissioners' verdict on the museums, which were so full that the curators were forced "to exhibit many specimens in highly inconvenient places". As an example, the report describes how "the collection of crustacea is situated between that of the reptiles and that of monkeys after which comes the rest of the collection of zoophytes and, while the whole collection of birds is on the upper storey, that of their nests is on the first floor, etc." This approach to exhibiting animal groups appeared unscientific, illogical and out of place, especially in a country that had pioneered the study of animal and plant taxonomy and evolutionary progression.

The situation in the hothouses and gardens, which held over 10,000 individual plants and 61,000 bags of seed, was no better; nor was the state of the living exhibits any less chaotic. The commissioners discovered that every shed and stable was overcrowded with animals in want of space, light, food, water, decent bedding and, in some cases, basic medical treatment. They were not, however, so much concerned that overcrowding was creating inadvertent cruelty in the menagerie as that it was costing the government a fortune to maintain so many animals in such a small area.

In this respect the Rotunda and its elephant enclosure were singled out for particular attention, the commissioners reporting: "We consider the maintenance of five elephants in the establishment as a useless expense which, however, for the present is unavoidable." They went on to advise the Jardin's administrators that they should endeavour "to effect an exchange of some of the elephants with some foreign menagerie".

The institution had developed a culture of expanding its collections, not shrinking them, and so was not keen on being told that it should lose some of its larger, more spectacular animals. The Minister of Public Instruction's report was ignored by the Jardin's managers but its contents were given wide coverage by the Parisian newspapers and it did not take long for word to reach the wider world. Soon there were others in foreign places who were taking note of the French government's criticisms and in particular its recommendation that the Jardin's elephant population be reduced. One person in particular believed he could use his French rival's uncomfortable situation to his advantage.

In London Abraham Bartlett, the Superintendent of the Regent's Park Zoo, was still in search of an African elephant for his collection and had taken the precaution of tracking down Jumbo's original owner, Lorenzo Casanova. Bartlett learned that the Italian was returning to Sudan for more specimens but that these would be the sole property of his financial sponsor, the German animal trader Carl Hagenbeck. Over the previous few years Hagenbeck's Hamburg-based business had expanded considerably and this had led him to look for further business opportunities abroad. In 1864 he made a trip to England during which he met Bartlett, and, finding that they had much in common, especially a genuine love of wild animals, they struck up a friendship. The relationship proved to be useful to both men: Hagenbeck had the rights to Casanova's animals while Bartlett had access to the Zoological Society's Purchase of Animals Committee, which had the final say on the acquisition of new stock.

It was Bartlett's hope that Casanova would return with further African elephants and that by the end of 1865 he would, at last, have his prize exhibit. While he waited Bartlett managed to score some other major successes, most notably an expedition to Calcutta in 1864 undertaken by members of the Zoological Society. This returned with a great many living animals, including three fine young Indian rhinoceroses which stood around four feet tall. With a rhino already in residence at Regent's Park, there was not room to house all these animals comfortably and so one was immediately sold to the Dublin Zoological Society. The other two were placed on show, to the public's delight, but one of them, a female, showed every sign of being bad-tempered, which was of concern to Bartlett, and to his staff, as he knew from personal experience how dangerous rhinos could be.

It was while the Superintendent was wondering what could be done with his grumpy rhino that news of the unfavourable inquiry into the Jardin des Plantes reached London. The part about its needing to shed elephants was of especial interest to Bartlett as the Jardin then held Europe's entire stock of African elephants. Word was passed up to Philip Sclater, the Secretary of the Zoological Society, who undertook exploratory negotiations with his contacts at the Jardin, and by early May 1865 he was able to report that the French had been instructed to exchange some of their elephants for other, hopefully less bulky, specimens from other zoos.

This sounded hopeful and so Sclater took the liberty of travelling to the Jardin des Plantes to meet Professor Henri Milne-Edwards, the director of the Muséum d'Histoire Naturelle. The two men discussed the possibility of an exchange and, although no deal could be struck, Sclater was able to return to London to report that he had "opened negotiations with respect to the acquisition of an African elephant from that institution which he trusted would lead to favourable results".

Two weeks later, and after much negotiation, Professor Milne-Edwards was able to confirm that the Jardin des Plantes was prepared to exchange one of its three African elephants, although he was not specific about which of them. The anonymous elephant was valued by the Parisians at £450 (£30,000 today), which was a high sum but justified by the rarity of the species in Europe. Sclater consulted with the Zoological Society's Purchase of Animals Committee, which at that time included Professors Thomas Huxley, John Gould and John Gray, three of the most eminent zoologists in the country. Perhaps on Bartlett's recommendation, the Committee decided to offer the French the recently acquired and bad-tempered Indian rhino, which was, Professor Milne-Edwards said, "a desideratum in my collection". When asked to value the animal, Bartlett assessed its worth as also £450, which was perhaps something of an overestimate. The Jardin was pleased with the offer of an Indian rhino but insisted that the London animal, of which there were other examples in Europe, was worth less than its own unique elephant. The matter was debated at length by Sclater and Milne-Edwards but in the end it was the Regent's Park authorities who gave way to the will of the French.

It was agreed by the Purchase of Animals Committee that, in exchange for an African elephant, the Zoological Society would offer not just the Indian rhino (which was still valued at £450) but several other animals as well, including two young dingoes, a black-backed jackal, a pair of wedge-tailed eagles, a possum and a kangaroo. The French seemed to be getting the better deal and yet, when the final agreement was drawn up, they chose to impose further conditions on the exchange: "In case of death of the remaining African elephants belonging to the Jardin des Plantes, the Jardin des Plantes is to have the right of repurchasing the elephant acquired by the Zoological Society of London at the price of £450."

The French had covered all eventualities, including the possibility that they might one day need to have their elephant back. The Zoological Society's desire for an African elephant was such that it did not seem to care about the unfavourable terms of the deal. On 7 June the Committee approved the agreement with the proviso that each side would pay for its own transport costs and that the exchange take place "as soon as the necessary arrangements could be made".

The British were the first to ship their animals and on 20 June the Indian rhinoceros, dingoes, birds and other exhibits were freighted across the Channel to Paris. The managers at Regent's Park had yet to be told which of the Parisian elephants they were to receive but if, by sending their part of the bargain first, they had hoped to engender a sense of goodwill in their counterparts at the Jardin des Plantes, they were to be sorely disappointed.

From the French point of view, choosing which of their three African elephants should be placed on the bargaining table had not been difficult. They certainly did not want to part with either Castor or Pollux as they were a male and female pair (and therefore capable of breeding) and also very popular with visitors. With these two out of the running, that left only Jumbo, who had languished in the Rotunda unloved and poorly cared for since his purchase from Kreutzberg over two years earlier. Jumbo had singularly failed to live up to the Jardin's expectations and, although around four years old, was not significantly taller than when he had first arrived. So it was Jumbo that was offered to the Zoological Society, which, perhaps unwisely, agreed to take the animal without having viewed him.

With the rhinoceros safely arrived in Paris, it was agreed that Jumbo would be delivered to representatives of London Zoo on 26 June 1865 at a location just outside the city. Bartlett was asked to pick a keeper who could be trusted to accompany the elephant on the journey by train and boat from Paris to London. The logical choice might have been Andrew Thompson, the Head Keeper, who was in charge of Chunee and Peter, the Zoo's two Asian elephants, but the Superintendent hesitated. He and Thompson did not get along terribly well as the keeper resented any interference from his boss, who, as a passionate observer of the species, was a frequent visitor to the Elephant House.

In fact, since learning that his zoo would be receiving a young African elephant, Bartlett had become enamoured of the idea that he would take personal charge of the animal and oversee its training and care himself. To do this he felt that would need to chose a keeper who would be subordinate to his will. As Head Keeper Andrew Thompson had had so much experience of the Asian elephants that he would have been bound to question Bartlett's methods, a consideration that led the Superintendent to give the job of caring for the new African elephant to a junior keeper. "I handed him over to Matthew Scott," he said later, "who I thought was the most likely man to attend to my instructions because he had no previous experience in the treatment and management of elephants."

So, on a cloudy morning in late June, assistant keeper Matthew Scott and a colleague from the Zoo stood at a French railway station being introduced to a young bull elephant named Jumbo, who until that point had spent the most of his short life crammed into the Rotunda at the Jardin des Plantes. On first seeing the beast Scott believed that the Zoological Society had made a terrible mistake.

"A more deplorable, diseased and rotten creature never walked God's earth," he recalled. "His condition was simply filthy. He had been in the care of Frenchmen for several years, and they either did not know how to treat the race of elephants, or culpably neglected his raising. I don't know which, but when I met him in France I thought I never saw a creature so woe-begone. The poor thing was full of disease, which had worked its way through the animal's hide, and had almost eaten out its eyes. The hoof of the feet and the tail were literally rotten, and the whole hide was so covered with sores, that the only thing I can compare it to was the condition of the man of leprosy spoken of in the Bible."

Bartlett had exchanged a consignment of healthy, well-tended zoological specimens for what was in effect damaged goods. It was evident that the French had managed to "effect that sort of fair exchange in which the advantage is all on one side" but the deal had been signed and there was no going back; like it or not, the Zoological Society was now the owner of the emaciated and debilitated Jumbo.

On seeing the state of the animal, one of Scott's colleagues suggested that they ought to give him up for "a bad job" and leave him in Paris to die, but Jumbo's new keeper would not hear of it. Scott was determined not only to return Jumbo to London but to see that he was restored to full health. Unlike his colleagues, he felt great pity at the manner in which Jumbo had been treated and an immediate desire to put right this wrong. "I undertook to be his doctor, his nurse and general servant," said Scott, and he was to be true to his word. For the next two decades he and Jumbo would rarely be apart for more than a few hours at a time.

∽ A True Vocation ∾

Behind every great celebrity there is a guiding figure who works behind the scenes, looking after the star's best interests and subtly controlling events. Sometimes this figure is a manager or agent; sometimes it is a mother, father or partner. In the case of Jumbo it was Matthew Scott, who played the part of manager, agent and father. Of all the people in Jumbo's life no one was more important than Scott, but their relationship was far from conventional and it would at times prove to be quite destructive. Scott's befriending of Jumbo was entirely true to his character but to understand this unique and complex man we must look back to his childhood, for his unorthodox methods of animal keeping were very much a reflection of his unusual upbringing.

Matthew Scott's background was humble and his origins partially feudal. His family was a member of one of the last generations of Britons to be born into the service of an aristocratic estate, a practice that was common in medieval times but much rarer by the nineteenth century. The aristocrats in question were the Stanleys, better known as the Earls of Derby, whose ancestral seat was in Lancashire, at the vast Knowsley Hall estate near Liverpool. The Stanley family were not just wealthy and well connected, they were active in many spheres of British life, including politics, charities and science.

In 1834, the year of Matthew Scott's birth, Edward Smith Stanley inherited his father's title and lands to become the 13th Earl of Derby. Before this he had been a prominent Member of Parliament and a member of the House of Lords but on receiving his inheritance the new Earl withdrew from political life and retired to Knowsley Hall. Edward Smith Stanley's real passion was not for politics (unlike his son, who would go on to become a British Prime Minister) but for natural history and wildlife.

Knowsley Hall had over 2,500 acres of parkland on which the new Earl had an ambition to create a private menagerie filled with all manner of exotic creatures from far-off lands. This was an era of exploration and discovery when every month brought ships back to Britain with holds full of strange animals, dead and alive. (For example, at the time when Smith Stanley started his collection Charles Darwin was collecting wildlife in the Galápagos Islands.) The Earl set aside over 100 acres of land for a new wildlife park and employed agents from around the world to catch and send him living specimens to populate it. Within a few years Knowsley Hall's zoological park had become one of the largest in Britain, with 2,000 animals representing 400 species of bird and mammal. Naturally these animals had to be cared for, but feeding them and cleaning their quarters quickly became a logistical nightmare, forcing the Earl to take help from wherever he could find it, even among his own servants.

Matthew Scott's family were housed on the Knowsley estate while they worked full-time for the Earl. In contrast with medieval feudalism, they were not legally bound to the estate and could move on at any time, although the cheap rent and steady employment provided by the Earl made it economically difficult to do so. Even so, there was almost no resentment of the Earl among his resident workers; instead many were grateful for the security that he provided their families. "The Earls of Derby were, and are, among the greatest statesmen of England," wrote Scott when reflecting on his childhood.

Scott's parents had been born, raised and married at Knowsley Hall, where his father was the estate's brewer and his mother a housekeeper. The last but one of 17 children (among whom there was just one daughter), Scott was not to know his father well, for, being over 20 years older than his wife, he died when the boy was aged four. Being raised by a single parent, Scott and his mother were close but he was judged by many to be wilful, naughty and sometimes rude. Often his mother despaired and described him to neighbours as a "rough, naughty lad, full of devilment".

In time Scott developed into a resourceful boy with a fondness for his own company and the outdoor life. His mother remarked that "if you take that lad and strip him naked, and put him on top of a mountain anywhere on the globe, he can get his own living; for, if there's nobody round the neighbourhood of the mountain, he will have the birds and animals feed him, like old Elijah and the raven in the wilderness, or, like John the Baptist, he will live on locusts and honey and clothe himself with the skins of animals".

With the family being supported by a widowed mother, Scott's education ended when he was aged 10 so that he could find employment. It was one of his elder brothers who, having spotted Scott's love of nature, found an opening for him in the Knowsley aviary as "keeper to the Earl's parrots". Working in the aviary was a job that most of the estate's staff strove hard to avoid, for although the birds' plumage was beautiful and their singing pleasing, few wanted to enter the cages to clean and feed them. Not so Matthew Scott, who accepted the job and was seen to fall in love with his feathered charges.

For the next five years Scott devoted himself to the parrots' care with extraordinary dedication, spending hours at a time in the aviary, day or night, talking to and stroking the birds. By his own admission he viewed them not as birds but as a substitute for the childhood friends that he lacked. He even developed the theory that any person who wanted to gain the total trust of an animal had in return to forfeit some aspect of their own life. "If I had not sacrificed a little comfort," Scott wrote, "and taken the trouble to feed them, they would not have had the confidence in me which to my mind they plainly exhibited. Nor would I have learned their ways. It is a fact that you cannot love, or have the affection of any bird or other animal, without attending to its wants, to some extent."

This servile attitude towards animals in captivity would remain with Scott for the rest of his days, but his success with the parrots caught the attention of his superiors, who took him away from his beloved birds to become keeper of the Earl's deer and antelopes. He immediately devoted himself to their care and formed a strong bond with them. The Earl was delighted and suggested to Scott that he might try to get the antelopes to reproduce, something that the previous keeper had been unable to achieve.

The teenaged Scott imagined that he would continue the family tradition by spending the rest of his life on the Knowsley estate, tending to the Earl's animals, but it was not to be. On 30 June 1851 the 13th Earl of Derby passed away, leaving his title and lands to his eldest son, Edward, an ambitious parliamentarian of many years' standing. The new Earl much preferred the Palace of Westminster to Knowsley Hall and had little interest in his father's zoological park, which cost £10,000 a year to run (£800,000 today). The old Earl had been aware of his son's indifference to the natural world and, rather than see his animals suffer through neglect, had made arrangements in his will for his park to be dismantled.

The Earl's stuffed animals, books and sketches (including many made by the poet Edward Lear during the 1830s) were given to the people of Liverpool, where they would form the basis of the city's first public museum. All the living specimens were to be sold by public auction, but before this Queen Victoria and the Zoological Society of London, of which the Earl had formerly been President, were to be allowed to take their pick from the animals at Knowsley Hall. The Queen chose two black-necked swans and five Impeyan pheasants while the Zoological Society took five elands, the largest species of African antelope. When auctioned the rest of the animals fetched just £7,000, a poor return on the vast sums that the Earl had spent acquiring and caring for his zoological collection.

This should have marked the end of Matthew Scott's career as an animal keeper and led to his transfer to duties elsewhere on the estate. However, the five elands chosen by the Zoological Society were not only in his care but were also his favourite animals. He had taken a keen interest in them and had not only persuaded a pair to breed but also been instrumental in raising their offspring. Given the problems associated with capturing and transporting African animals, Scott's knowledge of captive breeding and his husbandry skills were attractive to the Society, so it requested that the 17-year-old be allowed to accompany the elands to the Zoological Gardens in Regent's Park and care for them there.

Rather than face a career in domestic servitude, which would not have suited his gruff attitude and dislike of authority, Scott left Knowsley Hall and followed his elands to London. It was a tough decision for a country boy to make but in his mind the animals in his care came before friends and even family. He left promising his mother that he would return to visit regularly, but his assurance was false: he returned home just once, for his mother's funeral, the excuse being that his animals could not survive more than a day without him.

When Scott arrived in London in 1851 the city was alive with the excitement of the Great Exhibition and its famous Kensington Crystal Palace, an edifice that was a testament to Victorian engineering. The Exhibition had boosted London's tourism and had persuaded some of its more popular attractions to spruce themselves up for the influx of out-of-town visitors. The Regent's Park Zoological Gardens were no exception; an extensive phase of modernization had just finished that included the renovation of several of the animal compounds and the creation of a new Carnivora Terrace for large cats. As a result London Zoo was busier than usual, especially at weekends, most visitors coming away delighted with their experience.

"There are about twenty thousand animals in these Gardens," wrote an American visitor, "some free to roam as they please, some under the care of attending-keepers, others in yards, and others still in buildings and cages made expressly for them. Almost every rare and curious animal to be found anywhere on the face of the Earth is to be seen."

It was into this mêlée that the young Matthew Scott arrived in London; it was the first time he had ever visited a city (let alone lived in one) and the experience must have been a shock to his rural senses. The smell of smoke and the constant din of traffic and machinery would have been novelties to Scott, as would the noisy crowds of Londoners themselves, ranging from the hopelessly poor, who were numerous, to the unimaginably rich, who were not. Many other visitors drawn to the capital by the Great Exhibition were appalled by the extremes of London's social spectrum. "To look out upon human faces, pale, emaciate, wan, broken by disease, bearing expressions of faintest hope and darkest infamy and pollution," wrote the American William Drew, who, in 1851, encountered the city's slum dwellers. "Oh! What a sight! How cheerless, how loathsome. Can God's mercy reach them?"

Scott's position at London Zoo would have shielded him from the worst of this abject poverty, most of which was in any case to be found some miles away in the East End. He had joined the staff of the Zoo as a junior assistant keeper, at an annual salary of around £40. Such a lowly position was usually non-residential but as he was both young and a newcomer to London an exception was made and he was given a room in the Keepers' House. This stood in the Gardens and could house five unmarried men, most of whom would eventually wed and move out. Scott was an exception; he lived at the house for over 30 years, during which time he was never known to have had a sweetheart, let alone a prospective wife. For it was his animals that came first, leaving him little time for extracurricular activities such as romantic liaisons. In later life Scott's writings revealed his long-held belief that women were in some way perfect beings who could do little wrong yet often suffered through men's wickedness. "A woman would not do a dirty trick to Jumbo," he once remarked, adding that a wife was happiest when "baking the nice white bread and thinking of her dear husband". It is apparent that even from an early age Scott elevated women so high, and indeed was so introverted, that he would have been incapable of sharing his life with any living thing that did not possess a covering of fur or feather.

The work of a keeper at London Zoo was demanding and the rewards few: "the services required of the keepers are of a very special nature and their hours of attendance are long," acknowledged the Zoological Society, but for those in this largely unskilled and laborious profession the pay was not high. Being a keeper was hard, physical work: clearing out dirty stalls, preparing and moving large quantities of food and in some cases cleaning the animals. Prospects for promotion were poor (there was, for example, only one class of keeper when Scott arrived) and keepers could expect to be subject to the taunts and tricks of schoolboys and endless questions from the visiting public. Many became worn down by the work and took to the bottle or even vented their frustration on the animals. A keeper by the name of John Noble was twice found drunk on duty and eventually dismissed for beating a bear with an iron bar. Others were fired for embezzlement and one was even caught smuggling pigeons out of the Gardens, presumably so that he could eat them at home.

Matthew Scott and Jumbo shortly after their first meeting.

Among this rough-and-ready band Scott was a rarity in that his love of wild animals caused him to view his work as something more than just a job; to him it started as a genuine vocation and quickly grew into an obsession. Most keepers were able to pursue some form of social life but Scott, from the day of his arrival, was reclusive, spending hours alone with his animals and only occasionally leaving the Zoo to pay a solitary visit to a pub. Many of his colleagues, while regarding him as a loner, respected his ability to empathize with the animals in his care.

Details of Scott's early career at the Zoo are patchy and come mostly from his own writings or from snatched mentions in the Zoological Society's archives, but the two sources do not always agree. For example, Scott claimed to be on good terms with every animal at the Zoo and yet Abraham Bartlett noted that Obaysch the hippopotamus felt a passionate loathing for him. This animosity was given full expression when, a few years after Scott's arrival, the full-grown hippo (described by Bartlett as an "uncouth and powerful amphibious monster") escaped from his compound, causing great alarm.

"There came Obaysch down the long walk," wrote the naturalist Frank Buckland, "his huge mouth curled into a ghastly smile, as if he meant mischief. The cunning brute had contrived to push back the door of his den, while his keeper had gone for the carpenter to mend some defect in it. Having warned everyone to keep out of the way, Mr Bartlett called his keeper, who tried to coax the hippopotamus back with sweet hay. The brute munched the hay, but showed no sign of going back. What was to be done? Mr Bartlett is a man of unfailing resource. There was one keeper Obaysch hated, and he ran at him whenever he came in sight.

"'Scott,' said Mr Bartlett, putting a banknote into his hand, 'throw open the paddock gate, and then show yourself to Obaysch at the end of the path, and run for it.'

"Scott looked at the note, and then through the trees at the beast and, going into the middle of the path, shouted defiantly 'Obaysch!'

"'Ugh!' roared the beast, viciously, and wheeling his huge carcass suddenly round, rushed with surprising swiftness after the keeper. Scott ran for his life; with the hippopotamus roaring at his heels, into the paddock and over the palings, Obaysch close to his coat-tails; bang slammed the gate, and the monster was caged again. Just then, up drove a cab with a newspaper reporter.

"'I hear,' he said, 'the hippopotamus is loose!' 'Oh dear no,' innocently replied Mr Bartlett, 'he is safe in his den; come and see.'"

With the exception of Obaysch, Scott did put his animal husbandry skills to good effect at the Zoo. Under his care the Knowsley elands were soon siring offspring at an extraordinary rate; in time he would raise a total of over 40. It was noted that Scott had a flair for getting animals to breed and he was asked to work his magic on the collection of flightless birds, which included cassowaries, kiwis and ostriches.

Scott became emotionally attached to any animal placed in his care, showing a level of devotion that bordered on the obsessive. This was especially true of the Zoo's solitary kiwi, which one day he observed to be in bad health. The Head Keeper, Andrew Thompson, declared the animal "old and used up" and on the verge of death. Scott disagreed and said that it was probably just egg-bound, which greatly amused his colleagues as no males were in residence. They then openly laughed as Scott chose to spend entire days and nights sitting by the kiwi's side, talking to it and praying for its well-being. After 17 days the bird laid the most enormous egg, relative to its small body, that anyone at the Zoo had ever seen. Scott felt vindicated and suggested that, among other things, the male kiwi was probably responsible for incubating the egg.

The learned Fellows of the Zoological Society did not welcome the young keeper's interference in academic matters, which they saw as their concern. Scott was officially reprimanded for his behaviour and his outspoken views on the kiwi's biology. He was told that he could not possibly have known anything about the bird's breeding behaviour as he had "never been out of England". Overriding Scott's theory, the Society tried to settle the matter by paying for several Maori tribal chiefs to travel to London from New Zealand to offer their opinion on kiwi reproduction. Scott disagreed with their ideas and dismissed the Maoris as "savages" who were "ignoramuses on the subject". They returned home and in their place a male kiwi was sent to London. The bird immediately hopped on to the egg and began to incubate it, to the chagrin of Scott's superiors. Unfortunately it soon died after being attacked by mice.

Scott's belligerence, his dislike of human company and his superiority complex did not win him many friends at the Zoo, but he was an excellent keeper whose devotion to duty was remarkable. The appointment of Abraham Bartlett as Superintendent in 1859 seems to have been met with approval by Scott, who perhaps recognized similarities between himself and his new boss. Both had developed childhood obsessions with wildlife and, with no formal training, had forged careers for themselves in this challenging field. If nothing else, Bartlett would at least have been able to talk to Scott about their shared passion for animals, something that few other keepers wanted to do.

Certainly the relationship between the two men was sufficiently strong to give Bartlett confidence to entrust Jumbo to Scott's care. In doing so he may have hoped to exploit Scott's obsessive nature to help him care for and train the new elephant. If so, the decision was ill judged, for in appointing Scott as Jumbo's keeper, Bartlett was opening a can of worms that would eventually lead to a deep mutual loathing.

CHAPTER 7

∽ London ∽

When Jumbo first met Matthew Scott the keeper was in his thirty-second year and had been working at the Zoological Gardens for nearly 15 years. During this time Scott's boyish frame had filled out, turning him into a muscular, slightly stout figure, but he remained short at just five feet three inches. His clothing did not vary, consisting always of a dark suit, a waistcoat of a lighter colour and a tight-fitting bowler hat, below which was his somewhat plain-looking face with its bushy moustache.

After their meeting in Paris, Scott accompanied the unhealthy-looking Jumbo on an uneventful journey during which they took a train to the French coast, then a boat across the Channel and finally another train to London's Waterloo Station. At five years old Jumbo would have stood around five feet tall and weighed some 400 lb, which, although small for an elephant, was more than the average horse-drawn carriage could bear. For this reason it had been traditional for London Zoo to move its elephants about the capital on foot rather than use hired transport.

On arriving at Waterloo Scott would have walked Jumbo from the train to Regent's Park, a distance of some three miles. Given Jumbo's years of living in cramped confinement and the rotten state of his feet, this final stage of the journey may have been a slow, painful ordeal. The sight of such a miserable animal would not have impressed the public but it did appeal to Scott's sensibilities. There was nothing he liked more than to play nanny to a stricken animal and so, even though he and Jumbo had been acquainted for less than a day, keeper and elephant had already bonded.

When they reached the Zoo Jumbo was introduced to Bartlett and then given a separate stable where "a comfortable, clean bed" had been prepared for him. The little elephant did not spend his first night alone, for sleeping nearby was his new keeper, soon to be his best friend in the world. While Scott and Jumbo recovered from their journey Bartlett must have wondered what name they should give to their new guest.

Since the arrival of Jack in 1831 the Zoo's staff had named every elephant, but rather than choosing exotic or foreign names, as might be expected, they usually favoured English ones such as Jack, Peter, Jenny, Tommy and Alice. Indeed, when an Asian elephant arrived with the Hindu name of Katimeh, it was swiftly changed to Betsey. So it is somewhat surprising that Scott's new elephant was given the name Jumbo, which at that time was unusual and sounded distinctly foreign. In fact the origins of the name are unknown and are not recorded by Bartlett, Scott or any of the Zoo's other staff; in the absence of an official explanation many theories have arisen. One suggestion was that Jumbo's name derived from the Zulu word *jumba*, meaning a large packet, but this appears to have been inspired by the idea that the elephant was once a resident of South Africa, which was not so.

A better theory was that the name came from the slang phrase "my jumbo", which London's watermen, market traders and hackney-carriage men would shout at any person wearing tattered or heavily patched garments. Such ragged individuals were reminiscent of Mumbo Jumbo, a west African tribal holy man who would dress in bark and leaves. On certain nights the ragged figure of Mumbo Jumbo would enter a village and point out a wife who had allegedly been bad. The luckless woman would then be stripped naked, tied to a post and beaten with sticks. Stories recounting the sordid exploits of Mumbo Jumbo had circulated in Europe since the 1760s but they had become especially popular since the 1820s, when the published accounts of explorers of Africa became popular. It is conceivable that Bartlett may have taken one look at the sorrowful, diseased elephant with its infested, ragged skin and nicknamed him Jumbo in honour of the shaggy African divine.

But we should not dismiss the possibility that Jumbo did not receive his name in London at all, but while he was resident at the Jardin des Plantes. Unlike the British, who gave their elephants human names, the Parisians had a habit of naming their elephants after deities – after all, Jumbo shared an enclosure with Castor and Pollux – and stories about Mumbo Jumbo were also well known in Paris. This idea is pure speculation on my part, but it would explain why no one at London Zoo has ever taken credit for naming Jumbo and also why his name differs in its inspiration from those of the other elephants there.

Whatever the origin of his name, the truth of which is probably lost for ever, Jumbo was greeted with great joy by Abraham Bartlett, whose ambition of seeing a live African elephant had at last been realized. Jumbo's arrival late at night meant that Bartlett did not lay eyes on him until the following morning and, as soon as he did so, he too became concerned for the animal's health. He recalled that Jumbo "was in a filthy and miserable condition [and] the poor beast's feet for want of attention had grown out of shape".

Jumbo was also much smaller than Bartlett had been led to expect, the top of the elephant's head coming below the Superintendent's chin. This emaciated animal had cost the Zoological Society £450 and, although the purchase had fulfilled one of Bartlett's long-standing zoological ambitions, he was savvy enough to realize that the diminutive elephant would not impress many visitors. In his current condition Jumbo could not be mistaken for a marauding bull elephant and yet Bartlett needed to publicize his new acquisition in a favourable light. So, rather than try to sell Jumbo as a fearful giant, he decided to play on people's curiosity. Jumbo may not have been entirely awesome but he was still the only African elephant in Britain and that uniqueness brought obvious advantages.

Despite Jumbo's poor health Bartlett ordered Scott to place him alongside Peter and Chunee (who was formerly known as Jenny but probably renamed by Bartlett in honour of the elephant he saw killed at the Exeter 'Change), the two Asian elephants then resident at the Zoo. Jumbo was considerably smaller than both, causing Bartlett to estimate, correctly, that he was around five or six years old. But even given such a juvenile animal it was clear that African and Asian elephants displayed a number of striking physical differences. Bartlett judged that, like him, the public would be curious to see how the African species differed from the Asian and so he began to compile a list of their respective physical attributes.

The Superintendent's initial summary observed that "the most obvious peculiarity of the African species consists in the enormous ears, which cover the whole of the side of the head. The general outline of the two species is likewise very different, as is also the form of the trunk and the shape of the forehead." He used these observations in the Victorian equivalent of a press release which announced Jumbo's arrival, stressed his uniqueness as an exhibit and, crucially, hinted at his differences from Peter and Chunee. The newspapers took the information supplied by Bartlett and ran it almost word for word.

"The extensive collection of living animals belonging to the Zoological Society of London has just received an important addition in the shape of an African Elephant," reported *The Times* on 28 June 1865. "Although the Asian Elephant has for many years been well represented in the Society's gardens and in other collections of living animals, we are not aware that the African species, which is very distinct in form and particularly remarkable for the enormous size of its ears, has ever before been brought alive to this country."

Other daily papers followed suit but it was a popular weekly tabloid that offered the best publicity. The *Illustrated London News* offered to print a story on the new arrival and even sent an artist to Regent's Park to make a sketch of Jumbo in his enclosure. The result was a drawing of a young elephant which, while obviously not a calf, was far from being an adult. Jumbo's body, legs, head and trunk appear small and thin with few signs of the powerful musculature that is popularly associated with elephants of all species. And yet, protruding from beneath the trunk is evidence of Jumbo's emergent tusks, indicating that adulthood is not far off. However, as Bartlett correctly notes, by far the most striking feature is Jumbo's ears, which seem completely out of proportion to his head and body. The artist shows Jumbo in his wooden stable with straw on the floor, his long trunk tackling a meal of biscuits and bread.

Jumbo's first official portrait, July 1865.

Bartlett's text again entices the public to see Jumbo: "The African Elephant is very distinct in its outer form as well as in its internal structure from the Indian species; the council of the society have long been desirous of bringing the two elephants together side by side in the Gardens... The animal thus acquired is a young male, supposed to be five or six years old. He is nearly the same size as the smaller of the two Asian Elephants now in the society's collection."

This last claim was somewhat of an exaggeration. Jumbo was taller than Peter, the smallest of the Zoo's Asian elephants, but then again he was nearly two years older than him. Another exaggeration was the artist's impression of Jumbo, which showed a young animal in apparently perfect health. In reality Bartlett had grave concerns about the newcomer, so much so that those members of the public who were enticed to visit Jumbo were often disappointed. On Bartlett's orders he was not to be allowed outside and would be exhibited for only a short time each day, standing motionless next to Peter and Chunee so that the public could see that his ears were indeed bigger.

Both Bartlett and Scott were worried that Jumbo's condition was so serious that he might not recover. The Superintendent placed himself in charge of Jumbo's medical care and worked closely with Scott. Slowly the two men managed to restore Jumbo's health, but with each passing day the keeper became ever more attached to the elephant, refusing to leave his side for more than a few minutes.

"I watched him night and day," said Scott, "with all the care and affection of a mother (if it were possible for a man to do such a thing), until by physicking him from the inward centre of his frame I cleared out all diseased matter from his lungs, liver and heart. I then, by means of lotion of oil, etc., took all the scabs from the roots of his almost blinded eyes. I removed his leprous coat as cleanly as a man takes off an overcoat; and his skin was as fine as that of a horse just from the clipper's, after the hair had been cut off."

The healing process also required the "scraping and rasping" of Jumbo's rotten feet to give them back their natural shape. This task, carried out by Bartlett, continued for months and was hindered by nocturnal attacks from rats which attempted to eat away at the elephant's feet. Like the cartoon elephant that shies away from a mouse, Jumbo feared rodents for ever afterwards and would panic at the sight of a rat. (Rats have been known to kill captive elephants by eating holes in their feet.) In time Bartlett's and Scott's hard labour, patience and attention began to pay off; Jumbo's overall health improved, leading to a gain in weight and the emergence of a lively disposition. At the end of the summer preparations were made to move him from the temporary stables to more suitable accommodation.

Throughout September and October the Zoo's carpenters and blacksmiths made adjustments to the Giraffe House, converting it into what would become known as the African Elephant Den. The decision to house Jumbo separately from the two Asian elephants was not to Bartlett's liking; he had intended to display all the elephants together so as to highlight their physical differences, but there was simply not space in the existing Elephant

House for another resident. The Giraffe House, which was located close to the Elephant House, was the next-best alternative but it needed much work before it was ready to receive Jumbo. The wire netting and doors were reinforced, while basic repairs were made to the chimney, locks and windows. Although Jumbo was not yet well enough for public display, on 25 October label boards were fixed to the building which announced that it was occupied by an African elephant. By the end of October Jumbo had moved into his new quarters, but he did not like what he found and soon made his displeasure known.

On 11 November Bartlett and Scott arrived at the African Elephant House to discover that overnight Jumbo had used his trunk to smash several of the windows in his compound. The animal was unhurt and the damage quickly repaired but Bartlett was concerned that this bad behaviour could be repeated and ordered the blacksmith to prepare a chain with which to tether one of Jumbo's legs. It was hoped that by restricting his movement in this way, Jumbo would be able to cause less damage to his surroundings. For a while he remained calm but on Boxing Day he again went on the rampage and, after snapping his leg chain, charged at the wooden doors, damaging them so badly that it took the Zoo's carpenters and blacksmiths two days to repair them. With the cost of repairs mounting, Bartlett determined that the elephant should know who was boss at the Zoo. It would be Jumbo's first glimpse of the Superintendent's ruthless streak, but by no means his last.

"We found it necessary to put a stop to his gambols," recalled Bartlett, "and this we accomplished in a very speedy and effectual manner. Scott and myself, holding him by each ear, administered to him a good thrashing. He quickly recognised that he was mastered by lying down and uttering a cry of submission. We coaxed him and fed him with a few tempting morsels, and after this time he appeared to recognise that we were his best friends, and he continued on best terms with both of us."

Scott did not agree with physically punishing animals and so when writing about Jumbo's early days at Regent's Park he glossed over this unpleasant training technique. He preferred instead to remember the end product of his and Bartlett's efforts.

"I was rewarded by having a clean-shaven looking creature in a perfectly sound state of mind and body," he said.

Bartlett's thrashings had the desired effect and by early 1866 Jumbo was calm again and in almost perfect health. Bartlett decided that the time had come for the public to see the African elephant in all his glory and so for the first time Jumbo was allowed into the small, open-air paddock that was attached to his den. Even though it was the middle of winter, Jumbo resisted all attempts by Scott to drape him in an overcoat or a blanket. This led the keeper to speculate that wrenching Jumbo from Africa to England must have been akin to forcibly removing a native Englishman north to "Greenland's Icy Mountains".

Few people bothered to visit London Zoo in midwinter and so Jumbo's first public outing may have been witnessed by fewer than 40, but among the sparse crowd were some individuals who had been waiting months for the occasion. "It was my happiness to behold the animal I have never expected to see; a living African elephant," wrote the naturalist Theo Johnson.

By this stage Scott had formed a very close attachment to Jumbo and believed that he could empathize with the elephant, but in truth the relationship was very one-sided. Although Jumbo's behaviour had been modified, he was still suffering from the effects of his treatment at the Jardin des Plantes, which seemed to have left him with a dislike of confined spaces. He especially did not like being locked inside his den and was capable of throwing sudden tantrums or behaving in an unpredictable, immature manner. In the short term this did not matter as the undersized animal was being kept separate from the public but it did present worries for the future, especially to Bartlett, who as a child had witnessed the terrible rage and destruction that came before the execution of Chunee the elephant. While Scott had fallen for Jumbo's charms, Bartlett was not so sentimental; it was his policy always to keep an eye on the behaviour of his elephants, just in case they played up. The reputation of his zoo was far more important than the life of any one animal in it and, like Edward Cross at the Exeter 'Change, Bartlett would not hesitate to take whatever measures were necessary to keep control.

CHAPTER 8

∽ Alice ∾

It is often remarked that one can wait hours for a London bus only to have two arrive at once. The same would appear to be true of African elephants, at least as far as the Regent's Park Zoo was concerned.

Obtaining Jumbo from the French had been a real breakthrough for Abraham Bartlett and, given the lack of African elephants in Europe, appeared to be an opportunity that might not arise again for several years. In fact it was only to be a matter of weeks after Jumbo's arrival before the Superintendent was offered another young African elephant. This one was female and in good physical health, having been imported directly from the wild. At the time Jumbo was seriously ill and so buying a second African elephant seemed a sensible proposition, just in case the first one didn't make it. Besides, if Jumbo were to survive, there was the exciting prospect of having a male and female pair of African elephants. Not only did this make them easier to market to the public, but there was an outside chance that they might take a shine to each other and produce baby elephants, although, given they were both still calves, this possibility was some way distant.

Bartlett began negotiations with the female elephant's owner and on 9 September 1865 took a cab from Regent's Park to Whitechapel and the shop in St George's Street of Charles Rice, the animal dealer who had secured the animal. Unlike with Jumbo, Bartlett had been able to inspect the young female thoroughly before any money had changed hands and he was delighted at her rude health and amenable behaviour. According to Rice, the calf was very young, probably around a year old, and stood under four feet in height.

In fact so small was she that when considering how best to transport her back to the Zoo, Bartlett at first considered putting her into a cab, but this proved problematic. "Being anxious to remove her that same afternoon," he wrote, "I determined to walk her through the streets." However, St George's Street was located in one of the less salubrious parts of town – a quarter of a century later Whitechapel would be the haunt of Jack the Ripper – and as soon as word got about that there was an elephant abroad in the neighbourhood, Bartlett found himself surrounded by "a crowd of two to three hundred of the London mob, composed of a lot of dirty, ragged, noisy boys, and not a few of that nomad, the London rough, the curse to modern travellers about town".

The journey was painfully slow but the elephant was able to carve a path through the sea of people and as they progressed towards London's wealthier West End, so the ragamuffins dispersed. By sunset Bartlett was safely back at his Zoological Gardens and was pleasantly surprised that his dinner was waiting for him, laid out on a table in the open air. He sat down at the table; without being prompted, the elephant sat down beside him and the pair of them shared a meal of bread and apples. This was not the only surprise that Bartlett had for his staff, for during the long walk from the East End he had come up with a suitable name for the new arrival. "May I introduce you to Alice," he said, before tucking into his food. It seems that the great naturalist's choice of name may have been influenced by the literary sensation of the moment, Lewis Carroll's *Alice's Adventures in Wonderland*, which had been published only a few weeks before and was already a bestseller.

Shortly after this unorthodox meal, Alice was introduced to Matthew Scott, who was to look after her as well as Jumbo. Scott claimed that Alice's arrival was a source of great joy to his other charge and that on seeing the new arrival he put on a spectacular display. "When I passed by Jumbo's stable, where he roamed at leisure, the moment he saw Alice led along towards him, I thought he would have broken that stable front out to get at us. His delight and pleasure, expressed in the liveliest manner possible, and which I understood, exceeded that of any boy when he

71

meets his sweetheart. At least my Jumbo was more demonstrative and, I verily believe, possessed more real affection and love at first sight than most of the young men of the present generation do in a like situation."

This charming vision of elephantine love at first sight was, however, viewed more dispassionately by some of the Zoo's more scientifically minded staff. In 1865 both Jumbo and Alice were many years from reaching sexual maturity and, although they were unquestionably friendly and touched each other with their trunks, there was no sexual element in their original meeting.

"They always appeared quite indifferent to each other," wrote one regular visitor, but this did not stop Bartlett from advertising Alice as "Jumbo's wife", a title that soon stuck. Within months of Alice's arrival journalists were discussing the elephants' relationship in very human terms. On noting that Jumbo and Alice were housed in separate but adjoining stables, one bachelor writer commented dryly: "I am told by those who live in a world of which I know nothing that this is an attitude matrimonially correct in modern society."

That Jumbo and Alice could be friends without falling in love came of little surprise to the animal dealer Carl Hagenbeck, whose fascination with elephants had led him to take a particular interest in their love life. On one occasion he had an adolescent bull elephant that was fixated on a young female in a neighbouring enclosure. The male's affection was returned and Hagenbeck was touched to see that the two animals would spend hours caressing and stroking each other with their trunks. After a while the German's scientific curiosity got the better of him and he devised an experiment to test whether his bull elephant was suffering from love in the human sense or merely lust.

After waiting for the bull elephant to fall asleep, Hagenbeck led his lover away and replaced her with another cow elephant of a similar temperament. On waking, the bull elephant was immediately aware of what had happened and, ignoring the new female, he fell into a rage and remained agitated until his original love had been returned to him. On the basis of this and other observations Hagenbeck was able to make a startling declaration: "I have found that elephants 'fall in love' in the true sense of the word; that is, they conceive a truly monogamous affection for one particular cow, and are not merely actuated by a general predilection for the opposite sex."

Placing Scott in charge of both African elephants must have been an easy decision for Bartlett to make. After all, although not an elephant expert, the keeper was at the time devotedly restoring Jumbo to full health and, as others had noted, was making a good job of it. Having Alice placed in his care elevated Scott from a keeper whose responsibilities included Jumbo to the Zoo's full-time keeper of African elephants.

Scott had already shown himself to be capable of becoming obsessed with any animal in his care, be it a parrot or an antelope, but in the coming years he was to take this behaviour to an extreme. Lacking a social life or close friends as he did, there was always the danger that the responsibility of looking after what were arguably the Zoo's two most important animals would have an adverse affect on Scott's personality, inflating his already sizeable sense of self-importance. It was a danger that Bartlett was either not aware of or did not care too much about, but as the months passed Scott started to see his elephants not as animals but as his closest friends. The Superintendent should perhaps have been worried when, within only a short while of Alice's arrival, Scott had started to rewrite his African elephants' history, so that it was he, not the Zoological Society, who played a central role in their acquisition.

By contrast with Jumbo, Alice's exact path from Africa to Regent's Park was known to all the staff at the Zoo: she had been captured in the same part of Sudan as Jumbo and had been transported by Lorenzo Casanova to Germany, where they arrived in July 1865. The cargo suffered greatly, with only two of the many elephants that had set out on foot from Kassala reaching Europe, Alice being one of them. By this time Casanova was collecting exclusively for Carl Hagenbeck, the respected Hamburg-based menagerie owner and animal dealer. He already had buyers lined up for the lions, panthers, ostriches and other animals that Casanova had brought him. Alice had been promised to Charles Rice in London, who in turn had been in negotiation with the Zoological Society's Purchase of Animals

Committee; it took a month to settle on a price. For £551 the Zoo purchased Alice plus several birds, including a hornbill, a crow, a guineafowl and several finches, all of which were delivered to Regent's Park in September 1865.

This was the true story of how Alice reached London, but Scott would tell visitors a different story, which featured him as the Zoo's elephant procurement expert. "Having Jumbo entirely under my own care and management, I persuaded our Garden Directors to send to Africa for a female baby elephant," he wrote. "Men went down from London to the great sea, and arriving on the west coast of Africa, after a considerable search, they found such a specimen as they thought would answer my purpose. They brought it over safely and deposited it in my care and keeping."

Of course Scott, a junior keeper, was in no position to request an expedition to Africa, nor was the Zoological Society in a position to organize and pay for one. Besides, with only three months between Jumbo's arrival and that of Alice, there had not been the time for any such venture to take place. Fantasies like this were probably common among the keepers, who were continually approached by the public to tell stories about their animals.

With hindsight Bartlett realized that Scott's desire to make himself the centre of attention and to play down the role of his employers had been a warning that he was increasingly viewing himself as separate from the rest of the Zoo. The African Elephant House was becoming Scott's private domain, but by the time the Superintendent became of aware of the problem it was already too late.

CHAPTER 9

∽ Training Jumbo ∾

From the outset it was clear that Alice and Jumbo had entirely different personalities. Alice was young and, to judge by her health, had been well treated in the months following her capture; furthermore she was docile, compliant and free from bouts of ill temper. The same was not true of Jumbo, who could on occasion be surly and somewhat edgy; but even so, Bartlett was keen that he should be fully domesticated so that he could be walked about the park among the public, as were the Zoo's two Asian elephants.

No one in Europe had ever before fully tamed an African elephant and it was the firm opinion of some zoologists that the species was beyond domestication. This idea arose because of the greater size and aggressiveness of the African elephant in comparison with the Asian species and because none of the African tribes themselves had ever domesticated these animals (unlike in Asia, where domesticated elephants are a valuable source of labour).

"During nine years' experience of Central Africa I never saw a tamed creature of any kind, not even a bird, or a young antelope in possession of a child," wrote Samuel Baker. "The tame elephant would be especially valuable to an explorer, as it could march through streams too deep for the passage of oxen, and in swimming rivers it would be proof against the attacks of crocodiles. So few African elephants have been tamed in proportion to those of Asia that it would be difficult to pronounce an opinion upon their character when domesticated, but it is generally believed by their trainers that the Indian species is more gentle and amenable to discipline. The power of the African is far in excess of the Asiatic."

Bartlett subscribed to some of these ideas, declaring that everything in Africa was restless in comparison with its Asian counterpart. "Take the active and determined Chimpanzee of Africa as compared with the mild and inoffensive ourang of Asia," he wrote. Despite this, he held out hope that the African elephant could be brought under his full control: "I am inclined to believe that the African Elephant, if properly managed, would become quite as valuable and useful as the Indian species." Certainly the animal was intelligent enough to be trained; it was all a matter of devising a suitable training method that took into account the differences in temperament between the African elephant and the Indian. When thinking about this, he looked to the history books as an example.

"We must not forget that African elephants were regularly tamed and used by the ancients. That this was the kind used by the Carthaginians is evident from the form represented on the coins of Carthage... The great difficulty I see is the want of appliances at starting. In the first place, the African animal has far more courage, is much quicker in its movements, and is more determined and obstinate than its Asiatic relative. The two species appear to me to differ to so great an extent that the treatment that succeeds so well with Asiatic species would fail with the African."

After Jumbo's return to full fitness in early 1866, Bartlett ordered Scott to set about introducing him to the public. This was probably achieved by Scott and another keeper leading Jumbo about the Gardens, familiarizing him with their layout and with the general public, who would have been fewer in number during the winter. These excursions were successful and as the weather warmed up so visitors increased and gradually Jumbo became accustomized to crowds. After the young elephant's precarious start at the Zoo, Bartlett was pleased to discover that he was fond of human company and calm when surrounded by the public, even hordes of screaming children.

As summer approached it was either Scott or Bartlett (but probably the latter) who hit on the idea of periodically taking Jumbo out of the Zoo and leading him through the West End to the River Thames for an evening bath. Unabashed, the elephant and his keeper would stand at the water's edge and play together in front of a large crowd of amused onlookers. Despite the river's wretched pollution (this was only a few years after an excess of sewage in the Thames produced the "Great Stink" of 1858), Jumbo would suck in a trunk-load of water and send it shooting high in the air, drenching Scott and any passers-by stupid enough to be within range.

"I got all the shower and douche bath without the ability to return the kindness," wrote Scott. "I couldn't do more than splash a bit with my hands, or throw a few buckets of water on Jumbo's back."

The visits to the river were not just an enjoyable outing for Jumbo and Scott; they made up for the lack of a bathing pool in the African Elephant Den and were also an ideal means of pub-licizing the Zoo. The lack of a pool for Jumbo and Alice was of some concern; the Asian elephants had a bathing pool but during the adaptation of the Giraffe House there had been neither the time nor the space to build one for Jumbo and Alice. The Thames, it seems, was an adequate substitute, although there is no mention of Alice ever having been taken down to the river to swim with Jumbo.

As the first anniversary of Jumbo's arrival at the Zoo approached, so his owners and carers began to get a feel for the creature in their charge. Jumbo was subject to sudden changes in mood: he was happy and contented when in his outdoor enclo-sure or being led through the Gardens among the public, but if shut inside his stable he became restless and irritable. This was perhaps an enduring symptom of his ill treatment in Paris, when he must have spent weeks on end inside the cramped and poorly tended Rotunda. Occasionally his uneasiness when indoors would escalate into a towering rage during which he would throw himself at the doors in an attempt to batter them down.

A particularly prolonged and severe bout of bad temper struck in June 1866, when the enraged Jumbo spent several days charg-ing headlong at the doors, which buckled and splintered but, mercifully, did not give way. These assaults occurred only when he was locked up and so were usually nocturnal. Each morning for three weeks the Zoo's carpenters and blacksmiths were summoned to repair the African Elephant Den and to shore up Jumbo's quarters in preparation for another night of abuse. By the end of June steel plating had been fixed to the doors as well to the partition dividing Jumbo and Alice, and wooden window frames, benches and door handles had been replaced by their equivalents in iron. Jumbo was again put in chains, although this did little to prevent his outbursts.

Jumbo was starting to prove himself popular with the public so it must have been a relief to Bartlett that his violent tantrums mostly occurred at night and in the privacy of the Den. Indeed, by the late summer of 1866 Jumbo had become so acclimatized to the public that Bartlett considered that it was time for the young elephant to give public rides around the Zoo. In zoos across Europe Asian elephants had been trained to give rides but nobody had tried the feat with an African elephant. The move was a calculated gamble on Bartlett's part but if he were to succeed it would be a huge publicity coup for the Zoological Society as well as a money-spinner. The Superintendent was not known to shrink from a challenge and in the early autumn he ordered that a saddle be made for Jumbo and asked Scott to prepare the elephant for a new phase of training.

No record survives of how Bartlett and Scott went about training Jumbo to carry passengers on his back, but we can be certain that only the minimum of necessary force was used. Bartlett was fully aware that everything within his zoo was subject to close public scrutiny and that his compatriots would not tolerate any degree of perceived cruelty to an animal, no matter what the justification. This is not to say that Bartlett was against Jumbo's receiving the "occasional flogging" but this had to occur in private because "a multitude of protests from kind-hearted and sensitive people, in all probability, would have led to those concerned appearing before the magistrates at the police court charged with cruelty".

An idea of the manner and probable speed of Jumbo's training is provided by the memoirs of Carl Hagenbeck, perhaps the greatest of all the nineteenth-century animal tamers. In the years following Jumbo's arrival in Europe, Hagenbeck took delivery of five young African elephants, all untamed; they were temporarily housed in Berlin when they received a visit by the zoologist Professor Rudolf Virchow, who voiced the idea that the African elephant could not be tamed. Rather rashly, Hagenbeck remarked that if Virchow cared to return the following afternoon at 5 p.m. he would find the young elephants fully domesticated, taking passengers on their backs. As soon as the professor had gone, Hagenbeck, who had never trained an African elephant in his life, set about trying to break in his five exhibits.

"I had the elephants brought out and, selecting some of the most nubile keepers, I promised them rewards if they would clamber on to the elephants' backs and maintain themselves in that precarious position. The men were quite game, but the elephants by no means relished the part they were expected to play. They found the loads on their back uncomfortable and, rushing around with loud trumpeting, they shook themselves with such vigor that all the riders except one were sent flying into the sand. After the animals had been fed with bread and turnips they became somewhat quieter, and then the keepers essayed their task once more, this time with greater success. This procedure was continued until nightfall, by which time three of the creatures had been so far broken in that they would quite good-naturedly allow their keepers to ride them about the menagerie. The next morning their good example was followed by their two comrades… Professor Virchow arrived at five o'clock with some friends from the Geographical Society and was not a little astonished to see the wild elephants changed into domestic animals after a few hours' schooling."

One can suppose that Jumbo would have undergone a similar process but perhaps spread over a longer period. He too would have been coerced into accepting a human on his back and again we must suppose that the brave soul who first tried to mount Jumbo, if it was not Bartlett or Scott (and probably the latter), was probably another junior keeper.

We do know that the training sessions were successful but they did not leave Jumbo in the best of moods and perhaps even caused his first display of bad temper in public. On 4 October 1866, in the middle of his course of training, Jumbo was accused of knocking down and injuring a paying visitor to the Zoo. The man was Edwin Abraham, a Chancery clerk, who immediately engaged a firm of solicitors with a view to suing the Zoological Society for compensation. An investigation by Philip Sclater, the Society's Secretary, led him to conclude that "two keepers, and a third witness, who was near, all deposed that the elephant had not touched Mr Abraham, on the occasion in question". They declined to give any compensation to the clerk and the matter was dropped, but one wonders if there was more to the issue than the records reveal. Even Scott, who had nothing but praise for Jumbo, admitted that the elephant was capable of lashing out, although usually in response to ill treatment.

"He might get mad once in a while," his keeper admitted, "when some drunken fool tries to prick him with pins in a cake, or otherwise fool him. Jumbo always knows parties that try to play tricks upon him when he is being exhibited to the masses of humanity, and if ever any such parties should come within the reach of Jumbo a second time it wouldn't be good for him."

A few days after the incident with Edwin Abraham, Jumbo vented his frustration on the windows in the African Elephant Den and, having watched a workman repair the broken panes, promptly smashed them all again and, for good measure, damaged his door as well. Even with these fits of temper Jumbo was judged by Bartlett to be safe (and sane) enough to be allowed to give children pleasure rides around the Gardens.

After settling in at Regent's Park Jumbo had grown rapidly and by the end of 1866 would have stood just over six feet tall. Even so, he was still fairly small and unable to carry his young passengers about in a box-like howdah, as a larger elephant could have done. Instead a saddle was created for him which probably allowed the children to sit on his back with their legs astride. A set of wooden steps permitted the young passengers to mount and dismount in safety while at all times the temperamental elephant would be accompanied by Scott, who led him slowly through the Zoo using a collar and leash.

A ride on Jumbo cost a penny, for which each child would be issued with a ticket as proof of payment but also to remind them of their brief elephant-back journey. Bartlett placed Scott in charge of collecting the ticket money, a task that was not normally entrusted to junior keepers because of the risk of corruption. However, in this instance Bartlett rashly agreed that Scott could keep all the cash raised from Jumbo's rides. Why he should have done so is a mystery. Perhaps he did not know just how lucrative the trade would become; perhaps it was a reward to Scott for his work with Jumbo. Whatever the reason, Bartlett came to regret this decision and spent many years watching Scott pocket money that had been generated by an animal whose upkeep was entirely paid for by the Zoo.

For his part the poorly paid Scott soon realized that he had been handed a financial bonanza by his boss and he chose to grasp it with both hands. In some years the ticket money would provide Scott with as much as 10 times his annual wage, making him a wealthy man but, rather than share his good fortune, he became obsessed with protecting his privileged position from others. As an ordinary keeper, Scott was entitled to one Sunday off a month and he had taken this ever since starting at Regent's Park. However, Sunday was also the Zoo's busiest day, with visitors in their thousands, especially during the summer. Naturally, larger numbers of tourists meant greater takings for Jumbo's rides, and it seems that Scott from October 1866 chose to forgo his day off so that he could collect Jumbo's ticket money instead. For an unmarried man with few interests outside of the Zoo, this was perhaps no great sacrifice, but it is an extraordinary fact that over a period of 16 years Scott took fewer than five days of his holiday entitlement and no sick leave at all.

This jealous guarding of Jumbo's earnings was the first outward sign that Scott was manoeuvring to make himself the only gateway to the Zoo's African elephants. However, Bartlett still had ultimate authority over Scott and the elephants, a circumstance that did not suit the keeper's sense of self-importance. But this position would change thanks to an unfortunate incident that gave Scott exactly what he wanted and, in his own words, made him the "boss of the show". Bartlett saw it differently, saying that "it made everybody afraid of him".

⌘ Fever ⌘

On 19 December 1866 the Zoological Society gathered its staff together for a Christmas celebration and, in the midst of the festivities, announced that three keepers were to be rewarded for their success in "breeding foreign animals in the Society's menagerie". The fortunate men were Benjamin Misselbrooke, Henry Hunt and Matthew Scott, all of whom received the Landseer Bronze Medal and £5.

The decision to reward the men had been taken several months earlier and may have been a means of keeping them sweet in the wake of some major changes to the terms and conditions of all the Zoo's keepers. That summer the Society had divided its keepers into three classes, based not on their experience or skills but solely on their length of service. Misselbrooke and Hunt immediately became third-class keepers while Scott, who had worked at the Zoo for more than 10 years, became a second-class keeper. However, becoming a first-class keeper required 25 years' continuous employment, a prohibitive length of time. Furthermore, the keepers' pay had moved from a flexible system which included various expenses and benefits to a fixed monthly sum. Scott received £5 10s. (£5.50) a month (although his ticket money far exceeded this) while Misselbrooke and Hunt received £5. The Society valued Misselbrooke and Hunt because of their organizational skills and saw them as potential managers. Scott was certainly no manager but he was valuable because of his ability to get animals to breed.

The bronze medal was the design of Sir Edwin Landseer, who had engraved one side with images of some of the Zoo's larger mammals, including a rhinoceros, an Asian elephant and a giraffe, while the other side contained pictures of various flightless and predatory birds. The inscription on Scott's medal read: "To MATTHEW SCOTT, for his success in breeding Foreign Animals, in the Zoological Society's Gardens, London, 1866."

Detail from Matthew Scott's bronze medal.

It was one of Scott's greatest moments while at the Zoo: "It is a magnificent bronze medal, of which I am justly, I think, proud," he wrote some years later, adding that it was a just reward for "my trials, dangers and toils as the caretaker and breeder of the beast and bird".

If Jumbo was also proud of his keeper's award, he chose not to show it. On the night that it was given he again attacked his den and succeeded in bending the iron bars that reinforced his door, almost breaking the bolt. This display of displeasure at his quarters was well timed as only a few hours earlier the Zoological Society's Council had discussed the issue of its elephants' accommodation. Of the four elephants resident at the Zoo, three were not yet seven years old and were expected to grow considerably as they entered adolescence. Indeed, Jumbo, the eldest of the juveniles, was already gaining both height and bulk at an extraordinary rate and it was possible that he would outgrow his den within a few years. The committee could foresee the Zoo's being in possession of four adult elephants that could no longer be comfortably housed. Rather than risk leaving these popular animals in unsuitable conditions, as had happened at the Jardin des Plantes, it was agreed that the Zoo needed a new and bigger Elephant House which could accommodate the African and Asian elephants under the same roof. As a first step the Garden Committee was asked to "consider the best method of providing more accommodation for the Indian and African elephants in the Society's Gardens".

Six weeks later the Garden Committee came back to the Zoological Society's senior managers with the suggestion that a new and expanded Elephant House could be built on the site of the old Wapiti House. This would require the elephants to be moved from their quarters in the Zoo's central area to a site on its northern fringe between a public road and the Regent's Canal. The proposed site was well situated and offered plenty of room for a sizeable Elephant House with a large, south-facing open enclosure. With the Society's approval the Garden Committee was requested to ask the architect Anthony Salvin junior to draw up plans for the new building. As if to underline the point, a few days later Jumbo almost managed to break down the door to his enclosure, leaving it torn from its hinges. The Zoo's carpenters and blacksmiths had to remove both door and frame to make their repairs, which took three days.

Far from his settling down, as Bartlett had hoped, Jumbo's rages were getting both more frequent and worse. Nor did the elephant's mood improve when, in May 1867, the simple saddle that had been used to carry children about the Gardens was replaced by a heavier, more cumbersome device. This was a howdah, a centuries-old Asian invention used to transport humans in comfort on the back of an adult elephant. By now Jumbo would have stood around seven feet tall and weighed around 2,600 lb and was thought strong enough to support the weight of the howdah and several people on his back. Rather than use an ornate Indian howdah, which is box-like in construction and is often decked out with a canopy, cushions, carpets and ladders, Bartlett ordered a device of much simpler design.

Jumbo's howdah was open and step-like in profile, so that a line of passengers could sit on either side of his back, all facing outwards. This permitted up to six adults or eight children (or a combination of both) to ride on Jumbo at once, with Scott either walking beside him or, more usually, sitting astride his neck. To reduce the time between rides, a double set of wooden stairs was built which allowed passengers to mount and dismount on both sides of Jumbo simultaneously.

Jumbo was not the first elephant at London Zoo to carry a howdah as one had been previously used on the larger Asian elephants and always without incident. At first Jumbo reacted badly to the device, which was cumbersome and secured using a series of leather straps that run underneath his belly and round his back legs. On first being introduced to the howdah he reacted by damaging his den, but Scott and Bartlett persisted until he became accustomed to the sensation of wearing it and, in time, to the additional weight of passengers. Giving rides was not without benefit for Jumbo, as it took him away from the Elephant House, an environment he truly hated, and out into the open space of the Gardens and the crowds, which he loved. Each day at two o'clock sharp Jumbo, his howdah in place, would be led by Scott to the wooden steps by the Asian Elephant House. Then he would give rides continually until 6 o'clock, at which time he would be returned to his den, where the howdah would be removed and he would be prepared for bed.

The howdah greatly increased Jumbo's carrying capacity and so boosted Scott's income from the rides. The keeper's income from this source was, years later, calculated by Bartlett to have been as much as £800 a year, but nobody knows for certain as he was careful to keep the scale of this venture hidden from his colleagues and especially from his boss. Jumbo's rides had the potential to make Scott a wealthy man and gave him a good reason to exclude other keepers from exercising any degree of control over Jumbo. Scott made it clear to them that Jumbo and Alice were his concern and he did not want any help in caring for them.

Jumbo did not repay this loyalty and showed few signs of being emotionally attached to any of the Zoo's staff, even Scott, and continued to suffer from bouts of anger. In 1867 alone Jumbo's quarters needed repairing on at least 13 occasions, and as he increased in size so did his ability to inflict damage, the doors especially bearing the brunt of his rage. This could not be allowed to continue indefinitely, but every attempt to placate Jumbo or dissuade him from his destructive behaviour had failed. As winter approached, the situation looked hopeless, but a solution was to come from a most unexpected and unfortunate source.

In the days leading up to Christmas 1867 Jumbo exhibited signs of bad health and by degrees his condition declined until he was too sick to be taken from his quarters. Jumbo's illness was never properly diagnosed but it appears to have involved repeated fevers that gradually sapped his strength and reserves of energy.

"Too weak to do more than lean against the side of his den in helpless agony," wrote Theo Johnson, who witnessed Jumbo's decline, "his lack lustre eyes, which he slowly opened and shut, fixed on the ground; fallen away miserably, a mere mountain of skin and bone – Jumbo was indeed a wreck and ruin of his former magnificent self. It seemed as though his last hour had come."

This gloomy prognosis was certainly the opinion of Bartlett and the Zoo's veterinary surgeons, all of whom believed that Jumbo was beyond all earthly help. It was decided to let nature take its course, but not everyone was so pessimistic. From the shadows emerged Scott, who, with his typical brashness and self-belief, declared that he, and he alone, could save Jumbo's life. But to do so, he said, he needed to be left entirely alone with the elephant and receive absolutely no interference at all from others, including Bartlett. Given the consensus that Jumbo was close to death, this request raised no objection from either Bartlett or his vets. The task of nursing Jumbo therefore passed directly to Scott, a man with plenty of experience at handling animals but singularly lacking in formal medical training. To Bartlett the case must have looked hopeless, and as he left the African Elephant Den he probably expected never to see Jumbo alive again.

It may be remembered that some years earlier Scott had tackled a similarly hopeless case when the Zoo's kiwi had apparently fallen ill, although it was in fact egg-bound. On that occasion Scott had tended to the bird night and day until it recovered. He set about doing the same thing for Jumbo, forsaking his own comfortable lodgings for Jumbo's stark, straw-lined quarters. It was winter and so, while Jumbo lay in his weakened state, carpenters were called in to create some home comforts for Scott, including a seat and a stove. Apart from this, Scott and Jumbo were left entirely to their own devices over Christmas and the New Year, but the expected news that Jumbo had died did not materialize. Instead came rumours that the elephant had turned a corner and was regaining strength. Early in the New Year Scott was able to end his long vigil by Jumbo's side and announce that his patient was on the road to a full recovery.

Jumbo was indeed on the mend, to the amazement of Bartlett and the Zoo's vets, but how Scott had achieved the cure remained a mystery. Some talked of his having worked a modern-day miracle; others believed that he knew of some secret herbal remedy; there was even a theory that he had brought Jumbo back from the brink using some form of telepathy, hypnosis or "spiritual force". Others were more straightforward and asked Scott directly how he had nursed the elephant back to life but they only ever got one answer: "with bucketfuls of scotch".

Few believed that Scott had treated Jumbo using only whisky but there may have been an element of truth to the claim. In his memoirs Carl Hagenbeck recalled the time when several of his elephants were struck down with colic. "In order to cure them of this I gave them doses of rum. One of them, however, appeared to have had rather too much, for he became exceedingly hilarious and challenged his more sober neighbour to a duel. The jovial monster was disturbing the entire menagerie, so I saw that there was nothing for it but to repeat the dose, for the purpose of reversing the effect. I therefore supplied him with a large extra quantity of grog. He then became completely drunk and soon fell into a quiet sleep."

Exactly how Jumbo was cured has never been revealed but the process brought about a radical change in both the elephant and his keeper. "Since I brought Jumbo from his sick bed," wrote Scott, "he is like many a noble-minded man, who has been stricken down with sickness and raised up again, like old Job, to bless and magnify his creator."

In fact it was not the Creator that Jumbo took to magnifying but his keeper, whose days and nights of constant vigil instilled a child-like devotion in the elephant. Once back on his feet Jumbo took to following Scott about the Zoo in a puppy-like fashion and would become irritable and restless if the keeper left his sight for more than a few minutes. Popular opinion held that Jumbo was acting out of gratitude to Scott ("no one was more absolutely convinced that his life was saved by Scott than was the elephant himself") but the relationship had the side effect of removing much of Jumbo's latent anger. The episodes of wanton destruction virtually ceased, to the relief of the duty carpenters and blacksmiths: in the year following his recovery Jumbo damaged the doors to his enclosure just once and the year afterwards not at all.

We must suppose that Bartlett was pleased to see his African elephant bull returned to health and in a much calmer mood, but in time he became aware of another problem. The devotion that Jumbo displayed for Scott was so total that the elephant would not take orders from anybody else at the Zoo and would become restless and tetchy if the keeper was not around.

"When I go out of Jumbo's sight," said Scott, "or rather when I go away, he knows it, and if I don't come back at regular times he always makes me aware of it, both day and night. And he is selfish for if I am an hour or two overdue he commences to whine and cry and becomes very naughty, just the same as a child crying after its mother."

The realization that he was the only person who could control the great elephant gave Scott a measure of power that he had never before experienced. He had never been the easiest of men to work with but after Jumbo's recovery he became downright impossible and used his control over the elephant as a threat to his colleagues and superiors alike.

"Jumbo will do everything I ask him, good or bad," Scott would warn. "We're one – and woe be to anybody who tries to come between us!" The threat was not an idle one and it was with some alarm that Bartlett observed: "All the keepers had a fear of Scott, probably not without cause."

Life at the Zoo

The bond between Scott and his elephant may have been unconventional and even worrying, but it did lead to a period of extended calm in the African Elephant Den. Jumbo's violence ceased and his growth accelerated, transforming the elephant that was once considered a runt into an alarmingly tall and powerful animal. As Bartlett had hoped, his male African elephant was showing every sign of developing into an animal that was prodigiously larger and heavier than any elephant hitherto seen at the Zoo.

People also noticed Jumbo's increased size and were thrilled by the prospect of taking a ride on an animal whose species was being described by zoologists as "the largest animal on Earth". From lunchtime to dusk, winter and summer, children would queue for hours to ride on Jumbo's back. Scott may not have felt much affection for his fellow keepers but he did display a fondness for children, whom he would call "little folk" and with whom he had infinite patience.

As Jumbo returned from each tour of the Gardens, so Scott would gently help the "little folk" (and the occasional nanny) down from the howdah, then, after taking their ticket money, assist the next group of passengers up the wooden steps and into their seats. With all aboard, Scott would climb up on to Jumbo's neck and instruct the elephant to begin his progress. The tour lasted for 10–15 minutes and would wind its way through the drives and walkways of the older portion of the Zoo. The pace was slow and throughout the ride Scott would talk to the "little folk", encouraging them to sit quietly and requesting them to hold on tight. He too was enchanted by the experience, enthusing in the summer months about travelling through "magnificent gardens" which abounded with beautiful "grass plots, flowers, plants and trees".

In the course of a year thousands of children experienced the thrill of a ride on Jumbo, and a visit to the Zoo was considered incomplete without it. Before long Jumbo's fame was such that Alice, Chunee and the other elephants were considered inferior; parents, newspapers and guidebooks referred to Jumbo as "the elephant at the Zoo", ignoring his companions; some simply described him as "the children's friend". It was not just the off-spring of the Victorian middle and upper classes who benefited from a ride with Jumbo and Scott on Mondays, when the Zoo reduced the price of admission. The children of London's working-class population would also be waiting in the queue, their penny fare at the ready. It is even said that among Jumbo's customers were some of Queen Victoria's children (probably Prince Leopold and Princess Beatrice) as well as the young Winston Churchill. Indeed, Jumbo was a favourite of Queen Victoria, so we may assume that he received the occasional visit of Royalty.

It is claimed by Scott that in all his years of giving rides to children there occurred not one single accident and that the elephant, like his keeper, held the "little folk" in high esteem. To underscore Jumbo's gentleness Scott recounts an incident in which, while giving a ride, the elephant came to an unexpected halt.

"I shouted to him to go along," recalled Scott, who had been sitting on Jumbo's neck at the time, "but for once he did not obey the order. As I turned around to see what was the matter, there was a lady running over the grass plot on to the path, screaming and shouting: 'Oh, my poor child! My child, my child! Oh, he will be killed, he will be killed!' Well, I looked down from my elevation and saw Jumbo deliberately and coolly putting his trunk around the body of an infant that escaped its mother's apron-strings and had run and fallen in front of Jumbo. He just stopped right there, gently picked up the child by the waist with his trunk, and laid it on the green grass beside its screaming mother, more tenderly than the mother afterward took up the frightened child in her excitement."

Such legends enhanced Jumbo's reputation as the Zoo's gentle giant, but behind the scenes this gigantism was a cause for concern as the elephant's expanding frame started to look cramped in the confines of the African Elephant Den. In addition Bartlett did not want Jumbo to slip back into his truculent ways and wanted him settled in the new Elephant House as soon as possible, but progress on the building was frustratingly slow.

By March 1868 Anthony Salvin had drawn up a design which met with the approval of the Zoological Society's Council and so tenders were invited from several large building firms. Costs were foremost in the minds of the Council members, who instructed all those tendering to submit two quotes, one for the entire building, which would hold all four elephants plus the Zoo's large Indian rhinoceros, and one for the "centre and one wing only", to hold just the elephants. Five firms responded with quotes that ranged from £3,920 to £4,785 for the whole building and £2,596 to £3,092 for the other option. With money being the deciding factor, the commission was given to the builders Gammon & Sons, who had tendered the lowest quote. They were asked to construct the whole building and were given a £1,500 advance to get them going, but after a few months the project was already running so late that the Zoological Society threatened to levy a fine of £5 (around £330 today) for each additional day of delay.

The new Elephant House was eventually completed in June 1869 and it was with great ceremony that the Zoological Society's four elephants (and the rhino) were led across the Gardens, through a tunnel running underneath the public road and into the thin plot of land on Regent's Park's northern edge. For the first time since Jumbo's arrival, the Asian and African elephants could be viewed under the same roof. The new Elephant House was superior in all respects to the old buildings; constructed to mimic Swiss chalets, the new structure was made entirely from brick with sharply sloping slate roofs. It was divided into two main wings: a smaller eastern one with quarters for the rhino and a much longer western gallery for the elephants. Behind the building were two south-facing, fenced paddocks, each with a substantial bathing pool where the elephants and rhino could frolic in front of the crowds. When the animals were not in their paddocks, because of bad weather or maintenance, visitors were permitted to view them in their stalls from a gallery inside the building, entering at the rhinoceros end and exiting at the far corner.

The new building looked magnificent and received warm praise but it was not to Jumbo's liking and he expressed his displeasure in the only way he knew how: by attacking the doors to his new home. Bartlett had foreseen this possibility and given Salvin strict instructions that the doors to Jumbo's quarters had to be made impervious to the force of a charging elephant. Accordingly the builders were asked to add several layers of sheet iron to both sides of the doors, but this proved to be no match for Jumbo. Within days the doors were ruined, sending Bartlett into a towering rage. "The outer doors to the new Elephant House are useless," he wrote to the architect. "The African elephant has punched the sheet iron full of holes and the door has gone to splinters. I shall be glad to see you as soon as you can conveniently spare the time to come."

On Salvin's instructions the doors were further reinforced and Scott was instructed to pacify Jumbo, which he apparently managed to do. However, the elephant had not just damaged the Zoo's infrastructure, he had severely injured himself as well. While ramming the ironwork he had shattered and splintered both his tusks; this had occurred before but in this instance the ivory had fractured beneath the skin, close to the upper jawbone. Jumbo became calm again and little significance was placed on his damaged tusks but the injury was serious and would again put his life in danger.

The weeks passed and Jumbo's tusks began to grow again, but as the new ivory pushed its way forward the jagged ends deflected their path upwards into fresh skin. Instead of lying either side of the trunk and growing downwards, Jumbo's tusks emerged high up, breaking through the skin beneath his eyes. The resultant wounds became infected, producing abscesses that were not only painful for Jumbo to endure, but also affected his ability to eat. An alarming loss of weight followed, which Bartlett quickly linked to the infected swellings on his face. "Upon my going to him," he wrote, "he would allow me to put my hand upon these swellings, and appeared to me by the motion of his trunk to indicate the seat or cause of his suffering."

The infected wounds were beyond even the faith-healing skills that had previously been attributed to Scott and, with Jumbo's life evidently in danger, Bartlett took matters into his own hands: "I determined to cut through the thick skin in order to discharge the accumulated pus and enable the tusks to grow out of this opening. In order to accomplish this I had a steel rod made about eighteen inches in length, formed with a sharp hook at the end, the hook being flattened on the inner edge as sharp as a razor."

With his hook in hand, Bartlett issued instructions that he and Scott were on no account to be disturbed and then they entered the new Elephant House, bolting the doors behind them. The two men braced themselves and approached Jumbo, who by this time had become so weak that he was leaning against the wall for support. Bartlett positioned himself beneath the animal's lower jaw and set to work.

"I, with a sharp pull, hooking fast into the skin, cut it through, causing the most frightful discharge of very offensive matter. The poor beast uttered a loud shriek and rushed from us bleeding, shaking and trembling, but without exhibiting any anger. After a little coaxing and talking to he allowed us to wash out the wound by syringing it with water."

The operation was a success but Jumbo had been traumatized by the experience and it was judged too risky to carry out the same operation on his second abscess. It was agreed that Jumbo should be given the night to recover before any further surgery was undertaken. The next morning the two men returned and it was with some trepidation that Bartlett approached Jumbo with the hook; he expected him to back away or become violent and was surprised when he remained perfectly still even though he must have been aware of what was coming.

Bartlett used the hook to make a second incision, producing a sudden cry from the patient, but Jumbo remained stationary while the wound was incised and cleaned out as before. The effect of this amateur surgery was almost immediate; the tusks were able to grow through the holes created by Bartlett and all sign of infection vanished. Jumbo's appetite returned and he was soon consuming his usual diet of hay, straw, boiled rice, biscuits, mangel-wurzel and bread, along with whatever buns and cakes were given to him by the public. However, Jumbo's tusks never fully recovered and were always a disappointment to Bartlett; he had hoped that his male African elephant would be a famous "tusker" who could rival the ivories sported by the fabled Jack, but it was not to be. It became a habit of Jumbo's to use the sides of his den to wear away at his tusks, with the result that during his entire time at the Zoo they never grew more than a couple of inches long.

Bartlett and Scott lance Jumbo's face.

In the five years that they had known each other, Alice had never been a sexual partner to Jumbo but this did not stop the public calling her "Jumbo's wife". Scott did nothing to discourage this and would tell visitors that he had never before witnessed "more respect, deference and affection shown by a male to a female than Jumbo paid at all times to Alice, even during his sickness". When asked whether the couple had remained faithful to each other, Scott would even state: "I don't think that Alice ever deceived Jumbo; she certainly never flirted with any other elephants."

As the two elephants became sexually mature, they continued to show little interest in each other, but after their move to the new Elephant House rumours of a romance flourished again. These were prompted by the pair's antics in the new bathing pond. The joy of bathing was new to Alice but her companion had been quick to introduce her to the habit and, when not giving rides, Jumbo could frequently be seen in the pool, frolicking with his alleged wife. These occasions would attract a large crowd of spectators, who delighted at the elephants' games, which included chasing each other about the pool and much water fighting.

"Jumbo would, every now and then, turn right about and with his massive trunk throw up such a quantity of water as would make a shower-bath fall on Alice's back and then he would in the same way throw up to a great height a regular three-inch water-pipe gush. This would so tickle Alice that she would presently begin to reciprocate but as her trunk and powers were not so great as Jumbo's she could not make such a good job of it. It really is amusing to see Jumbo on his head trying to show his hind legs, just like the boys do when they are bathing."

With Jumbo behaving himself and living in apparent domestic bliss with Alice (at least in the eyes of the public), the Regent's Park elephants seemed settled and happy. Bartlett must have been pleased at the turn of events and might perhaps have dared to dream of an extended period of calm for the occupants of the new Elephant House. But the respite was to be short-lived and in the distance storm clouds were gathering; this time it was not just Jumbo's behaviour that was a cause for concern but that of his keeper as well.

∽ Heroes and Villains ∾

In the summer of 1870 the French Republic declared war on Prussia, an action that soon brought the invading army of Frederick III into France and, after several skirmishes, on to the road to Paris. By the end of September the Prussians had completely enclosed the French capital and were laying siege to the city; the unfortunate Parisians braced themselves for the period of starvation that would inevitably follow.

Within the boundary of the siege were Paris's two famous menageries, the Jardin des Plantes and, on the opposite side of town, the Jardin d'Acclimatation. As early as August the managers of these institutions had envisaged trouble and made a frantic attempt to evacuate their livestock to zoos in neighbouring countries. Many of the rarer species were removed but by the time of the siege both of the menageries still retained many animals, including most of their large mammals. As a temporary measure the animals from the Jardin d'Acclimatation were relocated to the safer surroundings of the Jardin des Plantes, but the lack of food and the bitter weather soon took their toll. The animals began to die from cold and starvation, and even plundering of the Jardin's extensive collection of trees and plants for food and fuel could not keep them alive. With the situation apparently hopeless and the people of Paris themselves on the verge of starvation, the Jardin's managers took the decision to begin selling off their stock to local restaurateurs, who, naturally enough, had designs on serving them up on a plate.

The commoner animals, such as the oxen, antelopes, gnus and camels, were the first to be eaten, but by mid-December the menu was being broadened to include the larger quadrupeds. Great attempts had been made to preserve the Jardin's two

African elephants, Castor and Pollux, who remained great favourites of the crowd and who, like their former companion Jumbo, would give rides to children in the nearby Bois de Boulogne. However, the elephants were starving and when a restaurant in the Passage des Princes offered to buy them for 27,000 francs the Jardin's managers regretfully accepted.

The best method of dispatching the elephants was a matter of some debate as it was suspected that at the first sign of injury they would go berserk. The first attempt involved the use of an explosive bullet which was aimed at Pollux's heart; it did not instantly kill the cow elephant but instead flooded her cage with blood and the unfortunate animal was observed to wait patiently and silently for her demise. When Castor's turn came, the bullet was aimed at the brain, producing near-instantaneous death.

That night Parisians who could afford it dined on elephant steak covered in *sauce Madère*. According to one diner it was delicious and a local newspaper declared: "We are in a mood to eat any number of strange animals and to declare their flesh sublime." The wish was granted when, two days later, meat from the Jardin's two bears was on sale at 14 francs a pound. "These poor brutes have done us no harm during their lives," said one Parisian, "and are serving us by their deaths."

The siege was lifted at the end of January 1871 but not before an extended period of artillery shelling killed many of the animals that had not been eaten, as well as several of their keepers. The Siege of Paris was a calamity that took the city's menageries many years to recover from and was a sober reminder of the role that fate had played in Jumbo's survival. Had the Jardin des Plantes refused to part with him or had they chosen to swap either Castor or Pollux in his place, then the venerable elephant at London Zoo would have finished his life inside a Parisian's stomach.

With the European stock of African elephants reduced by two, Alice and Jumbo were again a rare commodity, but despite the terrible happenings across the Channel the old rivalry between the London and Paris zoos persisted. A few months after the end of the siege Regent's Park received a juvenile Asian elephant named Tommy who proved to be even more restless than

Jumbo and was alleged to have been responsible for the death of his keeper, W.R. Paton. Rather than give Tommy to the Parisians, who were appealing for such animals, the Zoological Society quickly gave him to Dublin Zoo. Similarly, in September 1873 it agreed to sell Peter, its 10-year-old Asian elephant, to the zoo at Breslau in Germany (now Wroclaw in Poland) rather than the Jardin des Plantes, which, having received some renewed financial backing, was seeking to restock its menagerie.

The sale of Peter left Abraham Bartlett with three elephants under his control: Chunee, Alice and Jumbo. This must have seemed enough for an establishment the size of London Zoo, but an unforeseen sequence of events was to have terrible consequences for its elephants, and the man who would set these events in motion was Matthew Scott.

Since its completion in 1869 the Elephant House had played host at least once to Indian rhinoceroses, but over the years Abraham Bartlett had found these animals exceedingly troublesome and liable to display sudden and violent anger. Like Jumbo, the rhinos were apt to make running charges at their cages, sometimes inflicting terrible damage on their horns. One rhino had once ripped its horn clean off by charging at the railings in its paddock; another had to have its badly damaged horn removed, a delicate operation that required the animal's head to be wedged against the bars of its cage while Bartlett reached inside with a saw. It was far too risky for anyone to enter the cage.

On Saturday 21 November 1874 the Asian elephant keepers, Andrew Thompson and Richard Godfrey, were clearing out the stall of Jemmy, the Zoo's lone male rhino, while the animal frolicked in the paddock outside. This went against Bartlett's instructions; he believed that while cleaning took place Jemmy should to be confined to another stall in the Elephant House. But Thompson and Godfrey had become blasé about the danger posed by the rhino and, to save time, they would let Jemmy play freely outside, presuming that Scott, who worked next door, would alert them if the beast looked likely to return indoors.

That day Scott's mind must have been elsewhere, for as the keepers were sweeping out the old straw Jemmy came rushing in from the paddock, knocking them to the ground. With both men trapped on the floor Jemmy started to trample them, but their screams brought Scott running in. Without thinking, he grabbed a riding whip and started to thrash Jemmy about the eye, driving the enraged animal back into the paddock. He tried to drag the injured men into a fenced-off area of the stall but Godfrey had fainted and, before he could be pulled clear, Jemmy was back on him.

According to a newspaper report the rhino "tore the flesh off the man's leg from the thigh down to the knee, laying the bone bare", while Thompson was further trampled and received severe internal injuries. Using his whip, Scott was again able to drive the animal back and, the newspapers reported, carried both men from the enclosure to safety. "Scott escaped unhurt," wrote one journalist, adding, "he is a small man, by no means remarkable for his strength, but possessed of very great courage and presence of mind".

Other accounts were equally complimentary. "Mr Matthew Scott, the hero, is no ideal Guy Livingstone, with the strength of Hercules," wrote the editor of the *Daily Telegraph*, "but he pitted his life against odds so terrible that the boldest man alive might well think twice before venturing upon so forlorn a chance. There was no crowd to look on, no encouraging shout, no Victoria Cross to win; there were none watching during those terrible few seconds but Death on the one hand and Fortune on the other. And seldom has Fortune favoured a bolder or a worthier effort."

By contrast, Bartlett viewed the incident as something of an embarrassment for the Zoological Society (as did many of the headline writers) and made efforts to play it down. According to him the two keepers were injured but not as seriously as the newspapers had claimed; Godfrey's leg was not ripped open but merely bruised and both men had walked from the rhino cage and not been carried by Scott. As for the hero of the hour, he received no praise from his boss, who commented: "he ought to have been keeping the rhino entertained in the paddock".

Bartlett consistently refused to acknowledge Scott's heroism but readers of the *Daily Telegraph* made up for this by sending in sums of money for all the keepers. On 16 December Scott, Thompson and Godfrey applied to the Zoological Society's Council for permission to keep the cash that had been sent to them; the three men were allowed to do so and they may well have needed the money as their injuries kept them off work for some time.

The aftermath of the incident with the rhino was to reveal a ruthlessness in Bartlett that was rarely seen by the public. In January 1875 Andrew Thompson felt able to return to work and approached Bartlett about undertaking some light duties. "I was at once told to go to the cattle and deer sheds, the coldest place and the hardest work in the gardens," wrote Thompson in a letter of complaint to the *Daily Telegraph*. "At this time I was suffering from the shock to the system, and had a bad rheumatic attack. I had even to be dressed and undressed by others, and to go, therefore, to the new work would have been simply to send me back to bed."

Thompson refused the work and so Bartlett sacked him on the spot, disregarding the keeper's 30 years of service to the Zoo. The ex-keeper was bitterly upset at his dismissal, which included the loss of his pension, and especially at being separated from Chunee, the elephant that he had cared for since the early 1850s. The case was highlighted in the newspapers and brought a reply from a Fellow of the Zoological Society, who stated that "by refusing to work in the cattle sheds where Mr Bartlett sent him, [Thompson] had discharged himself, and so had forfeited his claim to a pension altogether".

The truth was more complicated. Bartlett had never got on particularly well with Thompson and had found him headstrong and unable to take orders. It was for this reason that the care of Jumbo had originally been given to Scott, a man who Bartlett thought was better at taking orders than Thompson (although he was later proved wrong). The injuries to the two Asian elephant keepers gave Bartlett the opportunity to reorganize the regime in the Elephant House, and when Thompson returned from sick leave he discovered that his job had been taken by somebody else. At the time of the accident Regent's Park held only one Asian elephant, the 25-year-old and much-loved Chunee. Perhaps reflecting on his earlier experience with Scott and Jumbo, Bartlett decided that Chunee's two new keepers should be men who had no experience of looking after elephants. In fact her new keepers turned out to have little experience with animals of any kind and were gardeners who had previously been in charge of a vegetable plot by the deer sheds.

The sacked Thompson was heartbroken at being separated from Chunee and, if the reports are to be believed, the elephant felt much the same way. "After Thompson's dismissal I noticed that the day after poor Chunee grew restless, irritable and melancholy, and so touchy that I was afraid to let my children go near her," wrote one regular visitor to the Zoo. There was certainly a marked change in Chunee's health; she visibly lost weight and became listless and ever weaker. On 7 July she sank to the ground and lay peacefully until, several hours later, she expired.

The Zoological Society recorded Chunee's death as being due to "consumption" (tuberculosis), a disease that is known to affect elephants, but others had their doubts about this. Remembering Thompson's dismissal, a newspaper correspondent noted that "beasts can die of a broken heart as easily as men, and no animal alive – not even a dog – conceives so strong an affection for his keeper as an elephant". Another letter writer was more blunt: "Chunee has died for want of that care and attention which Thompson used to bestow upon her."

Whatever the cause of Chunee's death, her body was dissected and distributed to various scientific institutions; the brain, which apparently weighed 12 lb, went to the Royal College of Surgeons. For the first time in decades Regent's Park had no Asian elephant in residence, a situation that reflected poorly on Bartlett and some of the recent decisions he had made. A frantic search for a replacement Asian elephant began but there was not one for sale or loan in Europe; fortunately, news of the Zoo's plight reached the Prince of Wales, who was then touring India. He purchased four elephants and arranged for them to be transported back to London, but they would not arrive until the following spring and summer.

After this disaster Bartlett's spate of poor decision-making continued when he attempted to use the death of Chunee to weaken Scott's power base in the Elephant House. He approached Scott and instructed him to relinquish one of his two African elephants into the care of the late Chunee's inexperienced keepers. Scott's reaction to this instruction can only be imagined but one suspects that the man who single-handedly fought a rhinoceros may have had something forceful to say about being made to give up one of his elephants. However, any protests that Scott may have lodged were in vain and it was with reluctance that he handed care of Alice over to the two new keepers, who had days earlier watched Chunee die. (It was, of course, out of the question that Scott should relinquish Jumbo, although Bartlett would doubtless have been keen to see him do so.) Disaster was not far off.

It is alleged that on receiving Alice the new keepers decided that the elephant was too frisky and needed to be broken in further. They set about this, it is said, by securing Alice with ropes and, having tied her up tightly, then left her overnight. At 9 o'clock the following morning Bartlett was in his office when he heard the terrible noise of an animal screaming in pain. Moments later one of Alice's new keepers came running in shouting that the elephant had torn off part of her trunk. Bartlett ran to the Elephant House and was horrified at the sight that met him.

"I found the end of her trunk in the middle of the den," he wrote. "It was warm and the nerves and muscles were still quivering and in motion. The poor beast appeared in great distress and agony, whirling and elevating her trunk and screaming; she would not allow anyone near her." Aware that elephants could bleed to death from a trunk injury, Bartlett ordered a bucket of cold water to be brought in. Alice was persuaded to place her trunk in it and, to the relief of all (including Scott), the bleeding stopped. For weeks afterwards Alice had to be fed and watered by hand but she was eventually able to use her trunk, which had lost nearly 12 inches in length, almost as well as before.

Like Jumbo, Alice was a family favourite at the Zoo and it did not take long for news of the injury to reach the newspapers. Coming so soon after Thompson's dismissal and Chunee's death, the injury to Alice looked less like an accident than neglect or abuse. In the wake of very unfavourable publicity, including a string of articles in the *Marylebone Mercury* which repeatedly referred to "the muddle at the Zoo", Bartlett gave an explanation for the accident. It was, he said, the result of Alice having got her trunk caught inside the leather strap that was used to secure her front legs while her den was being cleaned. In trying to pull her trunk free, she managed to rip off the end. This explanation, however, contradicted the story that was being officially divulged (on Bartlett's instructions) by the Zoo's keepers: Alice inadvertently trod on her trunk, they would say when asked by the public. The waters were further muddied by a rumour that the inexperienced keepers, to stop Alice hitting them, had left her tied up by her trunk and the injury occurred when the elephant struggled to free herself.

The adverse comments continued in the national and local papers for weeks, infuriating the Zoological Society and especially Bartlett, who was singled out for criticism: "The Resident Superintendent will probably upon reflection be disposed to admit that he has acted somewhat hastily," wrote the editor of the *Daily Telegraph*, who suggested that the disasters could have been avoided by judicious management and added: "It is to be hoped that the recent difficulties at the Zoological Gardens may, upon careful and temperamental consideration, be found capable of a final and satisfactory solution."

No member of the Zoo's Council was prepared to admit to any mistake and the criticism only served to harden their attitude towards the press. When, a few years later, one of the Prince of Wales's new elephants trampled a keeper to death, the incident was kept quiet until a whistle-blower within the Zoo alerted the papers. Accusations of a cover-up followed, especially when Philip Sclater announced that the elephant had been acting "more in play than earnest".

The year after the accident with the rhinoceros was one of the most traumatic ever endured by the Zoo as a whole but especially for its managers, who had been repeatedly accused of systemic incompetence. The troubles in the Elephant House had an effect elsewhere also. Scott had never been the easiest of men to work with but it would seem that the dismissal of Thompson, the death of Chunee and the injury to Alice all took their toll. From that time Scott started to despise his superiors at the Zoo and began to follow his own lonely path, shunning the company and affection of all with the exception of his beloved Jumbo, to whom he remained utterly devoted.

CHAPTER 13

Friction in the Elephant House

artlett's actions in the weeks following Scott's heroic rescue might suggest that he had tried to use the rhinoceros incident to effect a bungled coup at the Elephant House. If so, then he was only partially successful, for although Thompson and Godfrey had been removed, the intransigent Scott remained in place. The Superintendent was not happy with this outcome and made several attempts to undermine Scott's relationship with Jumbo.

After Jumbo's illness Scott had warned his workmates that he and the elephant were as one "and woe be to anybody who tries to come between us". This threat, it seems, was not an idle one, for it was clear that the elephant would not take orders, or even behave in an orderly manner, with anyone other than Scott. This gave Scott a strong bargaining chip with the Zoo's management and there was no question of moving him elsewhere in the Gardens or, indeed, of dismissing him. After all, who would control England's most famous elephant in his absence?

By the time of Chunee's death Jumbo was almost full grown and had reached the giddy height of nine feet and an estimated weight of around three tons. Bartlett's hope of possessing a gigantic specimen of African elephant had come true, and Jumbo was being advertised as the largest and heaviest elephant in all Europe, a claim that at this time was probably erroneous. Jumbo's size had not gone unnoticed by the visiting public, who welcomed the idea of their children riding on such an oversized but apparently gentle animal.

"Jumbo became the pride and glory of the Zoo, an immense favourite with the public," wrote Theo Johnson; and it was not just his height that thrilled the crowds but his cheeky personality as well. Jumbo was famous for having a love of music and in particular for his appreciation of the army bands that played each weekend at the Gardens during the summer. On hearing the band strike up, Jumbo would become highly animated and trumpet in time to the beat; in time he came to prefer the music produced by the band of the Horse Guards and became especially joyous when they were playing and sometimes annoyed if another ensemble took their place.

Also, in public Jumbo and his keeper had formed themselves into something of a double act. When Scott's attention was distracted Jumbo would extend his trunk and steal his keeper's trademark bowler hat, raising it high into the air. Scott would pretend to be enraged with his elephant and jump up and down until the trunk came down once more, placing the hat gently back on his head. For an encore Jumbo would reach across his fence to steal food from visitors' hands or, even more cheekily, drain their teacups and beer glasses. In fact Jumbo was noted for having something of a love for alcohol, and especially whisky, a habit that may have been a result of Scott's having cured, as he said, the elephant with it.

The public viewed Scott as a sociable, lovable character who was fond of clowning about with his elephant, but this was in contrast with the man's true outlook and behaviour. By 1880 Scott had entered his thirtieth year of working at the Zoo and showed every sign of wanting to continue until the day he died. This prospect pleased almost no one, least of all Bartlett, who had grown weary of his former protégé and was seeking a means of removing him from the Elephant House.

In contrast with the other keepers, Scott was in an extraordinarily advantageous position and, in the eyes of some, seemed to be able to operate outside the normal rules and regulations. For example, since 1871 the Zoo had been covered in notices which informed the public: "The keepers in the Society's service are not entitled to gratuities for the exhibition of animals under their charge. Visitors are requested not to offer gratuities to them." Scott, however, was allowed to keep the money generated by Jumbo's rides and he refused point-blank to share it with anyone.

Then there was Scott's celebrity status, brought about by his association with Jumbo, and which led the *Daily Telegraph* to remark that the keeper was "well known to visitors to the Gardens". Bartlett was keen to discourage his keepers from becoming recognizable public figures as it tended to produce situations such as had occurred with Andrew Thompson, whose acrimonious parting with the Zoo had become headline news. Again Scott seemed to be exempt from this unwritten rule, and while other keepers were routinely shuffled about the place Jumbo always retained his keeper.

The final liberty that seemed to have been granted to Scott concerned his attitude, which, while never entirely harmonious, became downright objectionable after Thompson's dismissal. When faced with the general public Scott would be sweetness itself and was especially noted for his patience with children and women. Behind the scenes he displayed a very different persona and was secretive, obstructive and rude to both his fellow keepers and his superiors.

"Matthew Scott was subject to that strange disease called 'cussedness'," recalled Theo Johnson. "This, like perversity, constrains its victims to do things the most contrary to their self interest." In Scott's case this included being outstandingly rude to his betters and, on several occasions, to visiting dignitaries as well. "He gloried in being as rude as he could possibly be – especially to those who appeared to be at all fashionable or distinguished."

Scott's celebrity status also affected his ego so that when he recounted stories from Jumbo's life history, the contributions of Bartlett and others would be removed in favour of himself. Had any ordinary keeper behaved in this fashion he would have been dismissed, but not Scott, whose unique ability to control the Zoo's gigantic African elephant seemed to place him above the law. The Zoological Society received complaints about his behaviour from many quarters but the dressings down that the keeper received had little apparent effect.

"The remonstrations made to Scott amused him and I need hardly say their effect was not a deterrent one," said Johnson. "And it must be confessed that to have a civil question replied to [by Scott] with a stony stare or a consignment to the realms of

Pluto, justified the complaints which through various channels reached the ears of the Society."

Although not the brightest of men, Scott had stealthily carved out an empire for himself at the Zoo and had done so under the nose of Bartlett, a man who prided himself on his ability to manage humans and animals alike. Scott even took to tormenting Bartlett at night by entering Jumbo's den and sharing a bottle of scotch with the elephant; as the pair fell under the influence of alcohol Scott would break into song, to which his elephant would provide a very loud trumpeting accompaniment. Bartlett's family home was only a short distance from the Elephant House and the noise was said to "effectively banish slumber from that of the Superintendent".

Bartlett did not take this threat to his authority lying down and in the late 1870s started to take steps to rein in his belliger-ent elephant keeper. He needed to find a means of splitting apart Jumbo and Scott even if this meant risking the wrath of the giant elephant. Bartlett correctly recognized that the best way to lessen Scott's monopoly over the animal would be to give him an assistant keeper. For many years Scott had refused to work alongside any other keeper, preferring to care for Jumbo entirely by himself, but some time around 1880 Bartlett told him directly that he was to have an assistant whom he would train to look after the elephant. Scott objected to this, so to sweeten the pill Bartlett told him that the choice of assistant would be his. On hearing this Scott realized that Bartlett was not going to back down over this issue and so acceded to the Superintendent's will, merely saying that he would prefer that the selection of an assistant be made for him.

This placed Bartlett in an awkward position, for Scott had no friends at the Zoo and was, by the Superintendent's admission, much feared by the other keepers. Nonetheless, some unfortu-nate keeper was assigned to the Elephant House with instructions to assist Scott in caring for Jumbo. For the first few days all appeared to go well, but less than a week after starting Scott's assistant entered Bartlett's office shaking with fear and declaring that "no earthly consideration would induce him to remain in a situation of such danger". The assistant keeper's resignation from the Elephant House was ruefully accepted by Bartlett but, rather than let Scott savour his victory, he immediately sent another man to fill the vacant post.

The issue of Scott's assistant precipitated a battle of wills between Bartlett and his keeper. A pattern soon developed in which a new assistant keeper would arrive and be allowed to go about his work until, a few days later, something would happen that would lead to his immediate resignation. These incidents were apparently terrifying and always originated with a display of bad temper from Jumbo. Theo Johnson portrayed the newcomer's plight: "To be knocked over like a ninepin by a wave of that mighty trunk while busied in some quiet employ; to be charged upon by an elephant ten feet high, whose hoarse scream must have sounded in terrified ears like the very trump of doom. These things must have been disconcerting to nerves not specially trained to surprise and shock."

There was little doubt in the mind of Bartlett, and of other members of staff, that Scott was the mastermind behind Jumbo's terrifying assaults on successive assistant keepers. It was later claimed that Scott intended no harm and that the elephant was just acting under instruction, but it had the desired effect. Bartlett saw that he could not compel any of his keepers to work with Jumbo, so by default Scott was able to maintain his lonely reign over the African elephant. The situation left Bartlett seething and so, the idea of separating Scott from Jumbo having failed, he determined that more drastic action was necessary, and in this he was greatly helped by a sudden change in Jumbo's behaviour. For the first time in many years Scott would find himself on the back foot.

In April 1881 the Zoological Society was forced to relinquish two of its male Asian elephants to Berlin Zoo when their owner, the Prince of Wales, gave them to his nephew, Kaiser Wilhelm II, as a wedding present. It was the first time in nearly a decade that the Zoo had removed a living elephant from its premises and a special platform had to be constructed to allow the adult bulls into purpose-built wooden crates. The removal of such large elephants had not been achieved during Bartlett's time at Regent's Park and may have given the Superintendent the idea of moving Jumbo to another British zoo or possibly even to one abroad. But to do so would have meant removing the Zoo's star attraction, which would have been unacceptable without good cause. Fortunately it was Jumbo himself who would provide Bartlett with the excuse he needed to get rid of both elephant and keeper once and for all.

On the night of 16 June Jumbo charged repeatedly at the doors of his den, causing considerable damage to the lock and bolts. It was a rare return of his old violent behaviour and was initially thought to be a one-off occurrence that was perhaps provoked by the clearing of the Elephant House's drains earlier that day.

Jumbo attacks his den.

All went quiet again until the first week of August, when Jumbo made another more concerted attack on his den; this time the damage was much more extensive. A week later Jumbo made another minor attack, but on 22 August he lost all control and during the night almost managed to destroy the entire Elephant

House. The sight that greeted Scott the next morning was quite unsettling: all the windows within Jumbo's reach had been destroyed, the doors were nearly broken down and the beams supporting the roof left in a perilous situation; he even managed to damage the public walkway outside, although exactly how he achieved this is not known.

For three days a nine-strong team of carpenters, blacksmiths and labourers worked to make good the damage, which included making props for the roof beams and the walls, but the repairs were not to last for long. One week later Jumbo began a prolonged onslaught of nocturnal violence; for five nights he attacked the doors, walls and windows, and it was as much as the carpenters and blacksmiths could do to keep the Elephant House standing, let alone secure. Iron plating was fixed to the doors, further props were placed under the beams and any excess furnishings were removed from the den.

Such behaviour had, of course, been seen in Jumbo's younger days but then he had been much smaller and the damage proportionately less. Now he was 11 feet tall and approaching five tons in weight; his giant size was threatening the Elephant House's infrastructure and, try as he might, there was little that Scott could do to calm his animal friend down. For the first time in a long while Scott could not claim to have total control over Jumbo and had to watch helplessly as the elephant ran amok, destroying everything within reach. The bouts were, however, confined to the night and during the day Jumbo was considered calm enough to be allowed to continue giving rides to children.

Bartlett watched the proceedings with a mixture of horror and interest. His knowledge of elephant biology led him to believe that Jumbo's bad behaviour could be related to "musth", a strange display of behaviour associated with sexual maturity in both African and Asian elephants. He sought the advice of Sclater, who agreed and explained that "after elephants arrive at the age of twenty-one, they behave dangerously at certain seasons called must or moost seasons". The phenomenon of the "musth elephant" had been known to elephant tamers and hunters for centuries and its symptoms fitted Jumbo's behaviour very well, as the Victorian naturalist John Wood explains:

"At certain periodical seasons the elephant becomes very unruly, and will not obey even his keeper, but is filled with a wild longing to attack anything or anybody. This state of things lasts a week or ten days during which time the elephant is called 'must'. Whenever a service or sport of great danger is on hand, must-elephants will be used if possible as they lose all sense of fear during their short madness, and will attack anything that is opposed to them. A very careful mahout is required to drive a must-elephant as his charge is quite as likely to turn his rage against friends as against foes."

In 1881 Jumbo was 20 years old but he would have only just reached full sexual maturity, which, in African elephants, generally occurs at around 18 years. Musth is closely associated with sexual maturity but in wild elephant populations it generally affects individuals in their late twenties or older. For some reason, perhaps related to his captivity, Jumbo experienced musth at an early age.

Although Victorian zoologists knew about the existence of musth and that it could turn a docile elephant into a raging monster, they were not aware of its main symptoms nor of its biological function. It is only in comparatively recent times that scientists have gained a better understanding of musth and its effects on male elephants, although the exact function remains a matter of debate. Studies of elephants in musth suggest that it is triggered by increased levels of the hormone testosterone in the blood. Concentrations of the hormone build up over several weeks, triggering physical and behavioural characteristics which are familiar to modern elephant keepers but which would have been unknown to Scott and Bartlett.

The early stages of musth would have caused some large glands in Jumbo's forehead (the temporal glands) to swell slightly and to start to secrete a watery fluid that would have run down his cheeks as thin, smeary streams. At this time Jumbo would also have started to dribble urine continuously, possibly spraying it down his back legs; this would have smelt distasteful and in modern zoos it has been observed that the floor of a male elephant's stall will foam when washed out. Scott may have inadvertently witnessed this, because in June 1881, when Jumbo would have been in the early musth stage, he ordered that the drains in his den be cleared out.

Over several weeks the testosterone in Jumbo's blood would have gone from a background level of around 1.0 nanograms per millilitre to perhaps as much as 65. The secretions from his swollen temporal glands would have become more sticky and would have smelt pungent, but the most striking symptom of the later musth stage is the aggressiveness displayed by the elephant, which, as evinced by Chunee at the Exeter 'Change, can be terrifying. Wild African elephants in musth have been observed to walk and behave in an overtly aggressive manner, to randomly attack other males and to use their heads, trunks and tusks to topple trees, to spray earth and to dig into the ground; they may also emit a low-frequency sound known as the "musth rumble". The exact function of musth is a matter of debate but it is generally thought to be part of a sexual attraction process in which the elephant marks its territory with urine and secretions, fights off potential rivals and attracts the attention of females with sounds and visual displays such as ear flapping.

This behaviour is all very well in the wilderness but in captive elephants the onset of musth presents a serious danger both to the animal and to its keepers. Bartlett understood that Jumbo's musth would be temporary but the elephant's violence reminded him of the death of Chunee, whose frantic behaviour threatened the safety of all at the menagerie in the Strand. Several questions posed themselves to Bartlett: would the Elephant House be able to withstand Jumbo's attacks? What if he ran amok inside the Zoo itself? Should the need arise, how could a five-ton elephant be quickly and efficiently killed? Bartlett had witnessed the firepower that had been needed to bring down Chunee in 1826 and shivered at the prospect of having to arrange a similarly protracted execution for the Zoo's star attraction.

Aside from the suffering that this would cause Jumbo, there were the British newspapers, which would make a big issue of anything other than a clean death. (A similar situation had faced Carl Hagenbeck, who had to kill a male elephant in musth which had attacked and nearly killed his keeper. He arranged to have the animal shot, but when the appointed hour came no one could

Above: A Nubian elephant hunter (or Aggageer) poses on top of a camel.

Right: Abraham Bartlett, the superintendent of London Zoo, a man with a passion for elephants.

Above: Matthew Scott and his beloved elephant Jumbo. The two were rarely apart for more than a few hours at a time.

Left: The "children's favourite" waits patiently while his passengers climb aboard.

Above: Jumbo greets some visitors as they pass by his den in London Zoo.

Left: Jumbo and Matthew Scott gave rides about the Zoo to thousands of children every year.

Jumbo's pitiful refusal to leave London Zoo tugged at the nation's heartstrings.

Above: After weeks of trying, Jumbo is persuaded to walk through the box outside his den.

THE ILLUSTRATED LONDON NEWS.

No. 2229.—Vol. LXXX. SATURDAY, APRIL 1, 1882. WITH (SIXPENCE TWO SUPPLEMENTS) BY Post, 6½d.

Left: The elephant is loaded aboard the *Assyrian Monarch* in the presence of a vast crowd.

Left: Phineas T. Barnum was arguably the greatest showman of all time – but was initially against the idea of buying Jumbo.

Below: Hysterical scenes greeted Jumbo's arrival in New York City.

Above: Jumbo in Madison Square Garden is shown as towering over his friend and companion, the elephant Tom Thumb.

Right: Thanks to the fuss surrounding his purchase, Jumbo became the star attraction of Barnum's circus.

Above: Jumbo lies dead on a railway embankment. News of the tragedy travelled around the world in a matter of hours.

Left: For decades Jumbo's stuffed hide continued to attract tourists – until the museum where it was housed burned to the ground.

pull the trigger and so the unfortunate animal was instead hanged by six men with a rope and pulley.)

For a few days in late September Jumbo appeared settled again but it was merely the lull before the storm and on 15 October the violence began again in earnest. Night after night the Elephant House sustained a ferocious assault and repairs were needed almost daily. In one memorable incident Jumbo used his head to ram an eight-inch-thick steel-covered oak beam and almost totally destroyed it. Bartlett was warned that if the elephant continued his assaults the entire Elephant House was in danger of collapse.

Jumbo had by this time been prevented from going into the rest of the Zoo, although he was still allowed into his paddock, but as his violent moods began to erupt during the day even this was not spared his anger. The raging elephant attacked the railings and churned up the yard with his feet; when he was confined to his den, the assaults continued there.

It was in the third week of November that Jumbo's musth ended; in the space of a few days his testosterone levels would have dropped back to normal, his temporal glands would have shrunk back into his forehead and his aggressive behaviour stopped. His last assault was on 18 November, by which time a total of 24 emergency repairs had been logged by the Zoo's retinue of handymen. According to one survey, the Elephant House had been brought dangerously close to collapse and so much iron plating had been used to reinforce Jumbo's den that it looked more like a prison cell than an animal pen.

"The door leading from the den into the open air is closed with massive beams of oak eight inches square; these are further strengthened by plates of stout sheet iron on both sides and are so heavy that two men can scarcely raise one of them from the ground. Nevertheless, these beams have not merely bent but positively broken through both iron and wood, by the muscular power of the animal. The sides of the den are everywhere strengthened by similar iron covered beams; but in spite of every precaution, the house is quickly being destroyed by the efforts of the animal during his fits of irritability."

As Jumbo's temper abated and normality resumed, Bartlett

(along with the rest of the staff) wondered how long they would have before the musth returned and whether it would cause Jumbo to be responsible for a death among the workforce or, more horrifically, the visiting public. Bartlett made his feelings about Jumbo perfectly clear in a report to the Zoological Society's Council:

"I have for some time past felt very uncomfortable with reference to this fine animal, now quite, or nearly quite, adult, and my fear of him is so entertained by all the keepers, except Matthew Scott, who is the only man in the gardens who dares enter this animal's den alone. I have no doubt whatever that the animal's condition has at times been such that he would kill anyone (except Scott) who would venture alone into his den, but up to the present time Scott has had, and still has, the animal perfectly and completely under his control. How long this state of things may continue it is quite impossible to say. At the same time, I consider that the matter is of so serious a nature that I feel called upon to draw the attention of the Council to the subject, for in the event of illness or accident to the keeper (Scott) I fear I should have to ask permission to destroy the animal, as no other keeper would undertake the management of this fine but dangerous beast. In conclusion, I may ask that I should be provided with, and have at hand, the means of killing this animal, should such a necessity arise."

The Council heeded the advice and provided Bartlett with a powerful rifle to be used "in the event of finding it necessary to kill him" but no conclusion could be reached as to what might be done in the long term with the troublesome elephant and his keeper. Bartlett did not believe that the Elephant House would withstand another battering and made plans to "chain Jumbo down and put him on half rations" if the musth returned. It was at this point that fate intervened and offered the Superintendent an unexpected and welcome lifeline: on 13 December he was handed a telegram from America which was to suggest an instant solution to all his problems. "What is the lowest price you can take for the large male African elephant?" said the telegram. It was signed "Barnum, Bailey and Hutchinson".

PART THREE

❧ ❧

THE JUMBO CRAZE

CHAPTER 14

✑ Piteous Scenes at the Zoo ✑

Phineas Taylor Barnum was one of the most flamboyant, colourful and controversial figures in America. From an early age he had proved himself to be a natural extrovert and entrepreneur who was happy to turn his hand to almost any venture, provided that it would make money. Born in 1810 in Connecticut, Barnum already had a string of business failures behind him when, in 1835, he purchased an aged and disabled African-American woman named Joice Heth, whom he exhibited as a 160-year-old wonder in a touring show (she was in fact in her eighties). This experience led Barnum to buy a museum in New York from which he built up a touring circus that included many human "freaks" such as the Bearded Lady, the diminutive General Tom Thumb and the Siamese twins Chang and Eng Bunker.

Fire and bankruptcy dogged Barnum's career but in 1871 the showman established P.T. Barnum's Grand Travelling Museum, Menagerie, Caravan and Hippodrome, a vast touring circus which boasted animal and human performers, a Zoo and, of course, his "freaks". The venture used the recently constructed railway network to move about the eastern United States, stopping in sizeable towns and cities; the circus was advertised as "The Greatest Show on Earth" and was wildly popular. In February 1881 Barnum merged his company with three others belonging to James Bailey and James L. Hutchinson; the result was P.T. Barnum's Greatest Show On Earth, and the Great London Circus, Sanger's Royal British Menagerie and The Grand International Allied Shows United. It was not the catchiest of titles and so the company was quickly renamed the Barnum and London Circus, with the resultant show, which retained

Barnum's format of a gigantic travelling circus, still popularly referred to as the Greatest Show on Earth.

Barnum's merger with Bailey and Hutchinson freed up a good deal of capital and it was agreed that the money should be used to seek out and buy some bigger and better exhibits that would attract the punters for the 1882 touring season. Accordingly, several agents were dispatched across America and Europe with instructions to "secure some great attraction" for the show, be it an animal, person or inanimate object. One of these agents was Joseph Lee Warner, an ex-mayor from Michigan, who was packed off to Europe in search of suitable exhibits; once there he travelled widely through England, France, Germany and Russia. While in St Petersburg Warner was enchanted with a boy named Jo-Jo whose face looked exactly like a dog's, but the young lad did not fancy a life in Barnum's circus. The agent returned to America empty-handed and somewhat dejected.

On 12 December 1881 Warner was summoned to the New York headquarters of the Barnum and London Circus, where he was interviewed by James Bailey.

"Find anything?" asked Bailey.

"No," replied Warner.

Bailey was disappointed to hear this but decided to pursue the matter. "What's the biggest thing you saw over there?"

"Biggest thing I saw was an elephant in London Zoo."

"How big?"

"Well, about so high," said Warner, raising his umbrella to arm's length and touching a spot on the wall.

Bailey expressed surprise at this. "Are you sure?"

"Yes. The elephant had to go under an archway to get out of his quarters and his back just scraped the top. I measured it with my umbrella."

"Eddie, get a stepladder and measure that," Bailey ordered Mott, his assistant. A few minutes later Eddie was able to reveal that by Warner's estimate the elephant was probably the biggest in the world.

"Can he be bought?" asked Bailey excitedly.

"Oh, yes," replied Warner, although in truth he didn't know whether he could or not.

"Well, I guess we'll get him then," said Bailey. Within hours a telegram from Barnum, Bailey and Hutchinson was on Abraham Bartlett's desk in London, to the Superintendent's wonder and delight.

Bailey's offer to buy Jumbo could not have come at a better time. Not only was Bartlett greatly alarmed at Jumbo's musth, he was also thoroughly fed up with Scott, who continued to challenge his authority almost daily. Selling Jumbo to Barnum would at a stroke solve both problems: a potentially dangerous elephant would be gone from the Zoo and it was more than probable that Scott would elect to go with him. But even if the keeper chose to stay, he would be without his great bargaining chip, Jumbo, and thus unable to blackmail the Zoological Society any further.

Bartlett did not wait for the Council's approval to sell Jumbo but made an immediate reply to Bailey's telegram: "Messers Barnum, Bailey and Hutchinson. Will sell him for £2,000."

Bailey was delighted and arranged a meeting with his business partners to break the good news. However, when told that Bailey had secured the purchase of a giant elephant, both Barnum and Hutchinson seemed less than delighted. Hutchinson objected on the grounds that the circus already had 30 elephants. "The necessity for another one is not apparent," he said.

Barnum's protest was connected to the company's financial arrangements. Because the three men had put differing sums of capital into the merger, the circus's profits were split unequally, with Barnum receiving half the money and the other two 25 per cent each. This meant that the purchase of Jumbo for £2,000 (£138,000 today) affected him disproportionately. Barnum complained that the cost of Jumbo was too high, especially when it was considered that the circus was laid up for the winter and not generating any money.

Bailey was disappointed at his partners' reactions and was perplexed by Barnum, who just a few years earlier had talked to an animal trader about making a bid for Jumbo.

"I am willing to pay a fortune for Jumbo, if you could get him," Barnum had said to William Jamrach, a London-based animal dealer who had secured many elephants for the Greatest Show on Earth.

"It is no use even to think about it," replied Jamrach. "Jumbo is as popular as the Prince of Wales and the Zoo wouldn't dare sell him. All England would be outraged at the idea; he is an English institution and is part of the national glory. You might as well think of buying Nelson's Column." This conversation warned Barnum off making a bid for Jumbo but later he confessed that the idea of obtaining the elephant had remained with him for ever afterwards.

Bailey's heart was set on having Jumbo and he fought hard to convince his colleagues that it was a good idea. He pointed out that their two rivals Forepaugh and Coup had both purchased large elephants for the 1882 season. This news brought Hutchinson round to his way of thinking and, after some further needling, Barnum also assented to buy Jumbo. A few months later this incident would be conveniently forgotten by Barnum as he took all credit for discovering and buying the elephant.

William Jamrach's advice to Barnum was given around 1874 and at the time he was perfectly correct: then Bartlett would have dismissed out of hand any offer to buy Jumbo, but things had changed markedly in the meantime. On 23 December Bartlett placed Bailey's offer in front of the Zoological Society's Council, together with a written report outlining his concerns about Jumbo's behaviour and the disproportionate power wielded by Matthew Scott. The matter was debated but it took only minutes for the Society to agree to the sale of "the male African elephant". The Society was not short of funds but the price of £2,000 did roughly equate to the Zoo's annual budget for animal feed. It was left to Bartlett to conduct any further negotiations with Bailey and to make arrangements for Jumbo's sale and departure.

Bartlett immediately telegraphed Bailey to confirm that "the large male African elephant will be £2,000 as he stands". He then added further conditions, the most notable requiring that, in addition to the sum paid for Jumbo, the Barnum and London Circus would be liable for making and paying for all transport arrangements. This was a sensible move on the Society's part and may have been inspired by the trouble encountered when moving the two Asian elephants to Germany the previous year. The Superintendent did not have to wait long for a reply; he received a short telegram from Barnum, who had taken over negotiations from Bailey, which read: "The terms for the big African elephant accepted. I will make arrangements for his shipment here. My agents will be with you shortly." So far all had gone according to plan, but now came the hard part; Bartlett would have to break the news of Jumbo's departure to the general public and, of course, to Scott.

Of Bartlett's conversation with Scott nothing is known as neither man chose to dwell on the matter in his writings. As for the decision to sell Jumbo to the Americans, Scott's account typically places himself centre stage, claiming that he consented to the deal only after "considerable persuasion". In truth the keeper had not been consulted at all about the sale and, given the breakdown in communication between him and his superiors, there is every possibility that he was informed of Jumbo's departure in the same manner as everyone else in Britain, via a small announcement made by Bartlett in *The Times* on 25 January:

"THE GREAT AFRICAN ELEPHANT – Barnum, the American showman, has bought, for the sum of £2,000, the large male African elephant, which has for many years formed one of the principal attractions in the gardens of the Zoological Society in the Regent's Park. The purchase has been made upon the understanding that the animal is to be removed and shipped to America by and at the risk of the purchaser. To those who know the size, weight and strength of this ponderous creature (certainly the largest elephant in Europe), the undertaking is one of serious difficulty and not unattended with some danger."

So keen was Bartlett to get rid of Jumbo that this proclamation was made several days before the Zoological Society formally signed the deal with Barnum's circus. Final permission did not come until 1 February, when the Purchase of Animals Committee signalled its consent to the sale, but by this time Bartlett already had the carpenters and blacksmiths engaged in constructing a wooden box big enough to hold Jumbo as well as making alterations to the Elephant House in preparation for his swift removal to America.

All was going according to plan and Bartlett received a further boost when Barnum asked if Jumbo's keeper might be allowed to accompany the elephant on his journey to the United States and remain with him for a short while until the animal became accustomed to his new surroundings. This was music to the Superintendent's ears and he at once approached the Society about the issue but found the Council more concerned with the unexpected financial bonus of Barnum's £2,000. In a meeting to discuss the money it was decided that it should be placed in a high-interest account at the London and County Bank while they decided what to do with it. Then, at Bartlett's insistence, the Council offered Scott six months' leave of absence so that he could travel to America with Jumbo.

For the first time in several years the centre of balance in the Elephant House had tipped away from Scott and towards Bartlett. The keeper reluctantly agreed to accompany Jumbo to America but if Bartlett thought that he had got the upper hand he was sadly mistaken. Scott might have lost that battle but the war was not yet over and he had decided not to take the matter of Jumbo's sale lying down.

In early February two of Barnum's New York agents arrived at Regent's Park with orders to facilitate the removal and transport of Jumbo in time for the opening of the circus's spring season in late March. The gentlemen concerned were William Newman, who went by the name of Elephant Bill and was one of Barnum's animal handlers, and Jim Davis, a legal agent for Barnum, Bailey & Co. As his nickname implied, Newman had much experience in handling large animals and it was he who would oversee Jumbo's removal and transport.

On their first meeting Newman did not endear himself to Bartlett when he suggested that he had sold Jumbo too cheaply. "It's a pity you didn't ask for £3,000," he remarked. "You might just as well have had it." Bartlett chose not to reply to the taunt: he knew that Barnum had bought an animal that was capable of unpredictably violent behaviour and whose destruction had been contemplated only a matter of weeks beforehand.

Newman and Davis were introduced to Jumbo and his keeper, and when they saw that the elephant would obey only Scott's instructions it was decided that it would be easier for all concerned if the keeper were left in charge of the elephant. This played straight into Scott's hands but the mistake would not be realized for some weeks.

During the first two weeks of February the Zoo's carpenters set to work building a gigantic wooden crate with wheels in which it was intended to house Jumbo for his journey to Millwall Docks in east London and thereafter for the duration of his sea voyage to New York. The crate was 14 feet long, 8 feet wide and 12 feet high; its design was based on that of a horse box, with its exterior made from pine planks and its interior lined with oak. The whole thing was bound together with thick bolts and massive iron bands which, it was hoped, would be able to withstand any fits of elephantine anger. There was no door to the box; this would be put on only after Jumbo was inside, with a gap of three feet left at the top so that he could see outside.

By Monday 13 February the crate was finished and a space had been booked onboard the *Persian Monarch*, which was due to depart London the following Sunday. The Monarch line, to which the steamer belonged, had been chosen because its ships possessed very long and wide hatchways as well as a great height between the decks; given the size of the crate, both attributes were necessary.

Few problems were envisaged by either the Zoo or Bill Newman and it was agreed that Jumbo should be placed inside the crate and moved to the docks on the Saturday so that, with favourable weather, he would be in New York by the end of the month. Barnum, who had sent the money for Jumbo on 8 February, made an agreement with Bartlett that as from the Saturday morning Jumbo was the sole responsibility of his company. Jim Davis, Barnum's agent, was not as optimistic as his boss and stated that in his experience "the African Elephant is more intelligent but more self-willed than the Asian Elephant. He cannot be coaxed or deceived into doing what he does not wish to do and is generally harder to handle." It was a very prophetic statement.

Early on the Saturday morning, before the arrival of the crowds, Scott entered the Elephant House and without ceremony led Jumbo outside into his paddock and towards the ramp leading up to the large wooden crate, which, without its doors, looked like a small square tunnel. All went as planned until Jumbo drew close to the box, at which point he became restless and agitated. Scott attempted to calm him and went to move the animal forward but he remained motionless. Several attempts were made to coax him towards the box but Jumbo would not be moved. He remained absolutely stationary for over an hour, during which time a small crowd of visitors accumulated at the fence to the paddock. Newman decided to take control of the situation and instructed Scott to place chains about the animal's forefeet; these were then wound round some stout rails in front of the Elephant House, the intention being to use them to haul Jumbo into the crate.

"He showed for the first time the unmistakable sign of fear," said one bystander. Jumbo used his trunk to touch and feel the chains and, on deciding that they were not welcome, he tried to pull himself free by shaking and jerking his legs. Finally he tried to break the chains by picking them up with his trunk and repeatedly throwing them to the ground. Scott advised caution to Newman but it went unheeded and the American took a series of heavier chains and ran them around Jumbo's neck and between his legs: these were to be used to secure him to the walls of the crate in case of rough seas during the voyage.

"Jumbo gave passionate vent to his alarm and anger," wrote a reporter at the scene. "His loud trumpetings and fierce assaults upon his iron bonds told a tale of something wrong to the elephants to the left and right of him. They joined chorus with poor Jumbo in bellowings of dismay. The female elephant Alice, Jumbo's 'little wife' as she is called, was most painfully agitated and cried piteously in her stall. Jumbo roared louder when he heard the sympathetic moans of his wife and friends."

The scene went on for hours, with repeated attempts being made to haul Jumbo into the box. At one stage the leg chains had several men on them engaged in a tug-of-war with Jumbo; they tried to use their strength and weight to pull the elephant forward into the crate but he dug his hind legs into the ground and resisted with ease. At six o'clock in the evening the leg chains were removed and Scott made one last attempt to lead him into the crate, but on mounting the ramp Jumbo stopped dead and could not be moved. It was a pathetic sight and one that was witnessed by many of the 1,200 visitors to the Gardens that day. Again and again efforts were made to persuade, cajole and drag Jumbo into the crate but each time the result was the same, provoking cries of disapproval and booing from the onlookers.

Newman was embarrassed and frustrated that the Zoo's elephant had got the better of him and ordered that Jumbo be returned to his stall. There followed a lengthy debate about what should be done, and at midnight Newman ordered that the wooden crate be taken to the docks without the elephant and that Scott should report for duty at 5 a.m. the next day.

Sundays were normally a day of rest for most of the Zoo's labourers but at dawn on 19 February over 20 of the maintenance staff were gathered at the Elephant House awaiting instructions from Newman. Outside the Zoo's main gate was a sizeable of number of sightseers; word of Jumbo's refusal to leave the Zoo had got around and had stirred people to come and witness his departure.

During the night Newman had formulated a new plan; he, Scott, Davis and several others would march Jumbo by road to Millwall Docks, a distance of about eight miles. It was Newman's hope that, once away from the Zoo, Jumbo could with luck be coaxed into the crate and then loaded directly on to the *Persian Monarch*. However, as the ship was scheduled to sail that afternoon the whole procedure would have to run like clockwork or they would miss the tide.

It was with some relief that Newman saw Jumbo emerge from his den still sporting his body chains. Encouraged by Scott, Jumbo made his way out of the Elephant House and round the building to a wooden side gate that led on to the public road. Within minutes a large crowd was gathered outside in expectation of watching Jumbo make his final exit from the Zoo.

The gate was opened and for a moment it appeared as though Jumbo might be about to walk through the gate, but after placing one foot on the road he came to a dead halt. Newman and Scott tried to urge him on but Jumbo refused to proceed and started to moan piteously. Scott approached him and talked to him in soothing tones; in reply the elephant embraced his keeper with his trunk and sank slowly to his knees, uttering a cry of distress that could be heard across most of the Zoo. A similar sound was heard to emanate from the Elephant House: it was Alice, who appeared to be lamenting the departure of her putative husband. On hearing this Jumbo sank fully to the ground and lay motionless on his side, making only the occasional grunting noise. In the crowd of onlookers many people were weeping at Jumbo's plight and cries of "Shame" and "Let him stay" were heard.

The minutes turned into hours and by mid-morning the public road outside the Zoo was thick with spectators, but Jumbo still lay motionless. All prospect of getting him to the boat by that afternoon had disappeared and so Newman agreed to return him to the Zoo. Scott ordered Jumbo to his feet and, to Newman's surprise, the huge animal obeyed and without hesitation began to make his way through the euphoric crowd to the Elephant House. Newman admitted to feeling humiliated; he knew that it would be another fortnight before the next suitable boat left for New York, although this at least gave him time to think of a new strategy to deal with Jumbo's protest.

The British newspapers had remained quiet on the issue of Jumbo's departure as it was not considered much of a story, but Jumbo's very visible protest would change all that. The first description of the pathetic scenes came courtesy of the *Daily Telegraph*, which had been notably hostile towards London Zoo in general and Bartlett in particular. The paper provided a detailed and sometimes overwrought description of the attempt to remove Jumbo from the Zoo but made little comment on the decision to sell him in the first place. This stirred other newspapers to give their own descriptions (some culled straight from the *Daily Telegraph*), including *The Times*, which, in addition to an account of Jumbo's behaviour, published a letter from an anonymous member of the Zoological Society who questioned the need to sell the elephant at all:

"In common with many fellows of the society, I have found my disgust at this sale intensified by the pathetic and almost human distress of the poor animal at the attempted separation of him from his home and his family. Our hearts are not harder than those of his keepers, and for his own sake, as well as for that of the rising generation, I venture to ask if it is too late to annul the bargain?"

The letter found sympathy with other readers and led to a flood of similar complaints, not just in *The Times* but in every newspaper across Britain. Many correspondents believed that Jumbo was being sold to help stem a financial crisis at the Zoo; this led to the suggestion that the public should buy Jumbo for themselves. "Surely there can be no doubt that the money can be easily raised by other means than the sale of the Zoo's chief attraction?" wrote an outraged Martin Skeffington. "Only let a subscription be started and plenty of people will be glad to send a guinea, as will I."

But Skeffington and others had missed the point entirely; Jumbo's sale had nothing to do with money but was instead a means by which Bartlett could get rid of both the elephant and his keeper. Besides, the elephant was no longer the property of the Zoological Society: the previous Saturday Bartlett had handed over all responsibility to the Americans. He had even taken the liberty of officially recording that the Zoological Society had lost, through sale, "one African Elephant, ♂; received in exchange June 26 1865".

Barnum's cheque for £2,000 had long since passed on to the Zoo's accounts department with instructions that it be placed on deposit at the bank. As far as Bartlett was concerned, neither Jumbo nor Scott was his problem and, given Newman's smug attitude on arriving at the Zoo, the Superintendent must have watched his failure to move the elephant with detached amusement. He had finally expunged his zoo of a long-standing problem and nothing would persuade him to take the elephant back, least of all the piteous cries being made by the general public.

CHAPTER 15

∽ We Won't Let Jumbo Go! ∾

On 22 February 1882 Philip Sclater was able to report that Barnum's cheque for £2,000 had cleared and that the money was resting in the London and County Bank. Even if he had wanted to, Barnum now had no means of cancelling the deal or of getting his money back and so, with the public outcry growing daily, it was decided that the Zoological Society should make a statement about the sale of Jumbo to an American circus.

When selling Jumbo Bartlett had specifically stated that the elephant was to be bought "as he stood", which meant that once he was out of the Zoological Society's hands, Barnum and his agents would take full responsibility for him regardless of any problems that might later arise. This precaution had been necessary for a number of reasons, not least Jumbo's violent behaviour the previous autumn, which, if due to musth, would be certain to recur. The public had not been privy to Jumbo's ill temper and Bartlett had neglected to mention it to Barnum when discussing the terms of the sale, but with Barnum's cheque safely banked Sclater decided that it was time to reveal to the public the truth behind the sale.

"It is not surprising to the Council of this society that so general a regret should have been expressed by visitors to our gardens at the prospect of losing the great African elephant," wrote Sclater in a letter to *The Times*. His letter went on to explain the reasoning behind the Council's actions: "Quiet and retractable as this fine animal generally seems to be, he has for some time been a source of anxiety to those in charge of him. It is well known to all who have had much experience with such animals in confinement that male elephants, when they arrive at the adult stage, are periodically liable to fits of uncertain temper.

Under these circumstances the risk of an outbreak on the part of so huge and powerful an animal in the much-frequented gardens of the society is not one which should be lightly run. The possibility of having to destroy the animal would be repugnant to the feelings of all who knew and admire him… Messrs. Barnum, Bailey and Hutchinson are understood to have upwards of twenty elephants in their possession. In so large an establishment any animal under temporary excitement can be withdrawn from exhibition and placed in seclusion, which there are no adequate means of doing in the gardens in the Regent's Park. It is hoped that the Fellows of this society and visitors to the gardens will feel that the Council have not been unmindful of their interests, or even those of Jumbo himself, when they, though very reluctantly, consented to part with him."

Sclater hoped that his vision of an enraged and uncontrollable Jumbo loose in the often crowded Zoological Gardens would let the Society off the hook by making the sale look like a matter of visitors' safety, rather than about money, as many were implying. Bartlett helped the Secretary's cause by writing an anonymous letter to *The Times* which gave the appearance of having come from a member of the public: "I have visited the Zoo rather frequently of late and I have noticed that Jumbo's temper is not so good as it used to be. If he were suddenly to get cross some day when a number of children were present some accident might happen. I venture to think the authorities have acted with discretion in parting with him."

The description of Jumbo as a rogue elephant was compelling but it did not wash with many of the Society's learned members. Privately some knew that the long-standing animosity between Bartlett and Scott had also played a strong part in the disposal of the elephant. "Manifestly the real reason was one that could not possibly be given," recalled Theo Johnson. "To say 'We were forced to part with him because in no other way could we get rid of his keeper' would have been humiliating and seemed absurd."

Others looked at the sequence of events behind the sale and wanted to know if the decision to sell Jumbo had been taken before or after Barnum's offer to buy him. Martin Skeffington, a vociferous critic of the sale, made an even more apposite point: "Is it or is it not a fact that during the last few days this dangerous animal has been allowed to mix with the little children and carry them on his back as he has done for many years past?"

The attempt by Sclater and Bartlett to explain away Jumbo's sale had little impact on the public, few of whom believed that the docile animal which ferried their offspring about the Zoo was capable of violence. By the end of February both the Zoological Society and several newspaper editors found themselves deluged by letters of complaint against the Society's actions. The issue of Jumbo's departure was not going to fade away as Britain entered a state of what would later be called the "Jumbo craze".

While the furore over Jumbo had been gathering strength, Bill Newman and Jim Davis were still deciding how the elephant could be made to leave the Zoo. After the disastrous public spectacle of the previous weekend Davis cabled Barnum: "Jumbo is lying in the garden and will not stir. What shall we do?" The showman was characteristically sanguine over the matter and replied: "Let him lie there as long as he wants to." Nobody in the world was better at exploiting the media than Barnum and even at this early stage the American showman sensed that Jumbo's reluctance to leave the Zoo had the potential to provide him with valuable publicity for his circus.

Meanwhile Davis had taken the precaution of booking a place on the steamer the *Lydian Monarch*, which was due to leave London for New York on 4 March. This gave him and Newman two weeks in which find a suitable means of crating and moving Jumbo to the docks. They agreed that Jumbo needed to be familiarized with his box and ordered that its wheels be buried so that the crate's wooden floor became level with the ground. It was hoped that by removing the small ramp they could persuade Jumbo to walk through the open-ended box as if it were a tunnel and in time be chained there.

Scott agreed with this idea but before putting it into action Newman asked for the box to be narrowed so that Jumbo's flanks could be better supported when inside. It was also decided to strengthen the box in response to complaints from the public that it resembled "a packing case made with planks". While the box was away from the Zoo being modified, there was little that Newman or Davis could do except await its return. Scott, on the other hand, kept himself and Jumbo busy by continuing to give elephant rides to the public, who were turning up to the gardens in ever-increasing numbers.

At the Zoo the first sign of the Jumbo craze came at the turnstile, which, on an average February weekday, would admit a few hundred visitors. Within a couple of days of Jumbo's public protest, numbers had started to climb, slowly at first but then very rapidly. On Tuesday 21 February 694 people visited the gardens, roughly double the usual number; the next day this figure more than doubled to 1,690 and, as the fuss over Jumbo spread, so the numbers climbed until on Monday 27 February there were 8,571 visitors (against 674 on the equivalent day the year before). The huge increase was doubtless helped by a spell of fine, clear, but cold weather that had settled over London and would remain for several weeks, but even so it was the Zoo's great African elephant that was drawing people in. After many years of being the children's favourite, Jumbo was rapidly becoming a celebrity with Britain's adult population too, but the increased popular interest and boost to the Zoo's takings did not put a smile on the face of Bartlett nor any of the other Council members. The failure of their plan to remove Jumbo quickly and quietly to America was about to bring them a great deal of trouble.

In the wake of the increased attendance came an unprecedented influx of letters to both the Zoological Society and every newspaper and topical magazine in the country. These were almost all against the sale and some addressed to Bartlett and Sclater were even threatening in their tone. At the other end of the scale were numerous letters from children pleading with the Superintendent to keep their "pet" in London. Offers of money were made to the Society, as were helpful suggestions about how best to persuade the elephant to go into his box. One correspondent suggested placing a mirror at one end so as fool Jumbo into thinking that there might be another elephant already inside; another offered to place Jumbo in the box himself for £10. The

Society's Council refused this kind offer for various reasons, not least because the gentlemen concerned, who lived in the countryside, wanted his fee and travel expenses paid up front.

Some were brave enough to voice support for the Zoological Society, most of them on the grounds that Jumbo might one day turn violent and kill a child. These opinions came mainly from members of the scientific community, one of whom, William Tegetmeier, a naturalist and the founder of the Savage Club, went to great pains to list previous catastrophes that could be attributed to aggressive captive elephants. His list included not only Chunee, whose death Bartlett had witnessed, but also elephants from Liverpool, Amsterdam, Versailles and Cologne that had allegedly killed one or more people before being shot or suffocated by their owners.

Such dire warnings fell on deaf ears, and this indifference seemed to be justified by the behaviour of Jumbo himself, who could still be found giving rides to children each day. By the beginning of March the Zoological Society was taking delivery of boxes of cakes, pastries and buns for Jumbo; one contained a selection of sponge cakes and gingerbread and was sent "from some nurses at London hospital, hoping Jumbo's future will be to remain in London". One gentleman even sent an enormous pumpkin, a vegetable not traditionally associated with the elephantine diet. Bartlett was at first reluctant to give any of the food to Jumbo just in case someone had poisoned it but he was later assured by Sclater that "experiments have previously been made with the object of poisoning a suffering elephant, and have failed owing either to some peculiarity of the animal's digestion or to the large portion of poison required to produce any effect on it". Even so, not all the delicacies went to the Elephant House for fear of unbalancing Jumbo's diet.

Of less suspicion were the many bottles of ale, wine and spirits that Jumbo received (and a dozen oysters), which, according to Scott, bypassed the elephant and instead were "put to where they would do more good". More sinister was a wreath of flowers that had been delivered to the Zoo with the message that it was to be placed about Jumbo's neck as "a trophy of triumph over his brutal owners and American kidnappers".

In a slack period for news, magazine and newspaper editors did not hesitate to prolong the Jumbo craze by pandering to their readers. "Have not the Managers of the Gardens been a little hasty?" asked the *Spectator*, thinking not of the many upset British children but rather of Jumbo's future novelty value. "It is nearly certain that in another century, when Jumbo has arrived at a green old age (elephants are believed to live 150 years, and certainly 130 years) the animal will, with the exception of a few in confinement, have totally have ceased to exist [in the wild]. When Jumbo is alone in the world, as he very possibly will be, he will be worth thousands, and be for naturalists an object of almost as much interest as a moa... It is a pity, in the interest of science as well as of the Gardens, to send him away."

The editor of *Vanity Fair* went a step further by starting a Jumbo Defence Fund, to which he personally donated £5, while his counterpart at the *Saturday Review* showed a somewhat better understanding of the situation: "it seems odd, to say the least, that [the Zoological Society] should be willing to sacrifice such a unique specimen as Jumbo for a sum of money which must really be a bagatelle for them. Indeed the question of profit and loss can hardly enter into their transactions ... were they a trading body, such a concession could never have been made."

Of more concern to the Zoo were the noises being made by clergymen, MPs and other influential people about the potential cruelty of crating and transporting a giant elephant across the Atlantic. Sclater did not want his zoo to be associated with such charges and so arranged for inspectors from the Royal Society for the Prevention of Cruelty to Animals (RSPCA) to be on hand during the next attempt to get Jumbo into his crate.

The allegations of cruelty were lent more substance by Bill Newman, who, in his frustration at Jumbo's non-cooperation, had told a journalist that the elephant was Barnum's property and that he had the right to shoot the animal if necessary. "Dead or alive," declared Newman, "Jumbo is to go to New York." It was a silly comment and one that further encouraged the notion that Jumbo's new owners cared little for his welfare.

With feelings running so high, there was a heightened desire in Bartlett and Barnum's agents (although possibly not Barnum himself, as we shall see) to see Jumbo removed from the Zoo as quickly as possible. On the afternoon of Friday 3 March the strengthened box was delivered to Regent's Park and, with the help of all 18 maintenance staff, was dug into the ground opposite Jumbo's den. Newman positioned it right in front of the doors so that Jumbo would have to walk straight through it if he wanted to get to his bathing pool.

"The newly constructed box, or van, is a massive vehicle," wrote a journalist. "The frame is composed of solid balks, morticed, bolted and all over heavily clamped with iron. The flooring is of three inch planks, and the sides and roof are lined with inch-and-a-half deal. The van is of such a strength that it is calculated to resist twice or trice the force that even this powerful brute could bring to bear against it."

The box was put in place before a crowd of over 6,600 people, a record number for the first Saturday in March, but if they were hoping to see Jumbo stroll nonchalantly through it they were to be disappointed. At Newman's request, Scott brought Jumbo from his den and allowed him to watch as Alice was led effortlessly and without fear through the open-ended box. Jumbo was brought forward and, with Scott leading him, he approached the box and was persuaded to stick his head inside it. He spent several minutes using his trunk and mouth to feel and sample the interior in minute detail, but when Scott was asked to lead him further inside, the elephant stood his ground. No amount of coaxing would work and, as before, Jumbo remained absolutely obstinate on the issue. The crowd thought that this was wonderful and cheered Jumbo on. Newman grew impatient and ordered that Jumbo be returned to his den for the rest of the weekend. In his absence delighted visitors, whose numbers rose to a staggering 16,000 on the Monday, were allowed to wander through the box to inspect "Jumbo's packing case" for themselves; many took the opportunity to carve messages of good luck into the wood.

The lengthy alterations to Jumbo's box caused David and Newman to abandon hope of catching the *Lydian Monarch*, which was departing that Saturday, but they hoped to be able to take the *Egyptian Monarch*, which was to leave five days later.

Davis had instructed Newman to get Jumbo on to the second ship regardless of the elephant's view on the matter. Newman duly told Scott that any further attempt to coax Jumbo into the box would be abandoned and that, when the time came, the elephant would be dragged inside using chains. Scott must have been alarmed to hear this, but so too were the newspapers. "Should this step be taken, it is probable that the Society will be proceeded against for cruelty," said *The Times*.

As it happened, any idea of getting Jumbo on to the *Egyptian Monarch* was abandoned when Sclater announced to Davis that several members of the Zoological Society had taken out a lawsuit against its Council. This was a serious turn of events and until the matter was resolved there could be no question of sending Jumbo to America. Davis and Newman were in despair about ever seeing Jumbo leave the Zoo and they fretted about the reaction of their New York bosses to this latest setback. They needn't have worried. Barnum was delighted at the way in which events were unfolding and had even had a hand in them.

A Weighty Foreign Topic

Phineas T. Barnum was a master at turning an apparent disaster into a triumph; he also firmly believed that there was no such thing as bad publicity. In the 1870s he had confided to a friend that he wanted to make a bid for Nelson's Monument, better known as Nelson's Column, which stood in London's Trafalgar Square. "I know they won't sell it," said Barnum, "but no matter. All I want is a big advertisement. It will furnish me a couple of columns of gratis advertising in every English and American newspaper for a couple of months and give my show the biggest boom a show ever had in this world."

When confronted with the issue of Jumbo's reluctance to leave London Zoo Barnum put into effect a similar plan. It would exploit the British public's anger for his own purposes and be a near-perfect demonstration of the art of manipulation of the media.

Barnum and Bartlett had struck their final deal over Jumbo at the end of January but at that time the American showman saw no need to publicize his new acquisition. His travelling circus was resting for the winter and not receiving paying visitors; it had probably been his intention to get Jumbo to the USA and settled in before advertising the elephant's arrival. That changed when he got wind of the headlines, editorials and letters that were filling the British press, many of which held two culprits responsible for Jumbo's predicament: the Zoological Society (for selling him) and Barnum (for buying him). Initially it was the Zoo that received the lion's share of the abuse, but when it became evident that money had already changed hands attention soon shifted on to Barnum. The sound of angry British voices was music to the showman's ears.

Thanks to the transatlantic telegraph cable, which could relay messages from London to New York in hours (as opposed to weeks by letter), Barnum was able to keep abreast of the situation at Regent's Park and thus to react quickly. It was the telegram from Davis on 19 February that first alerted him to Jumbo's refusal to be moved from the Zoo, and his reply, "Let him lie there as long as he wants to," was the first sign that Barnum was preparing to orchestrate a campaign of negative publicity against himself.

Barnum's first opportunity for mischief came on 23 February, when the editor of the *Daily Telegraph*, John le Sage, telegraphed Barnum on behalf of the British people: "Editor's compliments. All British children are distressed at elephant's departure. Hundreds of correspondents beg us inquire on what terms you will kindly release Jumbo. Answer prepaid unlimited. Le Sage, Daily Telegraph."

The showman had been to London several times and was familiar with the British national character, which he knew included a passionate love of animals. Le Sage's telegram told Barnum that the issue of Jumbo's sale was exciting the nation and the fact that the editor was prepared to pay for an unlimited reply (telegrams were charged by the word and were very expensive) made the showman's heart "gladder than it had been for many a day". Barnum set out to rile le Sage by returning a lengthy, rambling answer that not only refused the request to release Jumbo but cost the *Daily Telegraph* a small fortune in the process.

"My compliments to editors Daily Telegraph and British nation," he wrote. "Fifty-one millions [*sic*] American citizens anxiously awaiting Jumbo's arrival. My forty years' invariable practice of exhibiting best that money could procure makes Jumbo's presence here imperative. Hundred thousand [*sic*] pounds would not be inducement to cancel purchase. My largest tent seats 30,000 persons and is filled twice a day. It contains four rings, in three of which full circus companies give different performances simultaneously. In the large outer ring or racing track the Roman hippodrome is exhibited. In the other two immense connecting tents my colossal zoological collection and museum are shown. In December next I visit Australia in person with Jumbo and my entire mammoth combination of seven shows, via California, thence Suez Canal; following summer to London. I shall then exhibit in every prominent city of Great Britain. May afterward return Jumbo to his old place. Wishing British nation, Daily Telegraph and Jumbo long life and prosperity. I am the public's obedient servant. P.T. Barnum."

This giant advertisement for Barnum's circus had the desired effect as not only the *Daily Telegraph* but almost all British newspapers and magazines came out against him. In the coming days Barnum was accused of being vulgar, brutal, brash and a kidnapper; in a series of jingoistic articles and letters the British public fell back on their stereotypical view of the Americans as being uncultured, loud and obsessed with outsized objects. Delighted with this, Barnum immediately sent copies of le Sage's telegram and his lengthy reply to several New York newspapers in the hope that the American public could be inspired to back his bid for Jumbo. Again the tactic was successful and within days the American papers carried dozens of articles describing the distress in London while hinting that Barnum had engineered a great coup by having bought the elephant in the first place. However, some American journalists were bemused at the situation. The *New York Times*'s London correspondent, for example, reported: "Not withstanding the care of a possible European war, 'Jumbo' and 'Barnum' are on every lip. 'The Sale of Jumbo', 'Jumbo's Removal Postponed', are leading lines in the contents bills of all the daily papers."

Operating out of Bridgeport, Connecticut, Barnum continued to stoke the flames of publicity. He put about a rumour that Alice was pregnant, which spurred the *Daily Telegraph* to announce the forthcoming birth of an elephant at London Zoo. Bartlett was at pains to deny this but the rumour gained currency and was co-opted as another reason why Jumbo should stay put. Barnum happily released copies of all his correspondence regarding Jumbo, including the original telegrams between him and Bartlett about the purchase. He also released a letter that allegedly had been written to him by "a young English girl" (although the American spelling made some suspect that it had been written by Barnum himself):

MUTUAL ADMIRATION.
BARNUM TO JUMBO: "You are a *humbug* after my own heart. You have even beat me in advertising."

Barnum's behaviour was much parodied in the press.

"Dear Mr Barnum, I write on behalf of our dear old Jumbo. Do be kind and generous to our English boys and girls. We do so love him, and I am sure if you have children or little friends of your own you will be able to understand how their hearts would ache and their tears be shed should they lose the friend who has given them such delight, and who is one of their few pleasures in this great and sorrowful city... Dear Mr Barnum, you, who have so many famous animals, and among them so many elephants, surely will think seriously and kindly before you take from us our very dear friend Jumbo..."

By the first week of March the newspapers in America were participating in their own version of the Jumbo craze, which, although marginally more low-key than its British counterpart, had nonetheless become a daily feature of the US press. As various attempts were made to keep Jumbo in London, so the American print media expressed an increasing desire to see Jumbo in the USA. As Barnum had hoped, the American public were starting to clamour for a sight of Jumbo and were becoming frustrated with the delays being experienced in London. A few journalists were, however, wise to the showman's tactics: "Mr Barnum has obtained a fine advertisement in America and Europe out of the fuss," wrote one, "and the Zoological Society will find a certain solace for the abuse that has been heaped upon them in the thousands of pounds that have been paid at the entrance gates in the last few days."

For a while Barnum was able to ride this wave of free publicity, but the announcement that there was to be a court case over Jumbo was both unexpected and worrying. For the first time there was a genuine possibility that the elephant might be prevented from going to America and, on a judge's instruction, be forced to remain at Regent's Park. This outcome would have suited neither Barnum nor the Zoological Society and prompted an immediate telegram from Bridgeport to Davis in London which indicated just how much was riding on Jumbo's arrival at the circus: "Employ best counsel in London. Spare no expense. We must have Jumbo. Have expended $30,000 for engraving, lithographs and colored posters representing the largest elephant in the world standing beside little Bridgeport, the smallest elephant in the world."

Barnum may have had a playful and cheeky demeanour but he was a man who did not like to lose and he was determined that no British court should deprive him of his new elephant.

The lawsuit against the Zoological Society had been brought by one of its own members, Matthew Berkeley-Hill, a surgeon from University College London specializing in venereal diseases. The details are sketchy but it appears that, on hearing of Jumbo's sale, Berkeley-Hill had attempted to organize an extraordinary general meeting of the Society only to find that there was no provision for this in its by-laws. He then planned to raise the matter of Jumbo at the next general meeting, on 16 March, but then learned that it was the Society's intention to ship the elephant on the 9th. Rather than see Jumbo sail, Hill joined forces with Henry Burdett, another Society member, who agreed that there were sufficient legal grounds to sue the Council of the Zoological Society. News of their intention was announced in a letter from Burdett to *The Times* which appeared on 6 March.

"It has been decided to move the Court of Chancery to restrain the Council, their agents and servants from selling, parting with, or otherwise dealing with the elephant Jumbo, and to grant such other relief as the case may require," said the letter. It went on to set out Hill's grounds for bringing the suit, which included the allegation that the Society's Charter did not empower it to sell animals; that it was morally wrong to sell a dangerous animal; and that the Society's central purpose was scientific study, not trade. Legal cases are expensive and so it was announced that there would be a Zoological Society Defence Fund to which the public could contribute. "If sufficient funds are forthcoming," wrote Burdett, "there seems little doubt that Jumbo will remain a permanent inmate of the Zoological Gardens, Regent's Park."

The letter was published on a Monday but with Jumbo's place booked on the *Egyptian Monarch* on the coming Thursday, Hill and Burdett could not afford to wait for the public's money to flow in. On the day of the letter's publication they made an application to the Court of Chancery, through their barrister, Robert Romer, for an injunction which would stop Jumbo from leaving the Zoo until all legal proceedings had finished. The case was heard by Mr Justice Chitty, a judge whose experience and reputation for fairness suited both parties.

In court Romer outlined his clients' case to Justice Chitty and added the concern that Jumbo might be boxed and taken to the docks before the case could get under way. The judge agreed that this was a potential problem and granted an injunction against the Zoo's Council that restrained them "from removing the elephant from the Gardens" but did not prevent them from "allowing the elephant into the box". Romer's attempt to have the entire Zoological Society added as a co-plaintiff with Hill ("as he considered he represented a majority of the Fellows") was refused. Justice Chitty did, however, request that Barnum be added as a defendant along with the Zoo's Council. The case was then adjourned until the next day.

News of the suit drew forth many opinions from London's legal community, most of which held that Hill and Burdett had opened up a can of worms. One such commentator warned that "the Zoological Society have for these last fifty years been in the habit of selling duplicate and surplus stock. If the views of Mr Burdett and his friends are carried out, these animals must in future be killed."

It was amid such high feelings that, on the Tuesday morning, Justice Chitty opened the proceedings to decide Jumbo's fate. The plaintiff, Matthew Berkeley-Hill, was again represented by Robert Romer, while the defendants, the Zoological Society, its Council and Barnum were represented by Edward Macnaghten, one of the most experienced barristers in the country. Macnaghten's services did not come cheap, so in all probability Barnum's injunction to Davis that "no expense be spared" had been followed.

In his opening argument Romer asserted that under the Zoological Society's Royal Charter its Council had no right to sell any animals without first gaining the consent of its Fellows. He admitted that this right was invariably waived by the Fellows "as a concession to convenience". But he argued that "as long as the Council restricted their transactions to the sale of a gnu for £150, a giraffe for £200 or even an elephant for £450, the Fellows were content to acquiesce in the invasion of their rights but when it came to selling a unique specimen like Jumbo, it was time to assert the prerogative which has so long remained in abeyance". The basis of that uniqueness, said Romer, was Jumbo's gigantic size.

In reply Macnaghten summoned Philip Sclater and Abraham Bartlett as witnesses, both of whom stated that Jumbo had become dangerous and the Society had always sold off its surplus stock, including elephants. Bartlett added that he "was not aware of anything in Jumbo which gave him special scientific interest". Romer's reply, which argued that it was his size that made him unique, drew Macnaghten to comment that "whether Jumbo is larger than any wild elephant may be doubted, on the principle that there are as good fish in the sea as ever came out of it".

Justice Chitty agreed and said that he could not see the difference between selling Jumbo, priced at £2,000, and "his humble
fellow sold for a fifth of that price". He then cautioned Romer
that his case thus far seemed to be based solely on the public's
affection for the large elephant but that "sentiment may not have
a footing in a court of law". Furthermore, said the judge, the
Zoo's Council was the Society's executive body and had the right
to buy and sell any animals on behalf of its Fellows; only fraud
could be used as an argument against the sale of an individual
animal, and that was not the case here. This decision was a blow
to Berkeley-Hill but it was perhaps not unexpected. But the
plaintiffs had one further legal argument, and this was on a much
stronger footing.

A close study by Berkeley-Hill of the Zoological Society's
by-laws had revealed that five members of the Council had to be
present before any decisions could be ratified but, according to
the minutes, there were only three people in the Council when it
was decided to sell Jumbo to Barnum. Seeking to exploit this
technicality, Romer argued that the original sale was invalid as it
not had been ratified by the required number of Council
members and that Mr Barnum should therefore have back his
£2,000 and all expenses incurred.

For a while the Zoological Society looked to be in trouble, but
then Macnaghten pointed out that the sale had been ratified at a
later Council meeting at which five members were present.
Justice Chitty agreed that this second ratification validated the
sale and, despite further protests from Romer, the case was
settled in favour of the Zoological Society.

"The Council had the right to sell Jumbo," said the judge,
"and the right was validly exercised. Whether what they did was
advisable and considerate is another thing. The first is a matter
of law, the second a matter of opinion in which everyone has a
right to their own view."

The favourable outcome of the Chancery Court case left Phineas
Barnum once again free to export Jumbo to America but the
decision came too late to allow the elephant to be put on to the
Egyptian Monarch, which left London on the day of the Court's

decision. The next departure by the Monarch line was not until 25 March, which meant that Newman, Davis and Bartlett would have to endure another two weeks of Jumbo frenzy. Barnum did not complain; with the legal risk removed, he had another two weeks in which to talk up the elephant's arrival.

In Britain Jumbo's plight needed no additional hype; he was headline news to such a degree that when an assassin attempted to shoot Queen Victoria it was Jumbo that received the greater word count (at least in some papers). The issue was even raised in the House of Commons when Henry Labouchere MP asked the Secretary of the Board of Trade whether, given Jumbo's alleged foul temper, steps had been taken to ensure that passengers aboard the steamship would be protected from him. The Secretary answered that "The Board of Trade cannot possibly have any control over the uncertain temper of the elephant Jumbo." He did, however, promise that Government inspectors would be present at the embarkation to ensure that the cage was sufficiently strong for the voyage and to ensure that "the elephant should not be able to step on the deck".

Meanwhile the continuing publicity and good weather ensured that the Zoo went on receiving a record number of visitors, a state of affairs that required all the staff to be on duty to keep order. Unbelievably, Scott still managed to take Jumbo on his daily rides through the crowds, revelling in the attention, but the keeper and his elephant had only been given a reprieve from their deportation and in the background Newman and Bartlett were preparing to switch tactics. The time had come to get heavy with the elephant.

∽ How to Pack an Elephant's Trunk ∽

The collapse of Berkeley-Hill's court case saw several British newspapers retaliate against Barnum by accusing him of mistreating his circus animals. Mr Davis, his agent, denied this and was at pains to explain that Barnum had a tried-and-tested method of taming an elephant in musth ("fasten him up and keep him on a short diet"). The allegations of animal brutality did not subside and so in reply to his critics Davis decided to vent his spleen at the British public. "I observe that if a chain is put around an elephant's leg in this country an outcry of cruelty is at once got up, which shows that your definition of cruelty is not quite the same as ours. So far from proposing to treat Jumbo cruelly, we consider him the most valuable elephant in the world and propose to take the greatest care of him accordingly."

Jumbo's intransigence continued and led to heated arguments between Matthew Scott and Bill Newman, who continued to threatened that the elephant would be dragged into his box if necessary. The situation even began to concern Barnum, who knew that to exploit the wave of publicity he had generated in America, the elephant would have to be on board the *Assyrian Monarch*; if the animal arrived on a later boat Barnum risked losing the public's interest. The news the showman was receiving from Newman and Davis was not encouraging as both men had expressed their fear that Jumbo may yet force them to miss the *Assyrian Monarch*. Barnum sought to avoid this possibility by throwing money at the problem.

Bartlett had been largely uncooperative with Barnum's agents, insisting that the elephant was merely on deposit in Regent's Park and was no longer the concern of the Zoological Society. It was therefore with some reluctance that Davis approached the Superintendent to ask for assistance with removing Jumbo; as a sweetener he offered the Society £1,000 if it would "undertake to safely put Jumbo on board ship". The money was refused (perhaps because Bartlett did not want to again become legally responsible for the animal) but he too wanted Jumbo gone and undertook "to do their best to assist in carrying out the undertaking".

The nature of this undertaking is not entirely clear but it did require Scott to make a renewed effort to get Jumbo to walk through his box. The first such attempt was made early on Saturday 11 March, when few people were around to disturb the proceedings. Under his keeper's direction Jumbo was introduced to the box and, to Newman's amazement, was persuaded to walk through it from end to end without fuss. The agent insisted that Scott perform the manoeuvre again and he did so, taking Jumbo back through the box. The journey was made several more times until at last Newman was convinced that the animal was familiar with his prospective quarters. It was with some relief that he was able to inform journalists that "no trouble is now anticipated in getting Jumbo into the box when the decisive moment arrives within the next ten days". Given Jumbo's track record, many at the Zoo must have viewed this prediction as somewhat optimistic.

Later in the day Scott took Jumbo out into the Gardens, which were crowded with thousands of people, the majority of whom were there to see the elephant. Loaded with children on his back, Jumbo was taken from the Elephant House, through the tunnel and into the south part of the Zoo. As soon as he appeared crowds of people flocked about him, stroking and even kissing his hide. According to those who witnessed it, this was an emotional sight, with children and adults alike pleading with Scott to keep the elephant in London. As the sun began to set a light drizzle of rain started to fall on the Zoo, causing those near Jumbo to put up their umbrellas. After remaining calm all day, the animal took fright at this and, for a brief moment, seemed to be in danger of trampling the people standing in front of him. Scott managed to regain control but it was with some difficulty that Jumbo was coaxed back through the tunnel and into his den. There was alarm at this turn of events, so the following day, when the Gardens were again packed with people, Jumbo was confined to his paddock, where the public fed him dozens of buns, cakes, oranges, nut tarts and acid drops. Jumbo loved the attention that was being lavished upon him but he would become jealous if anyone in the crowd started to favour Alice. On several occasions he was seen to snatch food from her mouth, causing her to betray "irritation at the sparseness of offerings of food to her".

The following week Jumbo mania reached its peak. On Monday 13 March a record 24,007 people paid to visit the Gardens, some 22,000 more than on the same day the previous year. Even though it was the Zoo's cheap day, the turnstiles generated an astounding £592 in entrance fees and doubtless much more from sales of refreshments and souvenirs. At Newman's request, early each morning Jumbo would be walked through his box and made to accustom himself to it. On the Tuesday (when a mere 6,000 visitors were admitted) Scott was able to stand Jumbo inside the box and attach chains to him, all without the animal's distress or incident. After weeks of frustration the mood of Barnum's agents (and the Zoological Society's Council) was greatly improved. Even the poison-pen letters and death threats that were arriving daily on Bartlett's desk did not dampen their spirits. One anonymous lady wrote to tell Bartlett that Jumbo's removal "is not wise; and how often animals speak without words, but man will not listen to them!"

That Jumbo would board the *Assyrian Monarch* appeared to be a certainty and so on 15 March the Zoological Society's Council met to discuss how best to minimize the bad publicity that would doubtless follow the elephant's removal to the docks.

From the outset Bartlett had made it clear to Newman and Davis that Jumbo was ostensibly their problem, a policy that had resulted in Barnum's men being offered the bare minimum of assistance. Philip Sclater decided that in order to speed Jumbo on his way, this hands-off approach would have to stop. He instructed Barnum to "give Mr Barnum's agents every reasonable assistance in packing and moving out of the Gardens the male African elephant". Then, given the accusations of animal cruelty that were doing the rounds, he ordered that Jumbo be moved "in the presence of the Agents of the Society for the Prevention of Cruelty to

Animals. In case of their interference you are requested to withdraw all assistance immediately." As a further precaution the Zoological Society's Secretary also requested that Jumbo's box be yet again examined by a competent surveyor to ensure that it was strong and safe enough to get the elephant from Regent's Park to St Katharine's Dock, near the Tower of London. Like Barnum, the Society was displaying every sign of wanting to get Jumbo out of the Zoo and off to America but it still had to wait over a week before the elephant's departure.

Jumbo's final few days at the Zoo were hectic as visitors eager to see him arrived in their thousands. Each day he would be taken to the box, walked through it and then chained there briefly, all without fuss. In the afternoons Jumbo and Scott would go about the Gardens giving rides to children; the last was on Monday 20 March (when over 18,000 people visited the Gardens). Bartlett ordered that Jumbo be allowed to rest when this was over, to prepare him for his long journey at the end of the week. Both the public and the newspapers were aware that Barnum had won the battle and that the elephant would soon be leaving British soil, but a few brave souls continued to fight their corner.

"Why part with Jumbo?" asked the lyrics of a popular tune written in protest at the Zoo's decision. This sentiment was also reflected in other musical compositions, which included such titles as "Jumbo's Jinks" and "The Jumbo and Alice Polka". There was even a lament for Jumbo which summarized the public's mood:

> *"O why did the Council sell me?*
> *Why did 'cute Barnum buy me?*
> *Why did false Bartlett doom me*
> *To exile far away?*
> *What did my Alice tell me?*
> *Public with buns who ply me,*
> *Vote me a paddock roomy,*
> *Where I may rest or play!*
> *(Chorus) Why did the Council sell me?*
> *Why did stern Justice Chitty –*
> *Man who from the law ne'er flinches –*

Quash Romer's kind injunction
On my behalf? Bohoo!
Will they, devoid of pity,
Haul me away with winches,
Force me, without compunction,
Far from my well-loved Zoo?"

According to Barnum, whose account of events must always be viewed with caution, Queen Victoria was also outraged at the sale of Jumbo. She is alleged to have telegraphed Bartlett about the matter and it is said that the Superintendent was required to visit Marlborough House to explain himself to the Prince of Wales. The truth of this was never established but an official letter from the Colonial Secretary to the Queen's Private Secretary does record: "I am glad to hear that Her Majesty takes an interest in Jumbo. The poor brute has behaved with too much dignity to be consigned to the horrible vulgarity of Barnum and his 'mammoth show'." Barnum's reaction to such royal protestation was to claim that the Queen and her children had regularly ridden Jumbo and that he had once even been kept in the Royal Park at Windsor, where Her Majesty would make him sit and beg for sugar lumps – all untrue as far as is known.

With Jumbo's departure seemingly inevitable, there was great speculation as to when he would be caged and taken to the docks. The *Assyrian Monarch* was not due to depart until the Saturday but, given the previous problems, it was widely expected that Jumbo would be delivered to the docks a couple of days ahead of this, just to be on the safe side. The speculation was correct; Davis had scheduled Jumbo's removal from the Zoo for the Wednesday morning, but as the week progressed, so the elephant began to show an increasing reluctance to enter his box. To some it was almost as if Jumbo was aware that his time at Regent's Park was nearly up, but Newman had been closely observing Scott for weeks and had come to a different conclusion.

On the Tuesday Newman approached Bartlett privately and expressed the belief that, come the following morning, Jumbo would again refuse to enter his box. He based this prediction not on any instinctual understanding of elephantine psychology but on his theory that it was Scott who was the cause of all the trouble, not Jumbo. Newman accused Scott of being difficult and said that he was unwilling "to exert himself in the command he had over the animal". In fact, he said, "it was suspected that he was obstructing the work of removal and that his effort to box the elephant was a sham".

Nor was Newman the only one to think this; an acquaintance of Barnum named Gaylord had complained that during the original attempt to remove Jumbo, Scott had "manoeuvred the elephant" in order to promote sympathy in the assembled onlookers. "When it was time for him to leave and his box was ready, he got the order to lie down, and down he went, and the populace wept at the thought of the elephant's unhappiness. When he was told to come away, he came."

This idea made sense to Bartlett, who had encountered the keeper's intransigence on many previous occasions. It also explained why Scott had accepted the news of Jumbo's sale to the Americans with so little fuss: it had never been his intention to allow the elephant to leave the Zoo in the first place. If, as Newman expected, Jumbo were to put on yet another display of grief and reluctance, the public outcry might just ensure that Scott would get his wish. Bartlett had not undergone weeks of public abuse only to see his keeper get the better of him, so he determined a strategy that would use Scott's affection for Jumbo against him.

Having listened to what Newman had to say, Bartlett asked him if he thought he could handle Jumbo without help from Scott. Newman, who was Barnum's chief animal wrangler, replied that he was perfectly capable of handling Jumbo by himself. Bartlett then asked Newman to accompany him to the Elephant House, where Scott was, as usual, working in Jumbo's den.

The Superintendent called the keeper outside and ordered him to take some of his holiday entitlement (none of which had been used for over a decade) and to leave the Zoological Society's premises for a while. This sudden order took Scott by surprise; he asked Bartlett why he had given it. The reply was curt and honest. "It is my intention to send you away from the Gardens for a time in order that Newman should get accustomed to the habits and management of Jumbo before he leaves England," replied Bartlett. As an afterthought he reminded Scott that Barnum had offered to pay for his passage to New York and to allow him to accompany the circus for several months while Jumbo settled in to his new surroundings. The Zoological Society had given him six months' extended leave in which to do this; his place at the Zoo would be kept open so long as returned within that time.

Scott was aware that his scheme had been rumbled but, rather than risk sending Jumbo to the Americans alone, he begged Bartlett not to carry out his intention. "Please do not give me a holiday," he implored. "If you will only give me another chance then I will do my best to induce Jumbo into his box."

Bartlett, ever the politician, did not want Scott to remain at the Zoo and so although he appeared to be reluctant when he agreed to Scott's plea, it was actually the outcome he had wanted all along. After suffering the man's insolent behaviour for years, the Superintendent had regained control over his Elephant House and furthermore was confident that the next day would see Jumbo boxed and travelling across London to the docks.

The morning of Wednesday 22 March dawned to brilliant blue skies and a strong, biting northerly wind that had sent the night-time temperature plummeting several degrees below freezing. Scott awoke to find the Elephant House and Jumbo's box covered in a layer of fine, white frost that began to melt as soon as the sun's rays started to strike the Zoological Gardens. At 7 a.m. he went to Jumbo's den and gave him an abnormally large breakfast which, he hoped, would "put him in good humour". An hour later Jim Davis and Bill Newman arrived, followed soon afterwards by Bartlett and his son Clarence (who also worked at the Zoo) along with John Colam, the Secretary of the Royal Society for the Prevention of Cruelty to Animals, his chief inspector Samuel Tallett and the veterinary surgeon Professor William Pritchard.

It was hoped that starting at first light would make it possible to have Jumbo in his box and on his way before the opening of the turnstiles, but the harnessing process took longer than expected. This was not due to any obstructive behaviour by

Scott, who was being compliant, but to the need to be seen to be careful and methodical under the watchful gaze of the men from the RSPCA. At eight o'clock Scott and Newman were given consent to begin applying the necessary restraints to the giant elephant.

Jumbo's forelegs were already fastened to an iron bar in his den, a normal procedure to deter any nocturnal exuberance; these fastenings were raised to the higher part of his legs and a solid length of chain, known as a surcingle, was placed over his shoulders and fastened beneath his stomach. The elephant's head was then attached to the surcingle using a loop of chain that ran under his forelegs and round the top of his nose; this was designed to act in a similar manner to a horse's martingale (the strap that connects the noseband to the girth) by preventing Jumbo from tossing his head violently but at the same time allowing him some free movement and the ability to feed himself. During this process Jumbo was perfectly calm and waited patiently outside his den while his box was swept clean of the moisture left when the frost had thawed.

At 9.20 a.m. Scott led Jumbo towards the box, which had remained buried in the ground; he stopped momentarily at the entrance and for a short while it looked as though the elephant might once again put up a protest against his removal. A few words from Scott made him move forward again and, when the giant beast's body was completely inside the box, the keeper called out, "Whoa, Jumbo," bringing him to a halt. The chains on the elephant's forelegs were then taken through gaps that had been purposely left in the side of the box and made fast. On feeling this restraint being applied, Jumbo sank to his knees and, looking down at the ground, put out his trunk to Scott. To those viewing the scene it looked as though the animal was imploring his friend to release him from the chains: "There is something peculiarly human in this attitude," observed one of the onlookers, but Bartlett soon put him right by claiming that Jumbo was merely signalling that he had been beaten by a superior force.

This opinion was a little hasty, for within minutes the elephant was on his feet again and in fighting mood. It took over two hours to secure the remaining chains around his hind legs. Each

151

attempt by Scott and Newman was rebuffed by Jumbo, who kicked, stamped and sidestepped his way out of the chains. In the meantime the turnstiles had opened and the men found themselves working under the gaze of a small but growing crowd. When the restraints were at last applied Jumbo made one last bid for freedom by dashing his huge body against the sides of the box, hurling splinters of wood across the paddock; this behaviour continued as the Zoo's carpenters and blacksmiths placed strong wooden bands across the open ends of the box.

Jumbo ended his protest by ramming the box with his tusks, sending a shower of ivory fragments into the air. After this he appeared to recognize that the box would be his home for a while and settled down, occasionally reaching out with his trunk through the gap at the front of the box to find Scott, who remained there offering words of comfort and morsels of food.

It was not just Jumbo who had found this process distressing; in the neighbouring den was Alice, who, according to Scott, reacted to her mate's plight in a tragic manner. "The noise of the groans of Alice was at times of a wailing, plaintive, rather, musical kind. Then it would sound like a roar of thunder, and at times was as quick and successive as its peals. She tore about the stable in which she was confined, and dashed herself against its sides, till we expected every minute she would break loose and follow us. If she had, we should have had a nice time of it to separate them again."

It was noon by the time Jumbo was boxed and ready to go, and although the process had taken longer than expected it had at least taken place without serious incident. Bartlett was eager to hurry things along and went off to inform the men from the removal company Pickfords that it could bring its horses to the Gardens. This was done and in the early afternoon six powerful dray horses were led into the paddock in front of the Elephant House and harnessed to the box, which, it was estimated, weighed around 12 tons and was still buried in the earth.

Extracting the box from its hole was a dangerous and time-consuming task that required using the horses to haul it up a set of steel rails. It was an inch-by-inch process in which the wheels had to be periodically chocked with great lengths of timber. It took 45 minutes to get the box to ground level, after which progress through the Zoo was comparatively rapid until a soft gravel path was reached. The horses were negotiating this when a mischievous person in the crowd called out, "Whoa!", bringing the box to a halt in an especially awkward place. The wheels sank slowly into the gravel until the axles were covered, to the crowd's delight.

The Zoo's labourers were ordered to find several jacks and as many wooden planks as they could lay their hands on. Time and again the wheels were jacked up and the boards placed beneath them, but the loose earth and gravel proved unstable and it was another three hours before the box was fully extracted. By this time it was dark and the public had been turned out of the Gardens, but many had chosen to remain outside the main gates in order to witness Jumbo's departure. As they waited, some refreshed themselves with alcoholic drink which turned them into what one reporter described as a "rough crowd who stood there for hours, howling the beasts dumb".

With daylight gone, the work continued by lamplight but progress was far from smooth. A further stretch of gravel slowed the pace, as did the inconvenient siting of two trees on either side of the path, the gap between which was only fractionally wider than the box. The onset of night also sent the temperature plunging below freezing, necessitating the impromptu insulation of Jumbo's box with sacking and tarpaulins. Finally, just as the box looked to be on its way out of the Zoo, it sank into the earth again, this time within full sight of the "rough crowd", who shouted abuse at the staff and particularly at Barnum's men, while Scott was cheered and congratulated for his attempts to keep Jumbo in London. "Goodbye, Jumbo," called the crowd. "Goodbye, Scott, old fellow!"

Four more horses were harnessed to the box and by degrees the procession moved cautiously on its way again, creeping towards the main gates. At 1.25 a.m. the box was hauled out of the Zoo and on to the public highway. It had taken nearly 12 hours to travel the few hundred yards from the Elephant House, but from now on progress would be swift. As he passed through the gates Jumbo greeted the crowd with a loud trumpet and by shaking his box from side to side; in turn he was hailed with shouts of "The Yankees shall never have you" and "Hooray for Scott". With trouble always a possibility, a large number of policemen had been drafted in to keep order along the five-mile route to St Katharine's Dock.

The moment when the back axle of Jumbo's box touched the road marked the end of the Zoological Society's responsibility for the African elephant and his keeper. Bartlett was able to celebrate this by recording in his Daily Occurrences book the departure of "one African Elephant, ♂, 'Jumbo'; deposited by Messrs Barnum, Bailey and Hutchinson on 19 February 1882; returned to depositors". Newman and Davis also marked the event by nailing a board on to the box which announced Jumbo's new owners as "Barnum, Bailey and Hutchinson, New York, USA".

After 16 years and nine months at the Regent's Park Zoo, Jumbo was on the move again, as was his friend Matthew Scott, a man who had barely set foot outside of London since becoming an elephant keeper. The prospect of a lengthy transatlantic voyage to the self-styled "land of the free and home of the brave" must have looked very daunting to the introverted keeper and his pet.

CHAPTER 18

✍ Farewell ✍

Jumbo and his box were one of the largest loads ever to have passed along London's public roads. The surface may have been more solid than the gravel paths at the Zoo but there were still many problems to overcome. Chief of these was the inability of the dray horses to pull their load uphill, a factor that caused Newman to devise a wiggly route between Regent's Park and the docks which avoided steep areas such as Pentonville Road in favour of a flatter detour that eventually brought them to the site of the old Clerkenwell House of Detention, at the top of Farringdon Road.

The journey to this point had been far from straightforward; the box and horses were at first besieged by curious pedestrians and hansom cabs and then there were further problems with the wheels, which would repeatedly overheat owing to the great weight of their load. Water was continually applied to the axles but at one point sparks from the wheels caused a small fire which, although soon dowsed, led to calls to travel yet slower. All the while Scott rode on the front of the box, assuring Jumbo that everything was all right and stroking his trunk.

For his part the elephant remained mostly calm and it was only after the horses started down the steep hill between the former prison and the Thames that he began to display alarm, shaking his head in fear. Progress was slowed right down and it was not until just before 5 a.m. that the box clumsily made its way through the gates at the Mercantile Marine office at St Katharine's Dock, just east of the Tower of London. It was here that Jumbo was to be loaded on to a barge and floated downstream to the *Assyrian Monarch*, which was moored at Millwall Docks on the Isle of Dogs. The protracted process of getting

Jumbo to St Katharine's Dock had caused them to miss that morning's tide, but rather than leave him on the quayside, a prey to the crowds, it was decided to place him on the barge where he could spend a few hours in relative safety.

The barge that had been hired for the short river journey was the 60-ton *Clarence*, which had been specially ballasted to compensate for the weight and shape of the cage so that if Jumbo started to throw himself about the vessel would remain steady. Just before seven o'clock Jumbo and his box were winched upwards and swung across to the *Clarence* without incident; the dockers then set about making the box fast in the barge, shoring it up on all sides. In celebration Jumbo was given a hearty breakfast by Scott, supplemented with some beer given by a lady who had followed the box all the way from Regent's Park; as the ale was swiftly downed she cried piteously and wished the elephant *bon voyage*.

Three hours later the tide was sufficiently favourable to allow the barge to be towed from the dock into the river. By this time word of Jumbo's imminent departure had got around and the place was surrounded by thousands of onlookers. The main gates had been shut and were guarded by the police, so people climbed on to roofs, walls and bridges to gain entry into warehouses and offices, where they hung out of open windows. At one o'clock a tug was attached to the *Clarence* and the process of pulling the barge downstream started; a huge cheer went up from the crowd, causing Jumbo to shift his weight back and forth inside the box. For a moment the barge swayed in the water but the extra ballast kept it low in the water, minimizing its movement. The crowds continued to wave for several minutes as the *Clarence* made its way eastwards along the Thames.

As the tug rounded the bend of the river and passed Dundee Docks on the west side of the Isle of Dogs, Jumbo again took fright; he started to ram the bars on the front of his cage and, to Scott's horror, managed to loosen them. The keeper ordered the engines to be cut and spent several minutes calming the elephant before ordering them to be restarted. Just before three o'clock the *Clarence* entered Millwall Docks, surrounded by a flotilla of small rowing boats, one of which bore the name *Jumbo*, written in paint that was evidently still wet. At exactly 3.42 p.m. Jumbo was removed from the *Clarence* and put on the quayside, where he would remain overnight until the *Assyrian Monarch* could be brought alongside and the elephant loaded on board. As the box was dangling from the crane it was weighed at twelve and a half tons; given that the wood and iron were known to account for six and a half tons of this, Jumbo weighed six tons. Although his weight had been estimated at around this figure many times by Bartlett and Scott, this was the first time that their estimates had been confirmed mechanically. With Jumbo safely on dry land again, tarpaulins were slung over the box and it was left to Scott to keep his friend company overnight.

Before the start of Jumbo's Atlantic crossing Bartlett was required to perform one last duty with the elephant. On Friday 24 March the elephant's box had been swiftly lowered on to the *Assyrian Monarch* – the process took just eight minutes – and the load safely stowed. To celebrate the end of a difficult episode in the lives of the Zoological Society and Barnum's agents, it was proposed to hold a large lunch on the steam ship. This was a grand affair and attracted the owners of the various shipping companies involved with Jumbo as well as the American Consul-General, the Sheriff of London, several well-known businessmen and, of course, members of the Zoological Society, Bartlett among them.

Several speeches were made and toasts were given to the United States, to the City of London and to Bartlett himself. The Superintendent responded by saying that Jumbo had "many friends and few enemies" and that he hoped the elephant would one day return to the Zoo (although he almost certainly did not). However, the most surprising turn of events came when the Zoo's Treasurer, Frederick Trotman, stood up and formally presented Bill Newman with the Zoological Society's Gold Medal "in appreciation of his coolness and skill" when handling Jumbo. This was the Society's highest accolade and one usually reserved for exceptional endeavours; even Bartlett had yet to receive it. Awarding the Gold Medal to Newman was undoubtedly a snub (deliberate or otherwise) to Scott, whose many years as the African elephant keeper had gone entirely without official recognition.

After a speech by the Consul-General, who hoped that Jumbo would help cement a close relationship between Britain and America, the lunch broke up and the *Assyrian Monarch* made ready to depart early the following morning. Bartlett remained on board as he intended to sail aboard her down the Thames as far as Gravesend in Kent.

At five o'clock the next day the *Assyrian Monarch* at last slipped her moorings and made her way to Gravesend, where some 409 emigrant passengers were taken on board. Most were hopelessly impoverished and hoped to improve their prospects by moving to the New World; only 18 had paid for a cabin, leaving the remainder to sleep on the decks. Jumbo was, however, no ordinary emigrant and was given a special send-off by a delegation of senior politicians, military officers and aristocracy who had travelled down from London to wave farewell to the elephant. Among them was Lady Burdett-Coutts, the philanthropist and wealthiest woman in Britain, who shook hands with Scott and Newman before giving Jumbo a bun and wishing him a safe crossing. "You will find as warm friends in America as you have in England," she said before disembarking. The niceties had considerably delayed the ship's departure and it was six o'clock before she swung out into the tide and headed towards the Channel and into a strong north-westerly wind that was rapidly stiffening into a gale.

During the weeks of wrangling over Jumbo's fate the weather in Britain had been unseasonably fine and clear but the departure of the *Assyrian Monarch* coincided with a sharp drop on the barometer. Within hours of her setting off the skies were dark with rain clouds and the wind speed freshened into a gale, turning the sea into a mass of high, foam-capped waves. At first Captain Harrison attempted to punch his way through the storm but by evening conditions were so bad that the ship was put to anchor in the lee of North Foreland, at the eastern extremity of Kent, where it could ride out the storm. "The wind sung loudly in the cordage," wrote a passenger, "and in the midst of the roar of the gale Jumbo was once or twice heard trumpeting."

The elephant was understandably scared and had become

restless in his box, which lay exposed to the elements on the upper deck. As the spray lashed at the tarpaulins that covered the box, so Scott and Newman became increasingly worried about the tightness of Jumbo's chains, which were starting to chafe his neck and shoulders. It was decided that the chains should be taken off, which required the removal of the lower wooden bar from the front of the box to allow access. However, constant dowsing by sea spray had caused the wood to swell, jamming it within the iron reinforcing bands. Neither Scott nor Newman could shift it but, rather than let Jumbo suffer, Scott decided that he would climb into the box and free the chains himself; Newman disagreed with the plan, making it clear that one false move by the elephant and Scott would be crushed to death.

But Scott did not care and proceeded to squeeze himself between the wooden bars at the front of the box and, having done so, came to rest in the narrow gap between Jumbo's trunk and his breast. Newman implored silence from the small crowd that had gathered by the box and, working quickly, Scott sought to free the chains encircling the neck and belly of his elephant. This took several agonizing minutes, during which time Jumbo remained absolutely motionless. "He seemed fully to understand that the manoeuvres were for his relief," said one bystander. The task accomplished, Scott squeezed back through the bars to the applause of the crowd. With his head, neck and trunk once again fully able to move, Jumbo leaned against the side of the box and for the first time in several days fell into a deep sleep.

By morning the weather had calmed somewhat, allowing the *Assyrian Monarch* to make a brief stop at Dover, where the pilot and several other people, including Bartlett and Jim Davis, were landed ashore. It was the last time that Bartlett would see Jumbo but the parting was no great sorrow; the Superintendent had shown himself to be utterly unsentimental about Jumbo, a reflection of the emotional distance that he always maintained between himself and the animals he cared for.

Jumbo's departure gave Bartlett the opportunity to reassess the events of the previous few weeks. The positive benefit of the Jumbo craze was the unprecedented number of paying visitors who had attended the Gardens since the announcement that

Jumbo was going to America. The figures were incredible: in the month up to 18 March there had been 151,158 visitors (as opposed to 21,333 the year before), bringing in £3,077 4s. 6d. (£433 16s. 1d. the year before).

The selling of Jumbo had brought in a most unexpected windfall and certainly more than enough to buy a replacement African elephant for the Zoo. Bartlett therefore contacted Carl Hagenbeck, his old friend and Alice's former owner, to ask him what was available. To his surprise, the dealer was able to provide him almost straight away with a juvenile male African elephant and for just £300. Jingo, as he was already named, eventually arrived at the Zoo on 8 July and was housed in Jumbo's old den.

With Scott on six months' leave of absence, Bartlett also took the opportunity to make some regulatory changes that would pull him back into line should he choose to return. He felt that many of his problems with Scott had stemmed from his having been allowed to keep the money generated by the elephant rides. This, he felt, had made Scott reluctant to share Alice and Jumbo with other keepers, which in turn had allowed him to blackmail the Society. Furthermore, an audit by the Superintendent suggested that Scott had been making between £600 and £800 a year from the rides, an absurd sum for a keeper. The situation had to change.

Bartlett worried that Scott might not like America and choose to come back to London (as he was entitled to do under the deal with Barnum) sooner rather than later. This meant that the changes to rules governing elephant rides had to be implemented as soon as possible. Consequently on 5 April, when Scott and Jumbo were still in mid-Atlantic, the Council decreed that in future all those wishing to ride on an elephant must buy a ticket costing 2d. and that weekly takings would be subject to a close audit. By way of compensation, those keepers who were in charge of the elephant rides would be entitled to a small percentage of the takings.

On Monday 27 March the *Assyrian Monarch* steamed past the Lizard Peninsula, the most southerly point of the British Isles, and moved out into the Atlantic. As the boat passed close to the

Lizard Signal Station, Captain Harrison offered a semaphore message which read: "Jumbo well; very quiet; unchained." Then the ship moved into open seas and slipped out of sight; she would be out of contact for the next 13 days, although one enterprising journalist on board planned to seal his progress reports inside bottles which he would periodically drop overboard. If he did so, none was ever recovered.

On board all was quiet and calm; after the trauma of leaving Regent's Park and the stormy weather, Jumbo had settled down and was eating and sleeping as usual. A common protest during the Jumbo craze was that elephants suffered dreadfully from sea-sickness, an idea that was rubbished by both Bartlett and Barnum. Unfortunately for Jumbo, the assertion was true and whenever the sea became rough he would stop eating and stand stationary, his trunk hanging listlessly over the front of his box. Scott could do little for his friend other than offer him comfort. "Jumbo was somewhat alarmed at first by the noise of the machinery and the rolling of the steamship," wrote the keeper, "but I was always at his side, and managed to calm him so that he became quite a sailor when he got his sea legs on."

Elsewhere in the ship the senior officers and crew had formed the Jumbo Club, whose members were required "to look as wise as an owl, as meek as a newly ordained parson and as hypocritical as a temperance reformer". Scott, ever the loner, was not a member of this drinking society; he preferred to spend his spare time on the cargo deck with his beloved elephant.

As the *Assyrian Monarch* steamed westwards, Barnum prepared the American public for Jumbo's arrival. With his prize secured, the showman's objective was to create an exaggerated sense of expectation about the event. Thanks to the many column inches of newsprint that Jumbo had already garnered, there were few in America who were not aware of the elephant's existence. Barnum cashed in on this by using the newspapers to create a countdown to the *Assyrian Monarch*'s docking in New York, which was expected on or around 9 April. Prompted by Barnum, the papers would inform their readers how many days were left before Jumbo's arrival while giving the much-anticipated occasion all the razzmatazz of a royal visit.

The tactic worked and was helped by the unforeseen intervention of the New York Customs House, which informed Barnum that he would be liable to pay an importation duty of 20 per cent on Jumbo's value. This would add £400 to the already considerable cost of buying and shipping the elephant; it was not a pleasing prospect, but a careful examination of the Customs' regulations uncovered a potential loophole for Barnum to exploit. According to the rules, an animal could be exempted from duty if the importation "is for the good of the United States through an intention to improve the native stock". In other words, if Barnum could prove that Jumbo was being imported for breeding purposes, the duty would be waived.

Barnum's discovery that Jumbo could be exempted for breeding purposes led to one of the strangest news items of the entire Jumbo episode. In a lengthy article entitled "Home and Foreign Elephants", an anonymous author (but probably Barnum or one of his associates) complained bitterly about America's reliance on the importation of foreign elephants. "All the elephants that have trodden the soil of the United States have been brought from abroad," complained the author. "The reason is obvious. It is cheaper for showmen to buy elephants in Europe, Africa and Asia than it is to [breed] them here, and this fact is simply disgraceful to our legislators."

The article continued in a blistering tone, denouncing the free-trade policies of the government and the subsidy of other American industries such as blanket making, before descending into hysteria: "We now depend upon the Old World for our supply of those noble animals. Were we to be engaged in a war with all the rest of the world lasting, say, a hundred years, we should become absolutely destitute of elephants, and the misery that would result therefrom would be appalling. What would our children do without elephants to amuse them? What would the sick do without the sight of elephants to invigorate them? What would the Nation do when the loathsome press of Europe would sneer at us as an elephantless people? To be truly patriotic we must rid ourselves of this abject dependence on other nations for our elephants."

The solution to this problem was obvious: the United States

must bring in more elephants for breeding purposes. Unusually for an article about elephants, at no point is Jumbo mentioned (although Barnum's name crops up), but the timing of this impassioned plea was not coincidental.

There was further bad news for Barnum after it was revealed to him that his agent Jim Davis had left the *Assyrian Monarch* in Dover and had accidentally taken a vital piece of paperwork with him. Davis held in his possession the Bill of Lading, a document that had been issued by the shipping company following its receipt of Jumbo as a piece of cargo. The Bill was of vital importance as it stated that the only person to whom Jumbo could be delivered on arrival in New York was Barnum. This was simply a precaution against cargo being released into the wrong hands, but if the showman were to turn up without the Bill of Lading, the shipping company would be legally unable to release the elephant from the ship.

The problem came about because Davis had refused to travel on the *Assyrian Monarch* (probably because it was an emigrant ship) and had instead booked a passage to New York on the swifter and more luxurious *City of Brussels*. This ship left Liverpool on 30 March but was not due to arrive in New York until two days after the *Assyrian Monarch*, which left the possibility of Jumbo being stuck on the quayside as unclaimed freight until the arrival of Davis and the vital piece of paper.

This news upset Barnum's carefully laid plans for Jumbo's triumphant arrival in the New World and prompted him to travel directly from Bridgeport to the New York offices of the Customs House. Barnum held several meetings with the senior Customs Collector, a man named Robertson, during which it was agreed that the provision of an indemnity bond to the value of £4,000 would secure Jumbo's immediate release. On the provision of the Bill of Lading the money would be returned. After agreeing this, Barnum turned the conversation with Collector Robertson towards the 20 per cent importation duty payable on the elephant.

"Good thing, good thing, that law," said Barnum and, smiling broadly, added, "I'm bringing Jumbo over for breeding purposes, you see. Yes, Collector, for breeding purposes. The tariff is just right on Jumbo – just right."

The idea that a showman like Barnum should bring a famous elephant to America for breeding purposes struck the Collector as somewhat unlikely and so he wrote to the Secretary of the Treasury to ask his advice on this unusual matter. The Secretary was aware of Barnum's charm and of the stir that Jumbo's imminent arrival was causing. His advice was simple: if the showman was willing to issue an affidavit stating his intention to breed Jumbo and also to obtain a consular certificate to this effect, the elephant could be admitted free of duty. This good news reached Barnum on the afternoon of 8 April; it was well timed as at 11 o'clock that night the *Assyrian Monarch* steamed into New York harbour and dropped anchor a few hundred feet off Castle Garden Pier. Jumbo had at last arrived in the USA.

PART FOUR

AMERICA

CHAPTER 19

∞ New York, New York ∞

In the early morning of 9 April a small delegation of well-dressed gentlemen stood at the end of Castle Garden Pier, shivering in the raw New York wind. Among the party were Phineas Barnum and his co-partners James Hutchinson and James Bailey as well as several of their associates and a handful of newspaper reporters. All had their eyes fixed on the *Assyrian Monarch*, which lay at anchor in the harbour's midstream. Any news of Jumbo's state of health had yet to reach the shore and there was a sense of anxiety among everyone apart from Barnum, who regaled his friends with stories about a Swedish opera singer he once knew.

A few minutes later a small steamer pulled in at the pier head; it had been sent by Captain Harrison to take Barnum and the others to the *Assyrian Monarch* so that they could at last set eyes on the new addition to their circus. The captain personally greeted the gentlemen and was quick to tell them that Jumbo had weathered the voyage well and was perfectly fit and healthy. Then the party descended a gangway to what was called the shelter deck, where Newman was waiting to greet them.

Barnum shook his elephant trainer warmly by the hand and congratulated him for a job well done but as he did so the showman's eyes were searching about the deck, as if he had lost something. Finally he called out, "Where's Scott?" in such a forceful manner that the other visitors began chanting the same cry. The keeper appeared from below decks and was greeted warmly by Barnum and the others; he then led them to where stood Jumbo's immense wooden and iron box, from the front of which protruded his wildly waving trunk. The first view of him engendered a mixed reaction in the reporters: "The merest glance at the beast showed that he was of immense size, but upon closer inspection it was seen that he has extraordinary long legs, and that his height is due to their length."

Barnum's publicity blitz of the previous few weeks had perhaps led some of the people to expect a larger elephant than the one that stood before them. "What's the height?" called out one reporter. "Eleven and half feet," shouted back Newman. At this a murmur went up, with some voicing the idea that Jumbo was only marginally taller than some of Barnum's existing circus elephants. The showman responded to the mood of the crowd by telling them that "there is a considerable difference between the actual and the museum height of elephants: eleven and a half feet is the actual height of Jumbo!" This satisfied them, reported one journalist, and they "started to look at Jumbo with increased pride".

Newman commented on the amount of beer, wine and whisky that had been supplied by the public to Jumbo, much of which had ended up with him and Scott. This drew scorn from Barnum, who, as a teetotaller, disapproved of Jumbo's drinking. He looked at the keeper and said: "I am afraid Jumbo has been too liberally supplied with beer for many years." For a moment Scott looked flustered until his new boss added, with a smile, "That animal's growth has been stunted by the use of beer."

The ship's First Officer then piped up: "Why, Jumbo is as fond of whisky as he is of beer."

"Oh, no," replied Barnum. "Do not say that."

"If you don't believe it then I'll prove it to you," said the First Officer and immediately thrust a bottle of scotch at Jumbo. Without hesitation the elephant emptied the contents into his trunk and then curled the end back into his mouth, slowly pouring the whisky down his throat.

"I protest! I protest!" shouted Barnum, but it was too late.

As Barnum's impromptu press conference continued, so the first of many boatloads of invited guests boarded the ship. Despite the freezing-cold weather a party atmosphere developed in which Barnum was able to mix his various advertisements for his circus with anecdotes and humour. The morning progressed and on the shore a crowd of onlookers had gathered to witness Jumbo's disembarkation but by lunchtime both they and Barnum had grown restless.

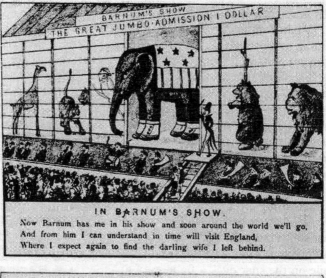

IN BARNUM'S SHOW.

Now Barnum has me in his show and soon around the world we'll go,
And from him I can understand in time will visit England,
Where I expect again to find the darling wife I left behind.

★ LOOK ACROSS THE OCEAN.

By Barnum I am highly prized and o'er the earth I'm advertised,
And I am better known of late than any other potentate;
So London folk once more adieu and mind my ALICE in the Zoo.

Jumbo's arrival in New York was greeted with joy by Americans.

Captain Harrison was asked what the delay was; he was some-what embarrassed to explain that the captain of the barge that was to take Jumbo's box to the shore was nowhere to be found. Barnum immediately ordered some of his men to set off in a tug to trace the man, who, it was alleged, was at home after being told his services were not required that day. Meanwhile the *Assyrian Monarch* went alongside the pier, allowing its many dis-tinguished visitors, including Barnum, to go ashore for a while.

It was not until 4.30 p.m. that the missing captain was traced and his barge brought alongside the ship. Chains were placed around Jumbo's box in preparation for his disembarka-tion. On the quayside the crowd had swelled from a few hundred in the morning to several thousand, many of whom had become over-excited in their wait to see Jumbo. As the box was lifted the *Assyrian Monarch* was invaded by what Captain Harrison described as "New Jersey desperadoes". The rigging filled with children shouting and screaming at the elephant while on the spar deck a fight started. The chaos and cacoph-ony startled Jumbo and, as his box was hoisted above the deck, it was feared that he would "break from his box and sweep everything before him".

Scott had chosen to ride on the front of the box and as Jumbo swayed nervously inside, he talked to him in low tones. "Be still, Jumbo," he said, patting him on the trunk as best he could while clinging to the wooden bars. It was several agonizing minutes before the box could be lowered on to the barge, during which time the alarming noise of cracking wood rang out several times, drawing gasps from the crowd. As the box touched the deck of the barge three ear-splitting cheers were raised; Scott stepped on to the deck to be warmly greeted by the crew. The keeper at first blushed but was observed to shed tears as Jumbo's howdah was lowered on to the deck next to the box.

By seven o'clock Jumbo's box was ashore and had been placed on a cart. An argument broke out between two of his new owners. The crowd, which was estimated at over 10,000, had been suit-ably appreciative after their first sight of Jumbo but now they were calling for the elephant to be allowed to walk up Broadway to his new home. Hutchinson was in favour of this idea and believed it to be safe but Bailey disagreed, fearing that Jumbo might panic and attack the crowd.

Accordingly, eight horses were attached to the box but the road was rutted and the wheels would not turn. Another eight horses were added but the box held fast and so the help of the crowd was engaged, but even the additional strength of another 500 men had no effect. Bailey ordered that some of the Asian elephants be brought from the circus but before they arrived one last pull made the box roll free from its rut. The crowd cheered and were treated to a loud trumpet from Jumbo. The cavalcade was reduced to eight horses again and was joined by Gypsy and Chief, two of Barnum's elephants, and then set off towards the city.

"It was the strangest procession which ever passed up Broadway," wrote one journalist. "First came the monster box, its eight horses, driven by Johnson, 'the best driver in the world'. Gypsy and Chief stalked solemnly after them on either side of their keeper. Behind them followed another eight horses and a long motley procession of men and women, boys and girls brought up the rear."

As with the journey from Regent's Park to the docks, moving the box produced a variety of problems, such as getting stuck in soft earth, the overheating of the wheels and a low bridge which was cleared with only two inches to spare. Gypsy and Chief were occasionally used to nudge the box out of a hole or up a minor incline. It was a slow process and it was not until the early hours of the morning that Jumbo reached the Barnum, Bailey and Hutchinson Circus in Madison Square Garden.

On 10 April 1882 New Yorkers awoke to find the front page of their newspaper adorned with an advertisement from Barnum which exalted Jumbo's arrival and proclaimed, in somewhat callous terms, that in obtaining him the American entrepreneurial spirit had overcome British absurdity. "Jumbo will be mourned by every child in Great Britain," gloated Barnum, adding that the elephant had been "torn from his home" despite the regrets of Queen Victoria. Readers were left in no doubt that New York was now home to the largest and most famous elephant in the world.

Jumbo's new home in Madison Square Garden had a long association with Phineas Barnum, who had first leased land on the site in 1873 for his Monster Classical and Geological Hippodrome. The venture was short-lived and closed in 1875, but a few years later the lease was renewed by the newly formed Barnum, Bailey and Hutchinson company, which in March 1881 started the first of many seasonal runs of the Greatest Show on Earth. The show was staged in a rectangular building which resembled a vast, open-plan warehouse and could hold 9,000 spectators and a three-ring circus complete with horses, elephants, camels, oxen, Chinese acrobats, Hungarian jugglers and a multitude of other performers.

This revival of Barnum's Madison Square Garden show met with the critics' approval: "The claim of Mr Barnum and his partners as to the multiplicity of their forces is not a vain boast, since it must be admitted that they undoubtedly control the largest, and in many respects, the finest exhibition of the kind seen here."

It was James Bailey's belief that each season's show should be bigger and better than its predecessor and so after the end of the 1881 season his agents set about acquiring new acts and a large number of new animals for the menagerie. Many of these were provided by Carl Hagenbeck, who, in January 1882, shipped eight giraffes to New York, only five of which arrived alive. Jumbo had also been acquired as part of this strategy and, in preparation for his arrival, Barnum and Bailey ordered that some alterations be made to the Madison Square Garden building. Even though the 1882 season had got under way on 14 March, all the auditorium's internal partitions were removed so that it became a gigantic open space in which Barnum could display his "Roman Hippodrome". This was a new show of which the centrepiece was a gigantic circular racetrack, over 40 feet in diameter, which ran almost the entire length of the building and within which were the circus's trademark three rings.

The alterations were made a week before Jumbo's arrival and took just one day to complete. Afterwards the crowds could thrill to the sight of horses, camels and elephants racing or parading round the Roman Hippodrome track while men and animal acts performed in the central rings. The effect was, by all accounts, stunning and even though the capacity of the building had been raised to 10,000, it was rare for there to be spare seats at the evening performances. The arrival of Jumbo would ensure that this trend continued.

After his nocturnal arrival at Madison Square Garden, Jumbo had been left inside his wooden box until first light, when the plan was to move him into his new quarters. Just before sunrise Bailey and Hutchinson met with their agent Jim Davis, who had just arrived from London; he regaled them with alarming stories of Jumbo's ill humour and wilfulness when at the Zoo, some of which greatly alarmed them. Immediately afterwards the two partners were told that the box was wider than the doors to the circus building and that Jumbo would have to be walked through the auditorium to his new quarters. Both men were suddenly nervous at the idea of letting such a grumpy animal loose but were told that there was no other choice.

Even after the bars had been removed from his box Jumbo treated his new surroundings with caution. He lowered a front foot on to American soil and then withdrew it again, as though the ground were too hot to touch. Soothing words from Scott eventually drew the elephant out of his box and into the auditorium; here he surprised everyone by suddenly rolling on to his back, waving his legs and trunk in the air for several minutes. After three weeks' confinement Jumbo was apparently stretching himself; no one dared approach and at length he returned to his feet, then followed Scott along the Hippodrome track, past the three circus rings and into the large elephant quarters at the back of the building. It was here that Jumbo gained his first glimpse of Barnum's other elephants, including the two-month-old calf Bridgeport and his mother, both of whom started at the sight of the giant African elephant. A separate area had been reserved for Jumbo and, at Bailey's request, his hind legs were heavily chained to a spike driven into the ground, but the confinement didn't suit him and within seconds the chains were free.

"He must be more securely anchored," said a nervous Bailey, aware that within hours the elephant would be on public display. Scott protested that Jumbo was at his most comfortable with

crowds but he was overruled by George Arstingstall, the head elephant trainer for the Barnum, Bailey and Hutchinson Company.

Arstingstall had been closely following Jumbo's progress since
the moment he arrived at the pier head and he was greatly dis-
pleased at what he had seen. When it came to training elephants,
Arstingstall took the opposite view to Scott; he did not regard his
elephants as pets or even domesticated beasts but as working
wild animals. "Mr Arstingstall has very fixed opinions about
elephants," commented Hutchinson. "He has no faith in the
good effects of being kind to them, and never attempts to romp
with them. He will soon subdue Jumbo."

Hutchinson was not joking; Arstingstall's training methods
were described as "emphatically sharp at times" and relied
heavily on a sharp iron hook that the gruff trainer carried with
him at all times. At the slightest sign of non-compliance
Arstingstall would jab this into an elephant's trunk or flank until
it reacted in pain. Needless to say, Jumbo was on the receiving
end of Arstingstall's hook several times before the end of his first
day at the circus and, as the trainer had promised, the newcomer
was both secured and subdued.

It must have been a rude awakening for Scott to discover that
he no longer had the last say in the matter of Jumbo's treatment.
He had to watch silently as Arstingstall ordered a team of blacksmiths to build an iron contraption which would secure Jumbo
in his stall. The job was finished just minutes before the doors of
Madison Square Garden were opened for the circus's afternoon
performance.

Midweek matinees rarely sold out but the attraction of Jumbo
ensured that on this occasion the venue received its largest-ever
audience. As soon as the gates were opened people rushed across
the hall towards the elephants' quarters; as Scott had predicted,
Jumbo proved himself to be quite content when surrounded by
people and gave an unexpected display of his ability to trumpet
along to the music that was drifting across from the Hippodrome.

The crowd thrilled at the sight of Barnum's transatlantic
acquisition and most agreed that he was indeed considerably
taller and heavier than any of his 21 elephants. The few people
who dared to suggest that Jumbo did not live up to Barnum's

promises were shouted down. One such was police chief Alexander Williams, who commented, "Pshaw, he isn't any taller than some of the other elephants here." Bailey overheard the comment and forced him to stand next to Jumbo, after which Williams withdrew his comment.

Outside the building children swarmed over Jumbo's box, invading its smelly interior, climbing on to its roof and carving their names into the wooden panels. Jumbo had been in New York for just over a day and yet he was already a bona fide tourist attraction. As the takings started to amass at the gate, so Bailey's and Hutchinson's many reservations began to subside a little. Perhaps the time, money and effort of importing Jumbo would be worth it after all.

∾ Grand Tour ∾

Separating fact from fiction is never easy when it comes to the statements and stories issued by Phineas Barnum. The great showman claimed, for example, that from the day of his arrival Jumbo increased the circus's takings by around £500 a day so that within a week of his arrival the expense of buying and transporting the elephant had been paid off. Whether this boast was true or not (and it seems somewhat unlikely), the presence of Jumbo certainly lifted Barnum's Greatest Show on Earth up a level and within two weeks of arriving, "England's Pet", as Barnum termed him, was the star of the entire circus.

Jumbo settled into circus life quickly and was said to enjoy his new environment. According to Barnum, Jumbo's introduction to his other elephants was a sight to behold. "The herd was drawn up in a column, and Mr Jumbo was marched along the line, saluting each one he came to. They seized each other's trunks, embraced, and altogether showed great delight at making a new acquaintance. Jumbo was soon at home, and it was not long before he selected his favourite of the other sex, and already he has shown a particular liking for three or four out of the females, and I have no doubt that before long he will be setting his cap at the others."

George Arstingstall had immediately set to work on Jumbo, the trainer's aim being to incorporate him into the circus show as quickly as possible. Using his loud voice and sharp hook, Arstingstall was able to bring Jumbo under his control with remarkable ease and speed. Snatched reports from behind the scenes at Madison Square Garden portray Scott and Arstingstall as having operated a sort of "good cop, bad cop" routine in which the British keeper was on hand to reassure the elephant after an encounter with the

American trainer's hook. The result was astounding and within two weeks Jumbo was a fully functioning part of the circus show, giving the crowds exactly what they wanted: a spectacular figurehead for an equally spectacular circus show.

Barnum's famous three-ring circus in action.

"Amid the music of sounding brass, hoarse horns and sonorous drums, a glittering cavalcade wound round the Garden. This was the grand entrée. The animals one by one came out from the caverns in royal purple and gold and sparkling gems. The menials and the dromedaries proudly waved elaborately wrought banners and devices. When the pageant had disappeared Jumbo came forth in all his modern magnificence with a troop of children on his back. At his heels was the baby elephant, and at his side a trainer in full evening dress. Following was a band of Sioux Indians from the plains and cowboys. Then came the curiosities from the museum. There were the giant and the bearded lady, the long-haired wonder, the white female moor and the tattooed man. In the ring performance great improvement was shown. George Arstingstall showed what his herd of elephants could do, even standing on their heads. The show was pronounced better than ever by the crowds. Jumbo was likewise satisfied with the crowds; he was kept busy all the afternoon and evening eating oranges and buns."

Against the odds the Barnum, Bailey and Hutchinson Company had found itself a mascot that was guaranteed to draw in a capacity crowd, even at the matinees. No wonder Barnum was seen rubbing his hands together during the performances he attended. This evident satisfaction was to increase yet further as the Greatest Show on Earth prepared to uproot itself from its base in New York and go on tour. Soon the whole of America would come to know and love the giant elephant from London.

Despite having the vast building in Madison Square Garden, Barnum's circus was not a permanent feature in New York; there were simply not enough people to sustain the show for an entire summer season, so, after a month in the city, the show would pack up and go on an extensive tour of the eastern United States and southern Canada. This was achieved by using the network of railway lines which criss-crossed mainland America, but moving an entire circus was always a logistical challenge.

Barnum's company owned its own rolling stock of 100 carriages and freight cars as well as four steam engines to pull them. Into these would be fitted the entire circus, including all its animals, performers and personnel and all their food and equipment. To maximize the display time the trains would travel at night so that they could arrive at their next venue early in the morning. At first light the equipment would be unpacked and, with consummate speed, the tents, cages and other paraphernalia erected ready for a performance that evening. After the final performance at a venue the circus would be swiftly dismantled and packed away so that the trains could set off before midnight and be at their next destination by early morning.

The schedule was punishing, a typical season taking in as many as 70 or 80 different towns, with some consecutive venues as much as 100 miles apart. The usual itinerary took the circus south from New York to Philadelphia and Washington and then inland to Cincinnati and St Louis. Finally, by the end of the summer, the circus would move north to Chicago and then into southern Canada, before returning to Barnum's headquarters in Bridgeport for a well-deserved winter break. In the smaller towns the circus would give only two performances (a matinee and an evening show) but even in a big city such as Washington it would stay for just a couple of days before moving on. The brevity of these visits was probably deliberate, designed perhaps to maximize audiences and instil a sense of urgency into those who wished to see the circus.

The question of how best to accommodate Jumbo during these travels had led Barnum and his colleagues to design a magnificent, purpose-built carriage that would house the elephant and Scott on their own. Jumbo's Palace, as it was called, was designed to highlight the elephant's uniqueness and was some 40 feet long, 13 feet tall and 8 feet wide. These were the maximum dimensions permitted by the railway companies; any larger and Jumbo's Palace would have struck low bridges and other obstacles; Barnum used this restriction to his advantage and invited people to see Jumbo before he grew too large to pass through the nation's tunnels. The outside of Jumbo's carriage was painted red with a gold edging, so as to create the impression of travelling royalty. Anybody who witnessed Jumbo's Palace would be left in no doubt that the world's largest elephant was housed within and that he was the sole property of Barnum, Bailey and Hutchinson. A set of double doors on the side, painted blue and gold, allowed access while inside there was a separate bed and toilet facilities for Scott.

Barnum used the occasion of Jumbo's departure from New York to parade his animals through the streets to the New Jersey ferry house. Jumbo led the parade with Scott by his side but Arstingstall had insisted that the elephant's hind feet be placed in chains, so that he could only walk, not run. Word that Jumbo was on the street soon got around and, within a few blocks of setting off, the procession found itself being followed by two or three thousand people, including dozens of street urchins. As the elephant passed the rows of brownstone houses, windows were thrown open and men, women and children leaned out to shout their goodbyes to the circus. The noise and confusion scared the horses and camels but somehow order was maintained.

To the surprise of the assembled crowd, Jumbo stepped on to the deck of the New Jersey ferry with little fuss and the remaining elephants were loaded in behind him. The paddle-steamer started on its way across the harbour and had travelled only a few hundred yards before Jumbo showed signs of unease. He began to reverse into the elephants behind him, causing them to shuffle backwards; those at the rear of the ferry were in danger of being pushed into the river, a fate that would kill them. Arstingstall leapt into action, shouting at Jumbo while thrashing him with his iron hook; even Scott was seen to use the whip on his pet.

Just as it seemed certain that one of the elephants would topple backwards into the water, Jumbo stopped still and then walked slowly forward again, relieving the pressure behind him. Some of the other elephants rubbed themselves up against him, as if to offer reassurance that everything was all right, and afterwards all of them remained calm. There was some relief when Jumbo was taken from the ferry and, in front of a large crowd, coaxed into his luxury railway carriage. The only casualty of the day was some of Newman's toes, which were badly bruised by one of Jumbo's misplaced feet.

Matthew Scott was proving himself to be a rather remarkable man. Given his reserved nature and dislike of travelling, he might have expected to find life with Barnum's circus exacting and unpleasant, but the reverse seems to be true. This most British of men found the American way of life very much to his liking. Perhaps the informality of the circus suited him better than Bartlett's rigid routines; or maybe the celebrity of being "Jumbo Scott", as the crowds called him, was pleasing to him. Whatever the cause, Scott certainly relaxed into his new role, to the extent that the idea of returning to London, as he was expected to do in October, was increasingly unattractive.

Jumbo, on the other hand, did not enjoy life on the road. He found the noise and constant movement of the train journeys tedious and frightening. With the majority of journeys being made at night, it was Scott's hope that his friend would use the opportunity to get some sleep, but this rarely occurred. "The shaking and jar of the train, the worrying noises, etc., keep him in a constant ferment of nervous excitement," the keeper complained, "and he gives me little chance for sleep."

Often during the night Scott would awake to find he was

sharing his bed with Jumbo's trunk, which would grope around for his face. When really frightened the elephant would dash himself against the side of the carriage, forcing Scott to rise from his bed and talk with him. More than once Scott calmed Jumbo by sharing a bottle of ale with him as a nightcap.

About a month after leaving New York the circus found itself in transit on the Erie Railroad when the train carrying Jumbo narrowly missed a collision with another locomotive. The screech of brakes, loud whistling and excess of steam terrified Jumbo, who made an accidental sideways lurch into Scott, who was standing in his carriage at the time. The keeper was pinned against the wall by the elephant's great weight and then pushed against the end wall by his trunk. Scott later laughed off the incident, saying: "Jumbo gave me such a squeeze that I don't want any more like it." In fact he suffered several injuries serious enough to confine him to the circus's infirmary for a few days. Thanks to Arstingstall's training, Jumbo was able to perform at night without Scott by his side, although it was said that he looked like "a little girl left without its mamma".

Night after night the circus travelled on and day after day the train would stop and the equipment and animals would be taken from the sidings to the showground, which was sometimes as much as two miles away. Many of the circus animals, including the elephants, horses and camels, would be used to haul or lug the poles, wires, canvas and other equipment but, at Scott's insistence, Jumbo was excused from this duty.

The impending arrival of the Greatest Show on Earth would be well publicized by gigantic posters that would be displayed on lampposts and in shop windows across the eastern United States. Before the end of the season these posters were dominated by just one figure, Jumbo, whose gigantic frame was drawn so that he appeared to be charging at the observer. Across the top was written the slogan "P.T. Barnum's Greatest Show on Earth and the Great London Circus combined with the Giant African Elephant Jumbo", followed by miniature diagrams of Jumbo's arrival in America and his forced removal from England. Within months of joining the circus Jumbo had become its biggest asset and had achieved an equal billing with Barnum himself.

When the train pulled into town crowds of children would flock round screaming, "Here's Jumbo! Here's Jumbo!" A sell-out performance was guaranteed, with those who could not get to see the great elephant perform being allowed to view him privately for 25 cents. "He's all we want to see," said one punter, "and we won't look at anything else. We don't care about the balance but oh, let us see Jumbo." Others would wait until the end of the show and then follow the elephant as he and Scott wound their way back to Jumbo's Palace, wishing him goodnight and good luck with his travels.

For Scott the adulation was rewarding and heart-warming ("the world has no idea of the joy and happiness I have experienced") but such an unrelenting schedule took its toll on both humans and animals so that come the autumn all were approaching exhaustion. In late October the circus would finish its season and retire to Bridgeport, where they would rest during the worst of the winter weather. This was a time for everyone to recharge their drained batteries and for the animal trainers and performers to devise and practise new tricks. The Bridgeport site abutted the railway line and covered 10 acres, much of which was taken up with lengthy warehouses that housed various workshops and the animals' quarters, including the Elephant House.

A reporter from the *Daily Republican* was invited by Barnum to come up from New York to see the Winter Quarters for himself. He was taken on a tour which passed through the black-smiths' shop, the harness room and a training area where he witnessed a baboon being taught to wear gloves and a cape while riding a horse. Across a courtyard lay the real objective of the reporter's visit: the Elephant House. "Jumbo, looking bigger and more good-natured than ever, stood in the corner towering above all the others. He has grown seven inches taller since last year, and his tusks now protrude about five inches. He extended his trunk to welcome us and to look for titbits. Mr Rose [a keeper] secured about a dozen loaves of bread. 'Up!' he cried. Jumbo obediently raised his trunk over his enormous head and opened wide his capacious mouth. Standing a few feet away Mr Rose just simply threw the loaves into the elephant's mouth, one by one."

By this time Jumbo was not just well known by the circus-going public, but by the whole of the American public. From the moment of his arrival in New York the American newspapers had closely followed his progress, giving periodic updates of his adventures while on the road with the circus. Perhaps inevitably, the elephant's catchy name and famed size soon led to his being used to analogize objects or people that were considered too large. A political spat developed in Pennsylvania when J.C. Delaney referred to an opponent as "Jumbo McClure", bringing forth the reply that this was "both impolite and inappropriate". By the end of the year tobacconists were selling "Jumbo pipes" and in May 1882 the *New York Times* announced the invention of "the Jumbo of Steam-Whistles", which could be heard from over 50 miles away. On a more pragmatic level were the street hawkers and souvenir merchants who had been busy creating models of the elephant in a variety of materials, including porcelain, rubber and glass; these were not just to be sold at the circus, but almost everywhere in the United States. By end of 1882 North America had gained a new superstar whose name was so familiar that it needed no explanation. Barnum attributed the elephant's success to his skilful marketing but even he must have known that luck had played a heavy part in the proceedings.

With his arrival at the Winter Quarters Scott cut his few remaining ties to his old home across the seas. The six-month leave of absence he had been offered by the Zoological Society's Council ran out in October, inspiring Philip Sclater to remind him that "unless he returned to the Society's service before the end of the year he would be considered to have resigned his situation". The keeper wrote back asking for his leave to be extended for another year. Sclater refused and on 17 January 1883 it was agreed by the Council that Scott's name "be removed from the books". This news must have been heartening to Bartlett, who had long wanted to see the back of his irksome keeper. In Scott's absence Jumbo's old den had been let to Jingo while a conspiracy of silence at Regent's Park ensured that Jumbo's departure was no longer a topic of popular conversation. Britain's Jumbo craze of 1882 had well and truly evaporated, but across the Atlantic it had only just begun.

❧ Fame, Fire and Brooklyn Bridge ❧

The Greatest Show on Earth started its 1883 season in much the same form as it had the previous year. On 21 March the entire troupe travelled down by train from Connecticut to perform its month-long stint at Madison Square Garden. Any doubts that Jumbo's popularity might have faded during the winter were dispelled by newspaper headlines which announced his arrival in terms such as: "Jumbo, the great and only Jumbo, who has received more attention and had more real greatness thrust upon him than any other existing quadruped, came down from Bridgeport to New York on a special train yesterday."

The circus announced its arrival by enacting an impromptu street parade between the railway station and Madison Square Garden, led, of course, by Jumbo. As an extra piece of showmanship, the press were allowed to see Jumbo taken to his separate quarters, which, it was noted, he was sharing at that time with a female elephant named Queen and her baby, Bridgeport. In what was doubtless a publicity stunt, reporters were informed that the great elephant had become very attached to Queen and her calf.

Journalists crowded around Barnum to ask him questions about his prize exhibit. Naturally, many of these concerned the elephant's size but Barnum refused to answer this enquiry directly, instead explaining that Jumbo had grown by at least seven inches since his arrival in America, that he weighed the same as a railcar-load of pig iron and that his trunk was as long as a crocodile. This refusal to give exact figures formed part of Barnum's new policy which held that no one at the circus was to attempt to measure or weigh Jumbo. In the absence of solid facts, it was his hope that the news media and public alike would exaggerate Jumbo's dimensions to ridiculous proportions.

This embargo even applied to the scientific community; in 1883 the zoologist and taxidermist William Hornaday asked Barnum several times if he might be allowed to measure Jumbo's height. Eventually he received a reply giving him permission on condition that "Mr Bailey consents". Hornaday travelled to Madison Square Garden with Barnum's letter in hand but received a frosty reception from James Bailey. "His indignation was as colossal as the great pachyderm," recorded Hornaday, who had been told by Bailey to leave the circus's premises. This routine whereby Barnum appeared to give a person permission to inspect Jumbo only for it to be withdrawn by Bailey was used on other occasions and may have been a strategy devised between the two men to minimize the bad publicity engendered by a refusal.

However, this was not the end of the story, for Hornaday later received word from two of Barnum's acrobats that they had estimated Jumbo's height at a shade over 11 feet. They managed this during their rehearsals by surreptitiously standing near the elephant with one of the poles they used in their act, noting the point on the pole which corresponded with Jumbo's height and later measuring it in private. This estimate was close to the figure of 11 feet that Bartlett had given a member of the Zoological Society earlier in the year and would tally with another clandestine measurement made two years later. In the meantime journalists were regularly describing the elephant as being well over 13 feet tall, just as Barnum had hoped they would.

In comparison with the previous year, the 1883 touring season of the Greatest Show on Earth proved to be highly troublesome. It began badly when, a few days after opening in New York, Barnum was arrested for alleged cruelty to two of his child performers. The charges were trumped up and soon dismissed but Barnum showed that there was no ill feeling by arranging for the judge and lawyers to visit Jumbo privately. A few days later a more serious issue arose when Pilot, one of the male Asian elephants, viciously attacked and maimed one of his smaller colleagues; Bill Newman attempted to intervene but the enraged Pilot turned on him and, using his trunk and tusks, knocked out several of the keeper's teeth. Pilot had at one time been a part of Edward

Cross's menagerie in London and had killed a keeper there; Barnum did not want a repetition of the incident and, perhaps fearing that Pilot was in musth, ordered the animal to be shot. It was a poor start to the season but everything settled down again when the circus left New York for a series of 12 performances in neighbouring Brooklyn. With Jumbo as the star attraction, the show brought in an astounding $62,750. The main tent was the largest in the world, capable of holding 20,000, and yet every night it was full and hundreds were refused entry.

Two months later the circus, in its usual breakneck progress across the eastern States, reached Chicago, where it would remain for several days. At 2 a.m. on 6 June an unattended lamp in the main tent set fire to the canvas, sending flames up to the roof and along the ropes and poles to the private boxes and seating areas. For a while the flames threatened to jump across to the tents that housed the horses and some of the wild animals but firefighters arrived in time to subdue the blaze and prevent this. The giant tent, which had covered six acres and cost $16,000, was a write-off, but by that evening the show had been reorganized and went ahead as usual.

However, the following day's matinee performance brought further trouble as one of the elephants, which was attached to a chariot, suddenly ran amok, sending other animals and performers running for their lives. The audience rose in panic and began to flee for the exits; a loss of life looked inevitable until the quick-thinking band struck up a tune that, miraculously, calmed both the wildlife and spectators, so averting any serious injury.

Further incidents followed, such as the one on 29 September when a chariot rider was severely injured during a performance. Just a few hours later an aggressive tiger escaped from its cage and was about to pounce on some of the animals when a cowboy used his lasso to ensnare it. Finally, on 16 October, as the season was drawing to a close, came a dramatic accident that almost spelled the end for Matthew Scott.

The keeper had been in Jumbo's "special tent" awaiting the start of the matinee when he heard a noise "like a bursting thunderstorm". He peeped out of the tent and was aghast to see 30 elephants stampeding towards him, smashing everything in their way. "If death ever stared me in the face," wrote Scott, "it did at that moment. On came the black mass of mad animals, and I thought there was no escape from being crushed beneath their heavy feet."

According to Scott, he felt Jumbo's trunk wrap about his waist, gently pull him into the tent and place him between his legs. "Jumbo then stood firmly and stretched out his trunk, as rigid as the limb of a large tree, and permitted not one elephant to get past it." The elephants were contained in the enclosure and in time the stampede subsided. "He repaid me for all the suffering he has ever caused me by saving my life," reflected Scott afterwards.

As the headlines detailing these misfortunes accumulated, so Barnum attempted to offset the bad press by announcing that he had obtained at great cost a rare white elephant from Thailand. He was quick to point out that these animals were considered sacred in the Far East but that, with luck, one would feature in his show by the end of the touring season. This plan also fell foul of the bad luck that was dogging Barnum when his Bangkok agent was forced to flee the country after receiving death threats from vengeful Thais who resented the thought of losing a white elephant to the Americans. Luckily the agent was able to obtain a replacement in neighbouring Burma but the elephant was deliberately poisoned before he could get it out of the country. Finally, the King of Burma, a man who had recently had all his wives murdered, agreed to sell Barnum a white elephant from his collection but by the time the arrangements had been made the animal could not be shipped in time for the remainder of the 1883 season.

It had been a costly and trying year for Barnum and his business partners but the presence of Jumbo had to a degree offset the ill fortune. However, as the season drew to a close it became evident that all was not well with their star attraction.

Towards the autumn of 1883 Jumbo was suffering from an unknown ailment. Over a period of several weeks he become withdrawn and went off his food; Arstingstall and Newman feared that this was prelude to musth but the aggression and irrational behaviour did not return. Instead weight started to fall from Jumbo's massive frame and he became listless and weak. All known elephantine illnesses were ruled out by the veterinarians and it was thought that the elephant might have been fed something unpleasant (such as rat poison) by a malevolent visitor to the show.

This was a worrying time for Barnum but he was nothing if not resourceful. Earlier in the year the showman had been contacted by Henry Ward, a professional taxidermist associated with the University of Rochester in upstate New York. Ward had preserved many of the circus's dead animals and had written to Barnum to offer his services in the event of Jumbo's death. Barnum had ignored the letter but by October the prospect of losing the star elephant seemed very much more real and he wrote back to Ward: "I shall have my managers understand that if we lose Jumbo (which Heaven forbid!) you must be telegraphed to immediately, and hope you will lose no time in saving his skin & skeleton."

Barnum had apparently hatched a plan whereby, should Jumbo die, his body would be stuffed and exhibited as part of the show. Another part of this plan was to buy Alice from London Zoo and have her exhibited next to the dead body of her "husband". It was a pretty morbid idea but one that would almost certainly have appealed to the paying public. As luck would have it, Barnum had to travel to London on business and while there he visited Bartlett to ask if he would part with Alice. The Superintendent was willing to do so but said that he would have to get the consent of the Zoological Society's Council. He duly wrote to Philip Sclater asking him to "authorise me to sell Alice the female African Elephant and at what price, I have seen Mr Barnum and I think I can manage to dispose of the elephant." But the Council was still smarting from the trouble caused by Jumbo's departure and refused Bartlett permission.

Barnum returned to America empty-handed but was pleasantly surprised to discover that not only was Jumbo still alive but there were signs that his health was improving. Throughout this period Barnum had been anxious that nobody should learn of Jumbo's ill health and had ordered that the elephant continue to perform to the public. The gamble had paid off and as the Greatest Show on Earth rolled into its Winter Quarters there was every sign that the elephant would make a full recovery.

This was just as well because the American Jumbo craze continued to reach ever more dizzy heights. In February 1884 the entrepreneur James Lafferty unveiled plans to construct at Coney Island a gigantic, Jumbo-shaped building 270 feet long and 122 feet high. Lafferty asked Barnum to loan him his elephant for the opening ceremony; the request was refused on the grounds that next to the building "Jumbo will resemble a very small and lean rat".

Late March 1884 brought the arrival of Toung Taloung, Barnum's much-advertised Burmese white elephant, which had come to New York via London Zoo, where it had spent a month being admired by the public. The newspapers acknowledged the novelty of the new elephant but declared that Jumbo was "ready to assert his superiority" over his rival; there was even a minor outcry when Barnum produced posters which placed the white elephant in a more prominent position than Jumbo.

The 1884 season got under way with the usual parade through New York that heralded the opening of the Madison Square Garden shows. Since the circus's last visit the city had seen the completion of one of the greatest civil engineering projects in the world. In 1870 work had begun on a vast suspension bridge that would stretch 1,600 feet across the East River, joining the boroughs of Manhattan and Brooklyn. This would be by far the world's longest bridge and, accordingly, it took 13 years to finish, with the grand opening taking place on 24 May 1883. Unsurprisingly, Brooklyn Bridge became an architectural icon and a symbol of the way in which America was overtaking Europe in terms of wealth, industry and technology.

For weeks before the opening of the bridge rumours had circulated that it was not strong enough to take the weight of traffic and would collapse into the river. Just six days after its inauguration the bridge was packed with pedestrians when a woman slipped down some steps, screaming as she did so. This simple event sparked an immediate panic during which the vast crowd surged along the walkways like a herd of cattle. The push became an uncontrollable stampede which crushed people against the barriers and trampled them underfoot; 12 people died and dozens were injured, including several children. For months afterwards the bridge's technological achievement was overshadowed by the horror of the disaster.

In May 1884 the Greatest Show on Earth, after performing in Philadelphia, returned to New York to begin its Brooklyn run. Before the show's arrival Barnum had been asked by Brooklyn Bridge's managers if he would walk Jumbo across the bridge, the idea being to use the largest elephant in the world to test its strength. It was hoped that the resultant publicity would convince the public that the bridge was perfectly safe. Barnum was ever alert to publicity opportunities and leapt at the chance.

On 17 May New Yorkers were invited to "see Jumbo, the largest known animal in creation, walking on the best and finest promenade in the world", but Scott was very much against the idea. He had heard the rumours regarding the bridge's integrity and became convinced that the weight of his elephant "would shake the whole concern down into the river". Barnum would have none of this and at 9.30 p.m. Jumbo led a minor parade of 21 elephants, seven camels and 10 dromedaries across the bridge, starting from its Manhattan end.

Brooklyn Bridge was lined with an estimated crowd of 10,000, who waved and cheered at the animals. "It seemed as if Noah's Ark were emptying itself," said one person, while others shouted, "Hooray! There's Jumbo!" as the elephant came into view. In reply the great animal flapped his ears and trumpeted but his keeper remained deeply unhappy and later claimed that of all the people on the bridge that day he was the only one who knew that any "antics" by Jumbo could cause the entire edifice to collapse. The predicted disaster did not occur but as the procession moved through Brooklyn a little girl was so anxious to glimpse Jumbo that she toppled out of a fourth-storey window and was killed. News of the accident greatly troubled Scott, who for months afterwards could not expunge the "thought of the poor mother's feelings when she raised up the shattered remains of her poor child".

This tragedy aside, the remainder of the 1884 season was less troubled than the previous year. Only two incidents of note occurred: one was a railway accident in June in which one of the elephant carriages left the tracks and rolled down a bank. Fortunately no person or animal was injured and Jumbo was employed to push the car back up the embankment and on to the tracks. The other was a small fire at the Winter Quarters which again caused no injury.

Jumbo had survived the entire season without illness or harm, and as Scott settled into his Bridgeport accommodation he decided that it was time to cash in on the elephant's new-found celebrity status in America by writing about his life with the world's most famous elephant. Although he was functionally literate, he was far from eloquent, and it was not until 14 January 1885 that he started to write his "humble and truthful history". The resultant manuscript was short and slightly rambling and, after its submission to a New York publisher, an editor tidied the rough phrasing and jumbled anecdotes into a coherent account.

At under 100 pages the finished book was slim but its style did preserve Scott's personality, including his earthy language and lack of grammar. It also reflected his egotism, and no opportunity was lost to place himself centre stage, especially where Jumbo was concerned. Major players such as Bartlett, Barnum and Newman are almost entirely absent, while all mention of Jumbo's illnesses and even of the tussles concerning his sale by the Zoological Society are missing. Above all, one gets the sense that after many years of playing second fiddle at London Zoo, Scott was happy with his new position in the circus and had fallen in love with the American people, to whom he continually refers in grateful terms. The book, entitled *The Autobiography of Matthew Scott, Jumbo's Keeper*, was ready in time for its author to be able to sell copies during the circus's 1885 season. Barnum was given a copy and evidently read it, for he would occasionally quote its more sensational stories to the press.

The autobiography finishes with Scott describing the scene inside the Elephant House at Bridgeport: "Jumbo is looking down with his wisest air at me: I am quite contented and so is he." He then makes a remark that, in the light of later events, appears to be remarkably prophetic: "The future is a sealed book; but I fear no danger, for we are all in the care of Him who marks even the sparrow's fall."

Scott's touching faith was to be sorely tested in the coming season.

☙ The Accident ☙

The Greatest Show on Earth started its 1885 programme with Jumbo and Scott in fine form. The winter break had brought many changes to the performance, notably the addition of a fourth circus ring. All who witnessed the new set-up agreed that it was the best, most spectacular show on earth. "Barnum outdoes himself", "the grandest Mr Barnum ever organized", "Barnum never gave a greater show" were just a few of the comments made by critics, each of whom took the time to mention Jumbo's role, which had been expanded to include his old job of carrying children about the showground in a howdah.

After four years with the circus Scott and Jumbo had become used to life on the road and by now were becoming familiar with many of the cities and towns through which the show passed. As ever, Barnum was not content with the status quo and had an ambition to use his star elephant's international fame by taking the show further afield. "The people of Texas, Colorado and California have yet to see Jumbo," said Barnum in July, adding that afterwards "he will visit Australia and Europe". Such promises had been made several times before but the excursions had never materialized and in truth were unlikely to do so while the eastern States proved to be lucrative.

The entire season had passed without major incident when, at first light on 15 September, the circus train stopped at St Thomas in the Canadian province of Ontario. The town had a population of around 9,000 and had been built up around a strategic meeting point of several important railway lines from other parts of Canada and the USA, earning it the nickname of Railway City. Indeed, it was difficult to escape the criss-crossing tracks in the town's centre and the site chosen for the show was located on a patch of ground halfway between two important rail junctions. As there was no direct access from the tracks, the circus equipment and animals had to be unloaded at a nearby level crossing and taken along a network of roads to the site. The task was tedious but by the early afternoon the troupe was ready to put on the first of two performances scheduled for St Thomas.

After months without mishap the matinee show brought the death of a bareback rider who slipped and was crushed by the weight of horses' hooves and chariots. It was a bitter blow but the show went on while the body was carefully removed without attracting the audience's attention. The evening performance was a professional and spectacular affair. The show now boasted 31 elephants, which were led through the big tent in a nose-to-tail procession with Jumbo at its head and the sacred white elephant following close behind. Although still the star of the show, Jumbo retained a role that was very much ceremonial and, other than carrying about howdahs of children, he was required only to be seen by the public. It was the Asian elephants that performed the tricks and stunts in the ring, with pride of place going to Tom Thumb. This dwarf elephant was also known as "The Clown" because of the foolish routines George Arstingstall had taught him, which included stealing objects from tables and replacing them when the trainer wasn't looking. Tom Thumb was a favourite of the crowd and, if the stories are to be believed, also a close friend of Jumbo, who shared a tent with him between the matinee and the evening show.

The nightly performance finished at around 9.30 p.m., after which the well-rehearsed task of dismantling and loading the tent and other equipment could begin in preparation for departure at midnight. Rather than load the carriages at the level crossing, the circus managers were told that they could remove a section of fencing and walk their equipment along 1,500 feet of track to the goods yard where the circus's train was waiting. This saved a great deal of effort and was only possible because, according to the railwaymen, no trains were scheduled to use the line for several hours. The operation proceeded smoothly, with Jumbo and Tom Thumb the last two animals to make the journey between the showground and the goods yard.

Scott and a railwayman took the two elephants through the

removed section of fencing and on to the railway line, walking them downhill towards the circus train. As they neared the goods yard Scott found that he was sandwiched between the circus train on his right and a steep embankment on his left. This forced Jumbo and Tom Thumb to walk gingerly along a narrow stretch of single track but no urgency was called for until Scott's ears picked up the distant rumble of a locomotive engine. Behind them, about 500 yards up the track, emerged the headlamp of a freight train which, to the railwayman's horror, was travelling on the same track as the elephants. He immediately shouted at the keeper to get the elephants off the line and then ran towards the train waving his red flag.

Scott found himself trapped between the steep embankment and the circus carriages; he tried to persuade the elephants to move off the line and down the slope but they were scared and refused to budge. Behind them came the shrill whistle of the freight locomotive, the driver of which had spotted the danger but, because the train was going down an incline, could not stop in time. Scott urged the elephants forward in a trot, shouting at them to keep moving in the hope that they would be able to pass in front of the circus train and escape danger.

The screeching of the brakes grew louder and louder until a collision between the engine and the elephants became an inevitability. Unable to do anything more, Scott threw himself clear and could only watch as, seconds later, the locomotive ploughed headlong into his treasured pets. Tom Thumb was the first to be hit but his smallness proved to be advantageous. The locomotive's cowcatcher struck him, tossing him sideways down the embankment, injured but alive. Jumbo was still fleeing for his life when the engine rammed him; at over six tons he had no chance of being thrown clear and instead his body took the full force of the impact. Jumbo gave a great roar as the locomotive struck his rear legs and knocked him to the ground. Both train and elephant went skidding together along the line for a short distance until the locomotive derailed and rode over his back. The great mass came to halt with Jumbo partially trapped beneath the locomotive and the edge of the first freight car; it was a terrible sight.

The noise of the brakes and the sound of the impact immediately brought a great number of people from the goods yard, among them many of the circus staff and railwaymen. Scott was the first to reach Jumbo, who lay prostrate on his side across the tracks; the keeper was relieved to see that his great friend was still breathing but it was clear that his injuries were many and serious. He sat by Jumbo's head, talking to him, encouraging him to be strong. Within a couple of minutes a dozen people had arrived with lamps and flaming torches; these revealed a number of deep wounds across the animal's legs and flank. Jumbo remained completely silent, as though resigned to his fate.

More men arrived and an attempt was made to free Jumbo from beneath the locomotive so that veterinary surgeons could get access to some of the more serious wounds. Scott remained by Jumbo's head and watched as a small trickle of blood left the elephant's mouth; his great friend drew a shallow lungful of air and then exhaled. It was his last breath, and as the giant body became perfectly still Scott fell upon it, weeping copiously and inconsolably.

With Jumbo beyond all help, the circus's veterinary team turned their attention to little Tom Thumb, who lay injured at the bottom of the embankment. They were surprised to discover that the little elephant's injuries, while serious, seemed not to be life-threatening. The unfortunate animal had received a broken left hind leg and some flesh wounds, both of which could be treated. He lay still while his damaged leg was dressed and heavily strapped; he was then helped up on to the track and led slowly back to his carriage.

The arrival of several railwaymen injected a sense of urgency. They pointed out that as other freight trains would pass along the line there was the danger that Jumbo's body and the derailed locomotive might be the cause of another accident. On this occasion the train driver, William Burnin, had been fortunate to escape injury; the next person might not be so lucky. The order was given for Jumbo's body to be removed as speedily as possible.

There were about 100 men at the scene, and ropes, planks and steel poles were brought from the nearby circus train. Moving and replacing the locomotive on the track proved to be a relatively easy task which took only a few minutes; it had been badly damaged by the impact and, although still working, would have to be returned to a workshop and largely rebuilt.

Moving Jumbo's body was not so straightforward. His weight and shape made initial attempts to lever him off the track useless and so steel cables were brought from the circus and placed round his body. With 50 men pulling on each cable and others using poles and planking to lever his back, the prone body was dragged off the line and down the embankment. Even with all that manpower, it took over half an hour. Afterwards Scott lay on Jumbo's body and wept inconsolably into the early hours of the morning. It was the first time in over 20 years that he would face a sunrise without the prospect of caring for his pet Jumbo. He was devastated and appeared ignorant of the growing crowd of spectators as he grieved by the elephant's motionless trunk.

By first light news of the accident had spread across the whole of St Thomas, drawing a sizeable crowd around Jumbo's body, which lay on its side on the embankment. Those who were first on the scene tried to take souvenirs from the body, clipping away tail hairs or pieces of skin from the damaged flank. One boy ran forward and deftly cut off a section of ear before being chased away; the arrival of several constables put a stop to such antics and after that the crowd was kept at a safe distance. A local photographer was permitted to take several pictures of Jumbo; in each one the great elephant is surrounded by members of the local community while the figure of Matthew Scott stands dolefully by his head, posing for the camera.

News of Jumbo's horrendous death was soon being telegraphed across the United States and the world. Phineas Barnum was staying at the Murray Hill Hotel in New York when word reached him. He was shocked and, somewhat uncharacteristically, immediately thought not of himself but of his British keeper. "Poor Scott!" he exclaimed to a reporter. "I don't know what he'll do without Jumbo. He cares nothing for human companionship. Jumbo was all the world to him. They loved each other dearly."

Barnum's mind then wandered to more practical matters. "The death of Jumbo will make necessary a complete change in our plans for the future." He mused on his much-publicized plans to take the show to California, Australia and Europe; these would have to be cancelled. "All Europe was waiting to see

Jumbo," he explained to the journalists, "but his death will not take away the life of the great show. We mean to make it better than ever in spite of Jumbo's loss."

"Was Jumbo's life insured?" asked one reporter.

"No, the loss is a total one," said Barnum, adding that he could perhaps sue the freight company for damages. The showman then took his leave of the newsmen so that he could begin to deal with the many issues that had been raised by the sudden loss of Jumbo.

Back in St Thomas local journalists had been busy interviewing all those who had witnessed the previous night's tragedy. By mid-morning the first accounts were being telegraphed to newspaper offices across the country, ready for the next day's papers. In turn these articles were syndicated across the Atlantic to England, France, Germany and other European countries. Readers picking up their daily paper on 17 September were greeted with the news of Jumbo's death, which had been conveyed in a variety of headlines.

"The Great Jumbo Killed!" revealed the *New York Times*, which went on devote two long articles to the story. Other American newspapers followed suit, their horror reflecting the level of stardom that the elephant had achieved in the United States.

In Britain the reaction was more low-key. The years since Jumbo's departure had seen a backlash against the hysterical scenes that had occurred at London Zoo. The Jumbo craze was viewed by many as a regrettable experience during which the British public had inexplicably lost control of its senses. The *Spectator* reflected on this when it talked of "the contempt with which the 'craze' about Jumbo is still spoken of. What was there contemptible about it? If one person had been interested in the huge beast nobody would have been annoyed; but because a million ones were interested, the interest was pronounced insane."

The British newspapers did not want to be held responsible for another bout of impassioned behaviour and so the news of Jumbo's death was generally passed on in small articles with unsensational headlines. However, many members of the British public were affected by the death and it was often opined that had Jumbo remained at London Zoo he would still be alive. Only the *Daily*

Telegraph expressed serious regret at Jumbo's loss; its editor had for many years pursued a vendetta against Abraham Bartlett and led its emotional obituary with the headline "Sad End of Jumbo".

All the early articles about Jumbo's death carried accurate reports of the accident and its aftermath which, to Barnum's annoyance, made the whole thing sound rather bungled and humdrum. His being in New York prevented him from controlling the journalists who were swarming into St Thomas. With no one to stop him, one reporter had made measurements of Jumbo's body which revealed his height to be exactly 11 feet and not the 14 feet that Barnum had been hinting at earlier in the year. To stem the flow of bad publicity Barnum dispatched to St Thomas a public relations man named Haight, who, on 17 September, held a press conference close to the spot where Jumbo died.

"The truth about the killing of Jumbo on Tuesday evening has not yet been published," Haight revealed. "The reason at first was not apparent. The baby elephant was in the rear and as the engine was closing upon them Jumbo raised on his hind legs as though to protect the baby. He then quick as thought dropped down and grabbed him in his trunk and hurled him with great force over all the tracks and against a freight car, twenty yards away, where he dropped down, whining like a puppy with a sore foot. Jumbo, in saving the life of his protégé, entirely neglected his own chance to escape. The locomotive struck him with force in the side, crowding him against some cars on the siding nearest him and fairly squeezing the life out of him."

This story was a product of Barnum's active imagination but it was carried by dozens of papers and was soon being quoted as fact. Barnum chose to play down news of Scott's fate. The keeper was devastated but this did not stop his being "pensioned off" by the showman, who could conceive no further use for him. Barnum was a hard man to whom death and injury were just everyday hazards of circus life. As the saying goes, "The show must go on," and on 17 September the Greatest Show on Earth rolled into the town of London, 20 miles north of St Thomas, and prepared for a matinee performance without Jumbo and his keeper.

CHAPTER 23

∽ The Comeback ∾

Within hours of Jumbo's death Barnum had announced his plans for the elephant's remains: "My wife suggests that I have Jumbo mounted and continue to exhibit him in the show for the present. That is what I shall do. If I can't have Jumbo living, I'll have him dead, and Jumbo dead is worth a small herd of ordinary elephants."

Just two weeks earlier Barnum had finished negotiating with the taxidermist Henry Ward as to what should happen in the event of Jumbo's death. As agreed a couple of years beforehand, Ward was to be in charge of preserving the body, with the mounted skin going to Tufts College in Medford, Massachusetts, where Barnum had established a museum. The fate of the skeleton was undecided but there was mention of its being sent to the Smithsonian Institution in Washington.

On hearing of Jumbo's death, Barnum's first action was to cable Ward at the University of Rochester instructing him to hotfoot it up to St Thomas. The taxidermist and two of his assistants set off immediately and arrived just one day later; Jumbo's body remained on the railway embankment, guarded by the police. On viewing the remains Ward decided that the task was greater than he had at first imagined and immediately hired six local butchers to assist him. Even with this manpower it took over two days to dissect the body and prepare its skin and bones; the fresh hide was found to weight over one and a half tons and the bones nearly two and a half. The most surprising discovery was made in Jumbo's stomach, which held hundreds of coins, a bunch of keys, several rivets and a policeman's whistle. "Jumbo was a bank all by himself," reported an amazed Ward.

Jumbo's hide, which had been removed in three parts, his

bones and some of his vital organs were freighted back to Rochester with Ward and his men. The remaining redundant flesh was gathered together by the people of St Thomas and placed on top of a wooden funeral pyre where it slowly burned up.

Ward estimated that it would take his assistants two months to stuff the skin for display as part of Barnum's show. (Tufts College, which had been promised the skin originally, was told that it would get it eventually.) The showman agreed to pay Ward a flat rate of $1,200 for the job but the taxidermist had underestimated the scale of the task. A new building had to be erected to house the project and the elephant's tusks proved to be damaged beyond use, necessitating the expensive creation of false ones.

As the work to preserve Jumbo entered its sixth month and took up ever more of Ward's time, he sent an inscribed slice of tusk to Barnum and asked him for more money. Barnum thanked Ward for the present ("My wife is delighted!") but refused him the cash, explaining that his underestimate "was no fault of ours, and you will surely gain thousands of dollars through the celebrity which the affair will give you".

While Ward struggled to stuff and mount Jumbo, Barnum set about enacting a failed plan of a couple of years earlier: he approached the Zoological Society of London to ask again if it would part with Jumbo's "wife", Alice. His request having been refused the first time, Barnum's hopes were not high and so he was mildly surprised when the Council not only agreed to sell Alice but asked just £200 for her. He immediately telegraphed Bartlett: "Will take Alice. Have sent money."

The sale of Alice occurred without a single murmur from the British press, but this did not stop Barnum from employing a lawyer, just in case the public became feisty again. In the event the only objection came from a London restaurateur who complained that after Jumbo's removal Barnum's men had left him with unpaid bills. The matter was settled and Alice departed in time to join the show, complete with Jumbo's stuffed effigy, at Madison Square Garden. She was to meet another old friend, her ex-keeper Matthew Scott, who had been rehired by Barnum to accompany Jumbo's remains as they toured the country.

The meeting between Alice and her late partner occurred on

20 April 1886 at 10.30 a.m. Jumbo was actually present in two forms: his stuffed skin, which, thanks to the use of 78,280 nails, was said to look remarkably lifelike; and his bleached bones, which had been mounted separately to form an articulated skeleton. The stuffed effigy seemed to be much bigger than the skeleton, which may have been a result of Barnum's instruction to Ward to make Jumbo "as large as possible" so that he might "show like a mountain".

In the circus's central arena, and without the presence of an audience, Alice was walked towards the stuffed Jumbo. She stood before him for a few moments, surveying the scene, before swinging her trunk round to touch his mouth and trunk. She then turned her back on Jumbo and gave a great groan. Bill Newman forced her round to face the exhibit again; Alice looked straight into Jumbo's eyes before turning and walking firmly away to her quarters. Some of those present were confused by what they had seen and turned to question Scott.

"Did she recognize Jumbo?" he was asked by James Hutchinson.

"Of course she did. She told me so," explained Scott, before informing him that he could understand elephant talk and repeating that "Alice told me that she recognized Jumbo." As the keeper walked from the scene to tend to Alice in her quarters it was observed that he was crying.

After the New York run Barnum's circus followed its usual tour of the eastern USA, where it met with success equal to that of the previous years. The presence of Jumbo undoubtedly contributed to this and led one newspaper to comment that "Jumbo stuffed is a greater attraction than Jumbo alive."

While the show undertook its tour Barnum started to sort out some of the legal issues that had resulted from the death of his former star. His first lawsuit had been against the *Globe* newspaper of Hartford, Connecticut, for suggesting that he had ordered Jumbo to be killed "for advertising purposes". Barnum was seeking $50,000 but the case was settled out of court. More complex was the issue of fault for the death. The circus staff insisted that the St Thomas railwaymen had told them that there were no scheduled trains on the line and that it was safe to walk along it. This was true inasmuch as there were no scheduled trains, but a great many unscheduled freight trains used the line, including the one that slammed into the elephant. In their defence the railwaymen stated that the circus had signed a contract which stated that its staff must load and unload only at the level crossing.

Faced with these complications, Barnum eventually launched a lawsuit against the Grand Trunk Railroad, whose unscheduled locomotive was the cause of the accident. As chance would have it, James Bailey had sold his share in the circus business only days before Jumbo's death and so the suit, which was for $100,000, was taken out by Barnum and Hutchinson. They wanted to prove negligence on the part of the freight company and as a consequence Matthew Scott, George Arstingstall and other members of the circus's staff were required to testify in court.

Barnum stated under oath that Jumbo had been worth around $50,000 a year to his business but the freight company hit back with the claim that his worth "was very slight". As proof it produced a deposition from Philip Sclater, who confirmed that Jumbo had been aggressive before his sale. The defendant's lawyers then highlighted a clause in Barnum's insurance which did not value any exhibit at more than $15,000. Finally, the freight company said that if it lost the suit it should be entitled to own Jumbo's stuffed hide and skeleton, at which point Barnum backed down and broke off the legal action, claiming that he "did not wish to part with the frame and outer covering of the great beast".

In October 1886 Barnum's circus found itself in the state of Virginia preparing for its return to its Winter Quarters. Since April Scott had been paid to stand next to Jumbo's gigantic frame with Alice, to act as a public guide and to talk about his adventures with the large elephant: "He never tired of telling of the peaceful disposition, the kindly nature and the altogether commendable habits of his late chum," noted one of his workmates somewhat sarcastically.

By the end of the season a number of things had become evident to James Hutchinson. The first was that Jumbo had entered American folklore and that his stuffed exhibit could be guaranteed to keep pulling in the crowds for a few years yet. The second was that Matthew Scott was still gravely traumatized by the loss of his elephant and his attitude was beginning to grate on others. "He is a restless, dissatisfied, pretty well broken up individual," complained Hutchinson. As Bartlett had discovered many years earlier, Scott was not an easy man to be around and so, with Jumbo transformed into an inanimate object, Hutchinson decided that the British keeper was surplus to requirements. For the sake of his staff's morale, he informed Scott that his services were no longer needed.

Unlike Barnum, who had been prepared to cast Scott out into the cold the previous year, Hutchinson felt some sense of duty to his keeper. On 23 October, after the show's last performance that year, he approached Scott to give him the bad news, advising him that he should return to England and ask to resume his old job at London Zoo (which suggests that he knew nothing of Scott's history there). To Hutchinson's surprise, Scott agreed that this was his best course of action and so later that day he was given his back pay, which amounted to $2,000, and enough money to buy a boat ticket back home. Hutchinson even helped him select a steamer and, after seeing him bid farewell to his colleagues, watched as Scott boarded a train for New York in order to catch the boat home.

The circus proprietor believed that this was the last he would see of the keeper, but several months later he found himself in Bridgeport for a snap inspection of the Winter Quarters and during his tour he was astonished to see Scott skulking in one of the courtyards.

"Halloa, Scott," he hailed. "What are you doing here? I thought you were in England with your friends."

"I rather like it in this country and thought I'd stay here for a while," Scott mumbled.

Then he made his excuses and sloped off, but Hutchinson was not satisfied and was especially worried by the man's demeanour: "He appeared to be a trifle ashamed of something, as if caught in a disreputable sort of proceeding." Hutchinson asked around about Scott but nobody knew of his presence except for the staff at the Elephant House. They claimed to have seen him every day since the show's arrival in Bridgeport the previous autumn.

"Scott had prowled about the barn," reported Hutchinson, "chatted with the elephant men and invariably wound up by a visit to the spot where the stuffed Jumbo and his skeleton are stored. After a short and, so far as is known, silent communication with his dead friend Scott would leave the place satisfied and go to his humble lodgings. If the deceased Jumbo travels this season Scott will want to, even if he isn't on the salary list."

Hutchinson was not fond of the idea of Scott hanging around the dead elephant and barred him from the Winter Quarters. The measure was only partially successful and when the circus travelled to Madison Square Garden for its opening performances Scott was again seen hanging around Jumbo's exhibit. It may have been at this point that Barnum and Hutchinson took steps to prevent him from bothering them any further. Scott was last seen with the circus at the end of March 1887 but on 12 April there was a newspaper report of his being aboard an England-bound steamer with George Arstingstall.

It is easy to envisage a scenario in which Hutchinson was forced to order the gruff, no-nonsense Arstingstall to manhandle Scott away from the United States and back to England. If this was the case the tactic may not have worked as a later rumour says Scott ended his days in America, eking out a living by selling copies of his autobiography. He certainly seems to be absent from Britain's Census of 1891 and there is no traceable British death certificate filed for him, all of which suggests that he may have spent the end of his life abroad.

This suggests a sad end for the keeper, whose dislike of human company, arrogance and unswerving affection for a giant African elephant did not serve him well. The enforced separation from Jumbo marked the end of his career as a public figure and after April 1887 "Jumbo Scott" or "Scotty", as he was known in America, vanishes from history. Scott was 53 and had led a rough lifestyle characterized by manual labour and long hours. He was only a few years away from his statistical Victorian life expectancy and one may suspect that it was not long before he followed his beloved elephant to the grave, although exactly where and when his death occurred is a mystery. Scott's unusual life history and his ability to turn potential allies into enemies echoes Hutchinson's view that "animal trainers, like old maids, are curious creatures".

With his former keeper off the scene, Jumbo's stuffed remains continued their tour of America for the remainder of the 1887 season and were as popular as ever. Alice remained faithfully by her husband's side but she was to fall foul of a curse that had stalked Phineas Barnum since his early days as a showman. On 20 November 1887 the entire circus menagerie was in the main building of Barnum's Winter Quarters, recovering from the strains of that season's tour. At around 10.30 p.m. a spark from a watchman's lamp set fire to straw. The flames quickly took hold and spread to wooden panelling and within minutes the whole building was ablaze.

Many of the staff were asleep or absent and by the time the alarm was raised the giant warehouse was beyond saving; the majority of animals inside were either heavily tethered or had been housed in wooden cages. There was no helping any of them and only those that could break free from their ropes and chains were saved. This included 30 of the elephants and one rhinoceros, who were able to use their bulk to crash their way through the side of the building and into the street. Six of them were terribly burned. "Great pieces of flesh fell from their side," said one witness, "and their blood splattered the ground as they ran."

The total losses were terrible; all the caged circus animals died, as did three of the elephants, including the sacred white elephant and Alice, both of whom were too scared to run from the building and so perished. It was third time in Barnum's career that fire had destroyed his business but he did not seem to have learned his lesson as it was later revealed that the circus was insured for only $100,000 against its real value of around $800,000.

Barnum always believed that the show must go on and, to everyone's surprise, the circus opened for its Madison Square Garden run the following March. The intervening months had seen Carl Hagenbeck and other European animal dealers working overtime to ship out dozens of giraffes, lions, hyenas and other exotic animals as replacements for the missing menagerie. One exhibit did not need replacing; Jumbo's hide and skeleton had been stored in a separate building and survived the fire unscathed. As the denuded circus made its way across America it was a relief for its owners to be able to use his familiar name in the publicity.

Back in the heady days of the Jumbo craze of 1882, Barnum had several times promised that Jumbo would one day be returned to London. It had originally been his hope that the Greatest Show on Earth would perform in Europe during 1887 but Jumbo's death stopped that idea and it was not until October 1889 that the circus finally crossed the Atlantic to perform in the English capital.

Perhaps because of the disastrous consequences of the fire, Barnum had started to show signs of being risk-averse. The veteran showman had been against the idea of exhibiting in London, believing that it represented too great a financial risk, but was persuaded to embark on the venture by Hutchinson. It took three steamers to transport the circus to its destination at the Olympia exhibition hall, where it spent the entire winter season. Despite Barnum's reservations, the show was a sell-out and a great success. Jumbo came too, but the lingering embarrassment of the Jumbo craze of seven years earlier led to his being completely ignored by the British press: it was an ignominious homecoming for the elephant who had at one time mobilized a nation in his support.

The sojourn in England was Jumbo's last outing with the circus. On returning to America Barnum and Hutchinson decided that his celebrity had run its course and that they should make good on an earlier promise to donate him to a museum. On 4 April Jumbo's mounted skin was delivered to Barnum's museum at Tufts College. Barnum was one of the college's trustees and it was his hope that the famous elephant would raise its profile. The mounted skeleton did not go to Tufts. It had originally been earmarked for the Smithsonian Institution but in the end Barnum chose to donate it to the American Museum of Natural History in New York.

JUMBO

It was one of the showman's final acts before bowing out from the spotlight. Two years later the curtain came down on Phineas Barnum, his death on 7 April 1891 sparking impassioned tributes across the world. Almost all those who reminisced on Barnum's achievements chose to mention his audacious purchase from London Zoo and acknowledged that the elephant's success had dominated his final years. "It was Jumbo here and Jumbo there – Jumbo everywhere," wrote James Bailey in memory of his former business partner.

Across the pond Abraham Bartlett, whose trademark beard had turned pure white, also acknowledged the showman's death and mourned his passing. Despite his advancing years and increasingly frailty, Bartlett remained the Superintendent at London Zoo and would continue do so until his death in 1897. His memoirs were published posthumously but in them he chose not to dwell on Jumbo and did not refer to him or to Scott in an affectionate tone. The African elephant that he had so longed to see in his zoo had ended up putting him to a great deal of trouble and was still being talked about at the time of his death.

Once placed on display at Tufts College, Jumbo's stuffed hide became a mascot and something of a good-luck charm. It is alleged that before sports games and exams students wishing for success would place a coin in the end of his trunk and then tug his tail. This latter practice proved to be so destructive that in 1942 the tail was removed and placed into storage.

The effigy of Jumbo remained at Tufts for over eight decades until 14 April 1975, when the lingering curse of Barnum's circus claimed it. In the early hours of the morning a small blaze started on the first floor of the Barnum Hall, where Jumbo was housed; it quickly got hold, engulfing the upper floor and roof in flames. The fire department was quickly on the scene but the heat and smoke left little that could be saved. A firefighter remembers seeing Jumbo moments before the flames rose up around him, but come morning all that remained were the four pipes that at one time supported his legs.

The loss of the college's good-luck charm was considered so tragic that a caretaker was sent to gather up some of Jumbo's ashes. To do so he used an old peanut butter jar into which he scooped a few handfuls of the elephant's charred remains. The jar was given to the director of athletics and to this day superstitious members of sports teams rub it for good luck. In 1999 the jar was subject to a "passing-of-the-ashes" ceremony between the outgoing director of athletics and his replacement. When asked if the jar really contained the elephant's ashes, the departing director replied: "We know that Jumbo was not cremated; he burned in a fire. Whatever burned, burned together. You gotta believe that these are Jumbo's ashes. He's in there someplace. I can't tell you which molecule, but he's in there."

Jumbo's skeleton fared somewhat better and is still in the vaults at the American Museum of Natural History. For many years the skeleton was on permanent display in the Mammal Hall on the museum's third floor but in 1969 the buff-coloured bones fell victim to a reorganization and were removed to storage. Since then the skeleton has periodically been seen as part of various exhibitions. It was last wheeled out in 1993 and in April of that year the Ringling Brothers and Barnum and Bailey Circus (as the Greatest Show on Earth was known after Barnum's death) paid tribute to their former elephant by marching 18 elephants, 34 horses, four zebras, two camels and two llamas past the entrance to the American Museum of Natural History. This parade, which was made in tribute to Barnum, began in Long Island and finished in Madison Square Garden; ironically the circus's plans to cross the East River using Queensboro Bridge (which invoke memories of Jumbo's crossing of Brooklyn Bridge in 1884) had to be shelved owing to structural repairs. Instead the elephants and other animals were walked through the Queens–Midtown Tunnel, leading to traffic chaos.

In the autumn of 1993 Jumbo's skeleton was returned to storage and has remained there but the Museum is frequently asked about the elephant's whereabouts. "People ask us all the time: where's Jumbo?" said a member of staff. "What happened to the skeleton? It's nothing macabre at all. People obviously still love it."

Jumbo touched the lives of many Victorians, but it was the advertisers who were to give this large animal his most enduring legacy within Western society. Within months of Jumbo's arrival in New York his distinctive but catchy name was being used as a quick and easy means of conveying any object's great size. Peanuts, cigars, pipes, hot dogs, foghorns and other items were all advertised as being "jumbo"; within only a few years the term had entered everyday speech across the entire United States: thanks to Barnum, Bailey and Hutchinson, American English had acquired a new slang word. Like all good American slang, "jumbo" crossed the Atlantic and, sometime before 1945, entered the British language as well. Later, and thanks to expressions such as "jumbo jet", it also became incorporated into the lexicon of other languages worldwide.

This slang may be Jumbo's most enduring legacy but it should not be forgotten that elements of his story featured in a children's book written by Helen Aberson in 1939. It was entitled *Dumbo* and told the tale of a circus elephant named Jumbo Jr, who is cruelly treated until it is discovered that his giant ears allow him to fly. Despite a small print run, a copy of Helen Aberson's book found its way into the hands of Walt Disney, who produced a full-length animated version of the story in 1941. It was a great commercial success and remains a favourite among Disney films to this day. There was also the 1962 Doris Day musical *Jumbo* (based on a Broadway show), in which a large elephant is at the centre of a battle between circus owners. Despite being well received by the fans, *Jumbo* was not as commercially successful as had been hoped, although Doris Day did get voted "The World's Most Popular Film Actress" later in the year.

From wild animal to the subject of a Hollywood musical: Jumbo was truly one of the most extraordinary creatures ever to walk the Earth. He was certainly a legend in his own lifetime but his influence has continued to this day. The next time you take a ride on a jumbo jet, shop at a Jumbo supermarket or eat a jumbo hotdog, spare a thought for the troubled animal whose international fame was also the cause of his demise. As P.T. Barnum himself knew only too well, the bigger they come, the harder they fall.

Bibliography

The following is a list of the published reference works commonly consulted during the writing of this book. More detailed sources and notes may be found in the next section.

Baker, S.W., *The Nile Tributaries*, London: Macmillan and Co., 1868

Baker, S.W., *Wild Beasts and their Ways*, London: Macmillan and Co., 1890

Baker, S.W., *The Albert N'Yanza*, London: Sidgwick and Jackson, 1962

Baratay, E. and Hardouin-Fugier, E., *Zoo: A History of Zoological Gardens in the West*, London: Reaktion Books, 2002

Barnum, P.T., *Struggles and Triumphs*, London: Ward, Lock and Co., 1882

Bartlett, A.D., *Wild Animals in Captivity*, London: Chapman and Hall, 1898

Blunt, W., *The Ark in the Park*, London: Hamish Hamilton, 1976

Bombas, G.C., *Life of Frank Buckland*, London: Thomas Nelson, 1909

Burgess, G.H.O., *The Curious World of Frank Buckland*, London: John Baker, 1967

Drew, W.A., *Glimpses and Gatherings during a Voyage and Visit to London and the Great Exhibition in the Summer of 1851*, Boston: Abel Tompkins, 1852

Fitzsimons, R., *Barnum in London*, London: Geoffrey Bles, 1969

Hagenbeck, C., *Beasts and Men*, London: Longman, Green and Co., 1909

Johnson, T., *Personal Recollections of the Zoo*, London: the author, 1891

Jolly, W.P., *Jumbo*, London: Constable, 1976

Lee, P.C., "Early Social Development in African Elephants", *National Geographic Research*, 1986, vol. 2, pp.394–401

Lee, P.C., "Family Structure, Communal Care and Female Reproductive Effort" in Standen, V. and Foley, R. (eds.), *Comparative Socioecology*, Oxford: Blackwell, 1989, pp.323–40

Lee, P.C. and Moss, C.J., "Early Maternal Investment in Male and Female African Elephant Calves", *Behavioural Ecology and Sociobiology*, 1986, vol. 18, pp.353–61

Lee, P.C. and Moss, C.J., "The Social Context for Learning and Behavioural Development among Wild African Elephants" in Box,

H.O. and Gibson, K.R. (eds.), *Mammalian Social Learning*, Cambridge: Cambridge University Press, 1999, pp.102–25

Mathieson, E., *The True Story of Jumbo the Elephant*, New York: Coward-McCann, 1964

Mitchell, P.C., *Centenary History of the Zoological Society of London*, London: Zoological Society of London, 1929

Moss, C., *Elephant Memories: Thirteen Years in the Life of an Elephant Family*, New York: William Morrow, 1988

Myers, A.B.R., *Life with the Hamran Arabs*, London: Smith, Elder and Co., 1876

Roca, A.L. *et al.*, "Genetic Evidence for Two Species of Elephant in Africa", *Science*, 2001, vol. 293, p.1473

Rothfels, N., *Savages and Beasts: The Birth of the Modern Zoo*, London: Johns Hopkins University Press, 2002

Russell, J.R., "Jumbo", *University of Rochester Library Bulletin*, 1947, vol. 3 (1)

Scott, M., *Autobiography of Matthew Scott*, Bridgeport: Trow, 1885

Sikes, S.K., *The Natural History of the African Elephant*, London: Weidenfeld and Nicolson, 1971

Sukumar, R., *The Living Elephants*, Oxford: Oxford University Press, 2003

Toovey, J.W., "150 Years of Building at London Zoo", *Symposium of the Zoological Society of London*, 1976, no. 40, pp.179–202

Twain, M., *Following the Equator*, Mineola, NY: Dover Books, 1999

Vevers, G., *London's Zoo*, London: Bodley Head, 1976

Zuckerman, S., "The Zoological Society of London: Evolution of a Constitution", *Symposium of the Zoological Society of London*, 1976, no. 40, pp.1–16

Sources and Notes

Abbreviations:
NYT: *New York Times*
TNA: PRO: The National Archives: Public Record Office, London
ZSL: Zoological Society of London Archives, London

1: The Elephant Hunters

Jumbo's origins: Some rumours held that this magnificent elephant started his life on the Zambezi River before being captured by Matabele hunters and sold to British colonials; others believed that he was one of twins that had been gifted to the French by the Viceroy of Egypt. There was even talk of Jumbo not having been a wild animal at all but of his being secretly born into a European travelling circus or backstreet menagerie. In fact Samuel White Baker describes seeing Jumbo in *Penny Illustrated News* (11 March 1882) but also relates the circumstances surrounding his capture, including Taher Sheriff's role, in his travel writings (see Baker, 1868, ch. 14). Following this it is possible to trace Jumbo's journey to Europe through Hagenbeck (1909), pp.8–9.

Hamran Arabs: The descriptions of Taher Sheriff, the Hamran camp, the Setite and Royan rivers and their hunting technique come from Baker (1868), chs. 14 and 17. For a later account of the Hamran tribesmen, see Myers (1876).

Johan Schmidt: Baker (1962), pp.20, 30–1; Baker (1868), ch. 14. Schmidt was later employed by Samuel Baker during his expeditions to Abyssinia. On 30 December 1862 Baker witnessed Schmidt's death from a progressive lung disease: "I sat by his bed for some hours; there was not a ray of hope; he could speak with difficulty, and the flies walked across his glazed eyeballs without his knowledge. Gently bathing his face and hands, I asked him if I could deliver any message to his relatives. He faintly uttered, 'I am prepared to die; I have neither parents nor relations; but there is one, she...' he faltered. He could not finish his sentence, but his dying thoughts were with one he loved." Schmidt was buried two days later and was much missed by Baker, who continually describes him as an excellent man.

Jumbo's age and weight: These were calculated using the mathematical functions given in Sukumar (2003), appendix 2.

Elephant biology and behaviour: See Lee (1986, 1989), Lee and Moss (1986, 1999), Moss (1988) and Sukumar (2003).

2: An Exotic Commodity

Elephant species: Roca *et al.* (2001).

"Better flavoured...": *The Penny Cyclopaedia*, London: Charles Knight, 1837, vol. ix, pp.350–3.

"The enraged elephant...": Goldsmith, O., *A History of the Earth and Animated Nature*, London: William Wright, 1824, vol. ii, p.176.

Saffron Walden elephant: *The Times*, 8 July 1851; 21 July 1851.

"far surpasses...": *The Penny Magazine*, 16 December 1837.

"This example...": *The Mirror*, 4 August 1832.

"I gazed on...": *The Times*, 6 July 1836.

"The doors were...": *Illustrated London News*, 19 June 1847.

"The Secretary be directed...": ZSL Minutes, 3 February 1858.

3: Crossing the Desert

The journey to Europe: The descriptions of Kassala, Suakin, Suez and the transport links between these may be found in Baker (1868), ch. 5. There is a full description of the logistics and problems encountered by Casanova in moving game animals from Kassala to Hamburg in *Land and Water* (25 July 1868) and descriptions relating to the voyage made by Jumbo in *Penny Illustrated News* (11 March 1882) and Hagenbeck (1909), pp.8–13.

"After their arrival...": Hagenbeck (1909), p.168.

The desert crossing: Baker (1868), ch. 14; Hagenbeck (1909), p.8; *Penny Illustrated News*, 11 March 1882; *Land and Water*, 25 July 1868.

The 2001 elephant sighting: *BBC Wildlife*, July 2003.

Lorenzo Casanova and Dr Josef Natterer: Hagenbeck (1909); Rothfels (2002), p.48.

Suakin and shipping: Baker (1868). Although the boat journey was risky, it was actually what made Kassala such an attractive place to animal traders such as Casanova. The town might be a long way inland but it was still the closest point to Europe where African game animals could be obtained. Other alternatives, such as capturing and transporting large animals from Kenya, Tanzania or South Africa, carried unacceptably high levels of mortality which had to be added to the costs of obtaining, feeding and transporting the animals.

"On the way...": Hagenbeck (1909), pp.12–13.

"could not afford...": Hagenbeck (1909), p.8.

Kreutzberg: Rothfels (2002), p.49; Foster, B., *The Upper Rhine*, London: G. Routledge, 1858, vol. ii, p.137.

4: The Superintendent

Bartlett's early life: Bartlett (1898).

Chunee and Exeter 'Change: Wright, J. (ed.), *A Natural History of the Globe of Man, of Beasts, Birds, Fishes, Reptiles, Insects and Plants*, Boston: Gray and Bowen, 1831, vol. 2, pp.195–209. On the demolition of the Exeter 'Change in 1829, the entire menagerie was sold to the Surrey Zoological Gardens but only after the authorities at the Zoological Society of London had turned down the chance to buy it.

"It was a business…": Bartlett (1898), p.2.

"The French authorities…": Johnson (1891), p.15.

5: Paris

Jardin des Plantes: Baratay and Hardouin-Fugier (2002).

"Entering by the gate…": *Chambers's Handy Guide to Paris*, London: Chambers, 1863, pp.128–9.

Rotunda and layout: Baratay and Hardouin-Fugier (2002), p.76; Gardner, A.K., *The French Metropolis: As Seen During the Spare Hours of a Medical Student*, London: E.T. Brain and Co., 1850, p.267; *Galignani's Messenger*, 12 April 1865; *The Times*, 21 April 1865.

Viceroy of Egypt's elephants: *Fraser's Magazine*, January 1872, p.20.

"The elephants are not taller…": *The Times*, 26 October 1863.

Exchange rate: The rate of 25 francs to £1 was taken from *Chambers's Handy Guide to Paris*, 1863, p.12.

"We consider the maintenance…": *The Times*, 21 April 1865.

Hagenbeck and Bartlett: Hagenbeck (1909).

"opened negotiations with…": ZSL Minutes, 17 May 1865.

Bargaining with the Jardin des Plantes: ZSL Minutes, 7 June 1865.

"I handed him over…": Bartlett (1898), p.45.

"A more deplorable…": Scott (1885), p.44.

"effect that sort of…": Johnson (1891), p.14.

"I undertook…": Scott (1898), p.44.

6: A True Vocation

Earls of Derby: Coward, Barry. *The Stanleys, Lords Stanley, and Earls of Derby, 1385–1672: The Origins, Wealth, and Power of a Landowning Family*. Manchester: Manchester University Press, 1983. Earl of Derby's will: TNA: PRO PROB 11/2140.

Scott's childhood: Scott (1885).

"There are about twenty thousand…": Drew (1852), pp.800–1.

"Oh! What a sight!": Drew (1852), p.164.

"A woman would not…": Scott (1885), pp.55, 59.

"The services required…": ZSL Minutes, 5 March 1873.

Errant keepers: ZSL Minutes, 2 January 1867; 17 July 1867; 19 April 1871.

Scott's social life: Johnson (1898), pp.20–1.

"There came Obaysch...": Bombas (1909), pp.250–1.
Kiwi: Scott (1885), pp.24–33.

7: London

Jumbo's name: See, for example, Jolly (1976), p.15.
Mumbo Jumbo: Bee, J., *Slang: A Dictionary*, London: T. Hughes, 1823,
    p.108. For descriptions of Mumbo Jumbo see, for example, M. Park,
    Travels in the Interior Districts of Africa, London: John Murray, 1816,
    vol. 1, p.42.
"was in a filthy...": Bartlett (1898), pp.45–6.
"the most obvious peculiarity...": *Illustrated London News*, 15 July 1865.
"The extensive collection...": *The Times*, 28 June 1865.
"The African Elephant is...": *Illustrated London News*, 15 July 1865.
"I watched him...": Scott (1885), p.45.
Giraffe House: ZSL Daybook, 20 September 1865; 6, 16, 20, 25, 30, 31
    October 1865.
Jumbo's attacks: ZSL Daybook, 11, 24 November 1865; 12, 27, 28
    December 1865.
"We found it necessary...": Bartlett (1898), p.46.
"It was my happiness...": Johnson (1891), p.15.

8: Alice

Buying Alice: ZSL Daybook, 9 September 1865; ZSL Minutes, 20
    September 1865.
Charles Rice: TNA: PRO RG9/275 fo. 61; p.21.
Moving Alice: Bartlett (1898), p.51.
"When I passed by...": Scott (1855), p.49.
"They always appeared...": Johnson (1891), pp.28–9.
"I have found that elephants...": Hagenbeck (1909), p.147.
Alice's purchase: ZSL Daybook, 9 September 1865; ZSL Minutes, 20
    September 1865; Johnson (1891), p.28; Hagenbeck (1898), p.11;
    Blunt (1976), p.167.
"Having Jumbo entirely...": Scott (1885), pp.47–8.

9: Training Jumbo

"The tame elephant...": Baker (1890), vol. 1, ch. 2.
"We must not forget...": Bartlett (1898), pp.61–3.
"I got all the...": Scott (1885), pp.54–5.
Jumbo's bad temper: ZSL Daybook, 5–7, 19–23 June 1886.
"a multitude of protests...": Bartlett (1898), p.46.
Edwin Abraham: ZSL Minutes, 17 October 1866; 1861 Census, TNA:
    PRO RG9/399 fo. 154, p.32; 1871 Census, TNA: PRO RG10/65; fo.
    20; p.34.
"He might get mad...": Scott (1885), p.59.
Ticket money: Bartlett (1898), p.49; Johnson (1891), p.16; ZSL
    Daybooks, 1886 to 1882.

10: Fever

Bronze medal: ZSL Minutes, 4 July, 21 November, 19 December 1866; 5 March 1873; 19 July 1876.

"consider the best method...": ZSL Minutes, 19 December 1866.

Jumbo's attack: ZSL Minutes, 6 February 1867; ZSL Daybook, 25–7 February 1867.

Howdah and rides: ZSL Daybook, 15–16 May 1867; ZSL: undated 1892 letter by Bartlett.

"Too weak to do more...": Johnson (1891), p.17. Frequent references are made to this bout of illness in the writings of Scott and Johnson but none states exactly when it occurred. Surprisingly, the ZSL's Daybooks, which are supposed to carry a record of any sick animals, do not list it either; this might add substance to Johnson's accusation that Bartlett suppressed "all mention of Jumbo's illness and recovery". Certainly Bartlett did not record other illnesses known to have affected some of the Zoo's elephants, including the prolonged one that led to Chunee's death in 1875. However, I have cross-referenced some of the descriptions of this illness against features recorded in the Daybooks and believe that Jumbo's illness started in December 1867 and continued into the New Year.

"with bucketfuls of scotch": Johnson (1891), p.18.

"In order to cure...": Hagenbeck (1909), p.226.

"Since I brought...": Scott (1885), p.56.

"When I go out of...": Scott (1885), p.62.

"Jumbo will do everything...": Johnson (1891), p.19.

"All the keepers...": Bartlett (1898), p.48.

11: Life at the Zoo

Rides: Scott (1885), p.57.

Winston Churchill, etc.: Barnum (1882), p.361.

"I shouted at him...": Scott (1885), pp.57–8.

Elephant House: ZSL Minutes, 4 March, 20 May, 21 October, 16 December 1868. *Illustrated London News*, 29 June 1869.

"The outer doors...": ZSL Letter Archive, Bartlett to Salvin, 8 July 1869.

Jumbo's illness and operation: Bartlett (1898), pp.46–8.

"more respect, deference...": Scott (1885), pp.50–1.

"Jumbo would, every now and then...": Scott (1885), pp.52–3.

12: Heroes and Villains

Siege of Paris: *Penny Illustrated Paper*, 14 January 1871; *Fraser's Magazine*, January 1872, pp.17–22.

"These poor brutes...": *Penny Illustrated Paper*, 14 January 1871.

Rhinoceros incident: *Daily Telegraph*; 25 November 1874; *Penny Illustrated News*, 5 December 1874; *London Clipper*, 5 December 1874.

"Mr Matthew Scott…": *Daily Telegraph*, 25 November 1874.
"He ought to have…": *The Times*, 25 November 1874. Bartlett made his
   views known to his friend Frank Buckland; see Blunt (1976), p.172.
Thompson's dismissal: ZSL Minutes, 16 December 1874; Blunt (1976),
   pp.172–4; Bartlett (1898), p.45.
Chunee's death: Blunt (1976), pp.172–3. Thompson's assistant Godfrey
   did not return to work until May 1875. He too was transferred to
   work elsewhere in the Gardens.
"Chunee has died…": *NYT* 16 August 1875; Blunt (1976), p.173.
Alice's accident: Bartlett (1898), pp.51–2; *The Times*, 5 August 1875; *NYT*
   16 August 1875; Johnson (1891), pp.31–2; Blunt (1976), pp.173–5.
"It is said to be…": Blunt (1976) p.176.
"More in play…": Blunt (1976), p.177.

13: Friction in the Elephant House

Jumbo and Scott: Johnson (1891), p.17; Scott (1885), pp.60–3;
   Mathieson (1964), pp.21–3.
Scott at the Zoo: ZSL Minutes, 21 August 1871; ZSL Daybooks, 1865
   to 1882; *Daily Telegraph*, 25 November 1874.
"The remonstrations…": Johnson (1891), p.20.
"To be knocked over…": Johnson (1891), p.22.
16 June and drains: ZSL Daybook, 16, 17 June 1881.
Jumbo's attacks: ZSL Daybook, 8, 18, 22, 23, 24, 31 August; 1, 2, 3, 5,
   6 September 1881.
"after elephants arrive…": *The Times*, 8 March 1882.
"At certain periodical…": Wood, J.G., 1885, *Sketches and Anecdotes of
   Animal Life*, London: Routledge and Co., pp.89–90.
Scientific view of musth: Sukumar (2003, ch. 3). It has been suggested
   by Sikes (1971) that Jumbo's bad behaviour can be related to the
   eruption of one of his adult molar teeth, the pain from which would
   have driven him wild. However, Jumbo's age and the prolonged
   nature of his bad behaviour make this unlikely.
Hagenbeck kills an elephant: Hagenbeck (1909), pp.153–4.
Bartlett warned…: *The Times*, 8 March 1882.
"The door leading…": *Land and Water*, 25 February 1882.
"I have for some time…": *The Times*, 9 March 1882.
Barnum's telegram: *The Times*, 2 March 1882; 8 March 1882.

14: Piteous Scenes at the Zoo

Barnum's life: See Barnum (1882); *NYT*, 27 February 1882.
"Find anything?": *NYT*, 1 May 1887; 19 April 1891.
"It is no use…": Twain (1999), p.639.
The sale of Jumbo: Bartlett (1898), p.49; ZSL Minutes, 1 February
   1882; ZSL Daybook, 26, 27 January 1882; *The Times*, 2 March 1882;
   Scott (1885), p.65.

"The Great African elephant...": *The Times*, 25 January 1882.
Scott's leave of absence: ZSL Minutes, 15 February 1882; Bartlett (1898), p.50.
"It's a pity...": Johnson (1891), p.18.
Jumbo's box: *The Echo*, 18 February 1882.
Assyrian Monarch: *The Times*, 21 February 1882.
"The African Elephant is more...": *The Times*, 21 February 1882.
The removal of Jumbo: *Daily Telegraph*, 20 February 1882; *The Times*, 21 February 1882; *Illustrated London News*, 25 February 1882; ZSL Daybook, 17, 18, 19 February 1882.
"In common with many...": *The Times*, 21 February 1882.
"Surely there can be no...": *The Times*, 22 February 1882.
"One African Elephant...": ZSL Daybook, 18 February 1882.

15: We Won't Let Jumbo Go!
Barnum's cheque: ZSL Minutes, 22 February 1882.
"It is not surprising...": *The Times*, 23 February 1882.
"I have visited...": *The Times*, 23 February 1882. The letter is signed "A.B.".
"To say...": Johnson (1891), p.24.
"Is it or is it not...": *The Times*, 24 February 1882.
"Jumbo is lying...": *Winona Daily Republican*, 11 April 1891.
New departure arrangements: *Daily Telegraph*, 20 February 1882.
Visitor numbers: ZSL Daybooks, 1881, 1882. Mondays are a cheap admittance day.
William Tegetmeier: *Land and Water*, 25 February 1882.
Letters and presents: *The Times*, 2 March 1882; *Animal World*, 1 March 1882.
"It is nearly certain...": *Spectator*, 25 February 1882.
Jumbo Defence Fund: *Saturday Review*, 25 February 1882; *Vanity Fair*, 25 February 1882.
RSPCA: *Animal World*, 1 March 1882; ZSL Minutes, 15 March 1882.
"Dead or alive...": *Daily Telegraph*, 22 February 1882.
"The newly constructed box...": *Illustrated London News*, 18 March 1882.
Jumbo refuses the box: *The Times*, 8 March 1882.
"Should this step...": *The Times*, 8 March 1882.

16: A Weighty Foreign Topic
"I know they won't...": Twain (1999), p.639.
Le Sage's telegram: *NYT*, 24 February 1882; *Daily Telegraph*, 24 February 1882.
"Not withstanding...": *NYT*, 8 March 1882.
"Dear Mr Barnum...": Jolly (1976), p.59.
"Mr Barnum has obtained...": *NYT*, 18 March 1882.

"Employ best counsel...": *NYT*, 8 March 1882. Bridgeport was a captive-born calf that had been produced by one of Barnum's Asian elephants the previous January.

"It has been decided...": *The Times*, 6 March 1882.

The court case: *The Times*, 6, 7, 8, 9 March 1882. The failure to secure Jumbo through the courts was a blow to Matthew Berkeley-Hill and settled the elephant's fate once and for all. It did not, however, mark the end of Berkeley-Hill's campaign against the Zoological Society, which continued in an unrelenting manner for several months. A week after the end of the court case the Zoological Society was faced with an official request from Berkeley-Hill to change its by-laws so that Special Meetings could be convened at short notice and the Fellows informed in advance of the intended sale of any important animals. The request was considered during several Council meetings but was thought to be impracticable. Berkeley-Hill would not be dissuaded and at a general meeting of the Society on 22 June his friend Henry Burdett requested that the matter be put to a vote. The Council responded by telling the Fellows that if the matter were pursued further they would resign and put forward a proposal of their own: "This meeting does not think it desirable to interfere with the discretion of the Council upon the question raised by Mr Burdett." It was carried by 145 votes, leaving Berkeley-Hill and Burdett again staring at defeat. "We are still firmly convinced that our proposals are reasonable, moderate in scope and beneficial to the Society's prosperity," Berkeley-Hill complained in his final letter to the Society. See his correspondence in the ZSL Letter Archive.

Parliamentary questions: *The Times*, 11 March 1882.

17: How to Pack an Elephant's Trunk

"I observe...": *The Times*, 10 March 1882.

"no trouble is now...": *The Times*, 13 March 1882.

"irritations at the sparseness...": *The Times*, 13 March 1882.

"Oh why did the Council sell me?": Jolly (1976), p.73.

Queen Victoria: *NYT*, 11 April 1882; Jolly (1976), p.71.

Scott's obstructions: Bartlett (1898), p.50; *Winona Daily Republican*, 6 December 1892.

The removal of Jumbo: *The Times*, 23 March 1882; *Illustrated London News*, 1 April 1882; *NYT*, 8 April 1882; Scott (1885), pp.68–9; ZSL Daily Occurrences, 22 March 1882.

"The noise of the groans...": Scott (1885), pp.68–9.

18: Farewell

Scenes at the docks: *Western Daily Mercury*, 24 March 1882; *The Times*, 24 March 1882; *Illustrated London News*, 1 April 1882; *NYT*, 8 April 1882.

On board the *Assyrian Monarch*: *The Times*, 25 March 1882.

Setting sail: *The Times*, 28 March 1882.

Jingo: ZSL Daybook, 8 July 1882. Jingo was initially popular with crowds but he did not grow to Jumbo's size and was said to be somewhat lopsided. He was also bad-tempered and in 1903 was sold to an Englishman living in America. He died on the crossing and was tipped overboard.

Changes to the rules: ZSL Minutes, 5 April 1882.

"Jumbo well...": *The Times*, 28 March 1882.

The ocean crossing: Scott (1885), p.73; *NYT*, 10 April 1882.

"We now depend...": *NYT*, 1 April 1882. I wondered whether this article was an April Fool's joke but it does appear to be serious.

"Good thing...": *NYT*, 5 April 1882.

19: New York, New York

Scenes in New York: *NYT*, 10 April 1882.

Madison Square Garden: *New York Herald*, 10 April 1882; *NYT*, 11 April 1882.

"The claim of Mr Barnum...": *NYT*, 29 March 1881.

The history of Barnum's show: *NYT*, 22 April 1880; 10 June 1880; 27 March 1881; 29 March 1881; January 17 1882; 14 March 1882; 2 April 1882.

Jumbo arrives at Madison Square Garden: *NYT*, 10, 11 April 1882; 23 April 1882; 22 February 1884.

20: Grand Tour

"The herd was drawn...": *Animal World*, 1 March 1884.

"Amid the music...": *NYT*, April 23 1882; 27 March 1883.

New Jersey ferry: *NYT*, 23 April 1882.

Life on the train: Scott (1885), pp.76–7.

Scott's accident: *NYT*, 20 May 1882; Scott (1885), pp.80–2.

"All we want to see...": Scott (1885), pp.78–9.

"Jumbo, looking bigger...": *Winona Daily Republican*, 6 March 1883.

Jumbo McClure/Steam-Whistles: *NYT*, 26 May 1882; 12 September 1882; *Animal World*, 1 March 1884.

Scott is sacked: ZSL Minutes, 17 January 1883.

21: Fame, Fire and Brooklyn Bridge

"Jumbo, the great and only...": *NYT*, 22 March 1882.

Hornaday and measurements: *Bulletin of the New York Zoological Society*, 1911; ZSL Letter Archive, Brine to Bartlett, 18 April 1883. For a further example of Barnum's deferring permission to Bailey see Russell (1947).

Barnum arrested/Pilot: *NYT*, 3 April 1883; 5 April 1883; 6 April 1883; 23 April 1883; 29 April 1883.

Chicago fire: *NYT*, 6 June 1883; 8 June 1883.
Scott saved by Jumbo: Scott (1885), pp.84–6; *NYT*, 17 September 1885.
White elephant: *NYT*, 9 June 1883; 6 December 1883.
Jumbo's illness: Jolly (1976), pp.139–40.
Ward and Barnum: Russell (1947).
"Authorise me to sell…": ZSL Letter Archive, Bartlett, 27 August 1883.
Coney Island elephant: *NYT*, 21 February 1884; 29 February 1884.
Arrival of Toung Taloung: *NYT*, 3 March 1884; 29 March 1884.
Brooklyn Bridge panic: *NYT*, 31 May 1883.
Crossing the bridge: *NYT*, 18 May 1884; Scott (1885), pp.86–96.
Scott's autobiography: Scott (1885), p.40. For Barnum quoting from the autobiography see, for example, *NYT*, 17 September 1885.

22: The Accident
"The people of Texas…": *NYT*, 12 July 1885.
Historical St Thomas: Elgin County Archives; *NYT*, 17 September 1885.
Jumbo's death: Many sources but especially *NYT*, 17 September 1885; *The Times*, 17 September 1882; *Daily Telegraph*, 17 September 1882.
"The contempt with which…": *Spectator*, 19 September 1885.
"The truth about the killing…": *Mariposa Gazette*, 25 September 1885.
Scott pensioned off: *NYT*, 18 September 1885.

23: The Comeback
"My wife suggests…": *NYT*, 17 September 1885.
Ward dissects Jumbo: Russell (1947); *NYT*, 18 September 1885.
The buying of Alice: *NYT*, 10 January 1886; 7 March 1886; 14 March 1886; ZSL Letter Archive, 8 January 1886; 22 March 1886; ZSL Minutes, 20 March 1886.
Alice meets Jumbo: *NYT*, 21 April 1886.
Globe lawsuit: *Winona Daily Republican*, 2 October 1885.
Railway lawsuit: *NYT*, 4 April 1887; 12 April 1887; 24 April 1887.
Scott and Hutchinson: *NYT*, 11 February 1887.
Scott in New York: *NYT*, 4 April 1887; 12 April 1887. I have checked without success various standard US and UK genealogical resources for any clue to Scott's fate.
Bridgeport fire: *NYT*, 21 November 1887; 22 November 1887.
Barnum's death: *NYT*, 12 April 1891; 19 April 1891.
Tufts College: *Medford Transcript*, 24 April 2007; Tisch Library archives; *Tufts Magazine*, Spring 2002. All that remains of Jumbo's original hide is his tail, which is kept securely in the college's archives, out of harm's way.
American Museum of Natural History: *NYT*, 22 January 1993; 4 April 1993.

Index